GOOD GIRLS GONE BAD

Other Books by Susan Nadler

The Butterfly Convention

GOOD GIRLS

GONE BAD
Susan Nadler

FREUNDLICH BOOKS
New York

Published by Freundlich Books
(A division of Lawrence Freundlich Publications, Inc.)
212 Fifth Avenue
New York, N.Y. 10010

Distributed to the trade by Kampmann & Company
9 East 40th Street
New York, N.Y. 10016

Library of Congress Cataloging-in-Publication Data

Nadler, Susan, 1947–
   Good girls gone bad.

   Bibliography: p.
   1. Female offenders—United States—Case studies.
2. Female offenders—United States—Psychology—
Case studies.   I. Title.
HV6046.N3   1987   364.3′74′0922   86-29155
ISBN 0-88191-048-1
9 8 7 6 5 4 3

For my mother and father

CONTENTS

AUTHOR'S NOTE

WHEN I FIRST decided to include a chapter about myself in this book, I called my father in Pittsburgh to tell him. His initial reaction was, "Oh no, Susan, I don't want to be in another book." I told him that the time I had spent in prison in Mexico had inspired my investigation of other middle-class women in crime. He understood that. He also understood that the addition of my chapter would explain my interest in the crimes and the characters of the women I had written about. Then we both agreed that the book was going to be painful for me as well as my family.

I was a good girl gone bad. Although I had grown up in an upper-middle-class family, was educated extensively here and abroad, and had all the advantages and comforts, in 1972 I served four and a half months of a potential twenty-seven-year sentence in a Mexican prison for drug smuggling. I have lived the life of an outlaw. I rebelled against everything and everyone, I self-destructed endlessly, and I hurt my family enormously. If I hadn't been busted in Mexico, today I would probably be dead.

I committed my first crime when I was ten. I shoplifted eye makeup from the five-and-ten, the long lost shoplifter's paradise of the fifties. By the time I was sixteen I was a full-fledged thief, had been suspended from private school for harassing the librarian, had used marijuana, and was considered a problem by my parents and teachers. I felt alone, isolated, yet also special.

My father owned a very successful business in Pittsburgh, my mother was an artist, we had live-in maids, my two sisters and I took music lessons and dance classes. I won poetry awards in both junior and senior years at my private girls' school. I could quote from Shakespeare and Dostoyevsky, I scored impressively on my college boards, attended the University of Wisconsin for three politically active years, and finished my degree in Jerusalem. But at the age of twenty-six, I was busted in La Paz, Mexico, for smuggling 500 kilos of hashish. I published an account of my experience, *The Butterfly Convention*, in 1976 and finally lay my life of crime to rest; but it has taken me a number of years of self-examination and interviews with women in prison to understand my attraction to crime.

This personal battle made me particularly fascinated with other contemporary criminals. Five years ago I interviewed eleven women at the Tennessee State Prison for Women, in Nashville. All were white, all were serving life sentences for murder. I wrote a series of articles about them for the Nashville *Tennessean*, and I organized country music performers to entertain at the prison.

Over the next several years, I began to realize that crimes like the one I had committed were being committed in ever increasing numbers by middle-class women. These were women who had had all the advantages of money, education, power, connections, travel, and ostensibly their family's support. These were women who could have made other choices in life. They often didn't need more money. Some were married to nice middle-class men in the suburbs, others had high-powered jobs in corporate empires. The world was open to them. But they chose crime, mostly the white-collar variety; embezzling, cat burglary, fraud, larceny, computer crime, and the con game. Many were not afraid of being caught. They were a mystery group to me.

Three years ago I began research for this book. I developed several clever theories to explain why the number of women in crime had doubled over the last decade. I got the facts. I read books on the subject, studied Federal Bureau of Investigation Uniform Crime Reports, poured over Justice

Department printouts, coveted every statistic I could find, and then attempted to synthesize all this information into one cohesive, giant blanket explanation.

The statistics are amazing. Crime has become a more acceptable way of life for women. The 1980s female felon is involved in far more serious crime than her predecessors; more white-collar crimes and more violent offenses that were formerly perpetrated only by men. According to the 1983 Federal Bureau of Investigation crime report, between 1969 and 1978 the number of female offenders for almost every crime listed has increased at a rate surpassing that of men. Although female prisoners make up only 4.3 percent of the nation's inmate population, their numbers are increasing at an alarming rate. Males still commit the greater absolute number of offenses, but it is the females who are now committing those same crimes at yearly rates of increases now running as high as six and seven times greater than those for males.

Over the last two years I traveled across the country and completed interviews with nearly fifty women in six maximum security prisons and one inner city jail. I have over thirteen hundred pages of transcripts. Some prisons would not let me in because of my past. It was not easy to get into prisons to interview because many officials thought I was going to write an exposé about prison life. This was never my intention. Although scheduling and last-minute changes often made my wait to be admitted to the prisons extremely tense, the officials for the most part were helpful and courteous, but also quick to get me out. The women were more than eager to talk to me and surprisingly forthcoming about their lives and motivations. Perhaps they sensed that I had more than a little sympathy and concern. But I was not to be hustled, nor taken in by their stories. I never excused their crimes nor accepted their rationalizations. Many were sly, others devious, and all were guilty. I understood where they were coming from, because unbeknownst to most of them, I had been there too. After a few early mistakes, I found it best not to share my past with either the officials or the inmates. I felt that the women might have had a different attitude toward me if I swapped crime stories with them.

There is certainly no question that the role of American women has changed in the last two decades, especially that of middle-class women. Important social structures have broken down, and women are facing not only the successes, but the stresses that men have always known. Women have become bold. For years, they have watched and heard about men who got away with white-collar crimes. Now they are going after the same power, the same stimulation brought on by crime, sex, and drugs. They want the same thrills as men. Some are more creatively competent criminals than their male counterparts. Many go about their crimes with the dispassionate, fearless single-mindedness we associate with such legendary bandits as John Dillinger and Belle Starr.

The day I began interviewing real women, my theories faded. I tried to fit the women into particular categories. This one turned to crime because she never had a resolved relationship with her father, this one was abused, this one was addicted to money, this one did it for love, this one was a product of the dissolution of the American family. But these women are real people, and real people are not archetypal chapter headings, but composites of their pasts, their genes, their dreams, the times they live in, and the fates.

What I held so dear the first year of research became irrelevant the second year. And by the third summer, I realized that my grandiose outline was just that, grandiose. The women's words and stories are stronger than any theories I could devise. They speak to all of us.

This book was extremely difficult for me to write. Aside from the overwhelming depression I felt at the various prisons, reliving my own past evoked memories I had tried to forget. I had constant nightmares about getting arrested and not being able to get away. I identified with some of the women's stories, and I worried that by dredging up my past I would be forcing my parents to relive theirs.

Prison is a stopover for the majority of inmates I interviewed. A miserable reminder of who they are and what they have become. From what I have seen, it is impossible to hope that prison can act as a means of rehabilitation, especially for bright, educated women.

Prison for women is as much a mind game as it is a physical isolation. Women try to manipulate each other. Female guards lord their power over female inmates. Female inmates rat each other out. They hurt each other the way they know best, with their tongues.

I consider myself lucky. I was a good girl gone bad gone good again. I have written since I was five years old and I found that through my writing I was able to duplicate the action I had been seeking on the street. I was also lucky that I was able to find a therapist to help me walk the bridge back into reality. Many of the women I interviewed will not be that lucky. There are not enough psychiatrists on prison staffs, and there is only limited job training and career opportunities offered to inmates. We need to work with ex-cons more closely so that the rate of recidivism will drop. We need to help these women reenter society, reintegrate with their families, their children, learn how to resist the thrills, fast money, and sense of power that "the life" offers. This is the problem that should be studied. Now. Before too many more good girls go bad.

GOOD GIRLS GONE BAD

CHAPTER I

COMING OFF THE PEDESTAL

*"After I've thought about it all this time, in a way I wanted
it to happen. I wanted to come off the pedestal. I wanted to
be myself, and it was kind of impossible the way people
looked at me. I've never felt better in my entire life since
I've been here."*
TERRY SAUNDERS
December 1, 1984
Western Correctional Facility

IT WAS GOING to be another gorgeous day in Santa Monica,
another morning of perfect weather, clear sunshine, salt
breeze, blue skies, and azure seas. The Santana winds had
blown the smog away overnight. The air was clean. It was
the type of weather that made people realize just how terrific Los Angeles can be. Terry pulled the floor-length
drapes open and gazed out the French doors to her patio,
greeting the morning with a yawn. She grabbed the one
dirty ashtray in the otherwise immaculate sunken white living room, and carried it with her to the kitchen, where she
emptied it into the garbage compressor. Humming an unre-
cognizable tune from the fifties, she turned her tiny break-
fast-nook TV on to the "Today Show," and walked out into
her small but well-landscaped backyard to pick a dozen
oranges from one of her trees to squeeze for the family
breakfast. The smell of the Señor de Noches was still so
overpowering in the early morning dew that for one moment

3

she buried her head in the blossoms, and then, carrying her twelve perfect oranges in the battered old bucket, she returned to her kitchen and her automatic juicer to begin the meal.

"John will probably want waffles this morning," she said to no one in particular, as Jane Pauley began an interview with Jane Fonda.

"Now, there's a superwoman for you," she continued, smiling up at her oldest son as he stumbled into the kitchen to grab the first glass of juice.

"What's for breakfast, Mom?" he asked as he kissed her perfunctorily on the cheek.

"Anything you want, Honey," she answered, wiping her hands on the apron he had given her for Mother's Day. WORLD'S GREATEST MOM was emblazoned on the front in big red letters. As Terry ran down the list of what he might want for breakfast, the youngest son, Joel, came ambling in.

"I want sausages," he announced, flipping the TV dial to a cartoon show and turning up the volume.

"Joel, please," Terry began, the sound of the juicer, combined with the loud voices of the Flintstones, too much for even her early morning ears.

"Come on, you're the world's greatest mom," Joel joked, kissing her on top of her small head and ruffling her shoulder-length auburn hair, which she kept cut in a stylish, but modest, do. "You can't complain about us," he laughed as his dad, Chuck, hurried into the kitchen, partially dressed in his gray suit, tie in hand, late as usual, hectic, as is an architect's wont.

"No, you certainly can't complain. What would we do without you, Honey?" Chuck smiled distractedly, waiting for his bacon and eggs, as he turned the station back to NBC. "Sorry I can't make it with you to the PTA meeting tonight, Terr. I have too much work to do today. We're starting a new shopping mall in Tarzana, and I need to meet the contractor."

"That's all right, Honey." Terry tried to hide her disappointment from showing in her sad, dark eyes. "I'll just run over there after work and be home in time to make your dinner."

"That's my girl," Chuck said, already picking up the paper to read the morning headlines.

"I'm everybody's girl," Terry thought as she fried eggs, made waffles, and considered what she would wear to her office today. She had to stop in Brentwood to check in on her new paralegal business, pick up more checks at the bank for her boss at the construction company, drop off Chuck's clothes to the cleaners, call her mom, send flowers to her girlfriend who had just had a hysterectomy, go to the PTA meeting at Santa Monica High, and be home in time to make dinner. It was a rough schedule, even for Superwoman. But Terry had plans. Challenging plans. Plans no one would ever believe she had concocted herself. Plans that would make her successful, without being successful. Secret plans that only she knew about.

The new girl Terry had hired in her offices was young, fresh, and just out of college. Her name was Nancy, and she would make an excellent paralegal for all the successful attorneys in Brentwood who handled their wealthy clients patronizingly and were more concerned with the way their secretaries and paralegals looked than with the quality of their work. "Everything is very image oriented around here," she had explained to Nancy on the first interview.

Terry had opened her offices only last fall, with encouragement from her family and friends who knew that she could do anything she wanted. The prospect of running her own business, and continuing to head up Dale McClintock's giant construction office had at first frightened Terry, but the

belief of everyone she cared about in her ability to do everything had buoyed her spirits, bringing a rosy blush of excitement to her normally sallow skin. The belief of everyone but
Dale, who was afraid that he would lose her, his buffer
against the world, his beard with those whom he cheated so
coldheartedly, day after miserly day.

Terry believed in being totally fair with her employees,
paying them what they were worth. In fact she was totally
fair with everyone in her life, especially her husband and
children. Sometimes she felt that her husband expected her
to do too much, take care of too many responsibilities. But
he had always been financially and emotionally supportive of
her and the boys. As supportive as a man could be. They had
never wanted for anything. Terry had all the material things,
all the clothes, kitchen appliances, cars, and jewelry she
ever asked for, or dreamed of. But she had reached a certain
point of boredom. She had gone back to school after twelve
years of marriage and added to her list of credits and her two
BA's the acquisition of a paralegal degree from UCLA. At
first working as the administrative assistant for Dale had
been enough. She liked the responsibility of running the
show, making sure that all the jobs came in under budget,
making sure the books were right. Hell, the only time Dale
even looked at the books was at the end of the month to
check the final bills. After she had mastered the job and
learned to juggle the roles of wife, mother, lover, cook,
chauffeur, tutor, gardener, maid, and daughter she had decided to open the business. Not for the money. Hardly. Between her and Chuck, they had all the money they ever
needed. But the business was a challenge. And she had con-
quered it. Her tiny paralegal company was going into its second year of operation, and it was thriving. Sometimes at
night in bed in Chuck's arms she laughed at just how much
money she really was making. Still in Chuck's arms, she suddenly thought. It was amazing that after seventeen years the
love between Terry and Chuck was so good, so sweet. He

was a wonderful man. But now she was facing a new challenge, one that ate at her constantly.

Terry's reverie was broken by the insistent ring of the private business telephone line.

"Hello," she answered in that round, melodious voice that seemed to fit with the rest of her: sweet face, docile mouth, trim, athletic body. "Yes, Daddy, how are you? Gee, I'm sorry to hear that. No, I'm not too busy to talk," she sighed into the receiver. After all, it was her duty to honor her mother and father; they had been terrific parents—supportive, positive, instilling in her and in her siblings a strong sense of Christian values. "Well, if Kelly can't decide what to do, why doesn't she ask her husband, I'd ask mine." She put her dad on hold to answer the other line.

"Saunders' Girls," she said switching her voice to a more authoritative, professional tone. "Yes she is here. I'll get her if you can hold for a moment, please, sir. Oh, Jack," she laughed in a tinkling soprano, "how are you? Good. I'm so glad it's working out."

"Linda," she called to the tall, dark girl sitting at the far desk, "it's Jack James from the law firm. Honey, you must be doing wonders there; they are very pleased."

"Hello again, Dad," she pushed back onto her father's line. "Yes, of course. Well, what about the school counselor? Kelly wants me? OK, I'll try to make time to talk to Kelly and Jim tomorrow night. Wait a minute, Dad, it's Joel's basketball night. OK, after the game . . . yes, no it's not too much. It's just that if Kelly is having trouble with her son . . . OK, I know she depends on me. I love you too, Dad. At ten. Send Mom my love."

Terry put the receiver back slowly. She had always kept everything together in the family. She had been the one to collect the money from her sisters and brothers at holiday times to buy the family presents. She had been the one to coach her brother in French. She had been the one her mother had depended on to push her brother Joseph into

med school. And now Kelly and Jim were having trouble
with their eldest boy; he was using drugs. Like every other
teenage boy from a wealthy home in Beverly Hills. It was
Chuck's opinion that because Kelly's husband, Jim, was
never home that much the boy just ran rampant. And Kelly
and her husband drank. A lot. It was beyond social drinking.
Everyone who walked into their home had to have a drink
first thing. Even if they didn't want one. As if that was the
acceptable social custom. And those kinds of needs didn't
escape children. Terry said a quick prayer to herself to thank
God that both of her boys were still so good, seemingly drug
and alcohol free. She and Chuck never argued in front of
them. Maybe it was unnatural, but she and Chuck hardly
ever argued at all. The phone rang again and Terry got up
quickly, grabbed her leather briefcase, applied more lipstick,
wiped the corners of her mouth for traces of her powdered
donut breakfast, and set off for her other job, running a large
construction firm in San Fernando Valley.

Dale McClintock was a large, handsome man who looked
like a much taller version of Alan Ladd. He had the kind of
detached blond, Viking smirk that women could not resist.
And he knew it. But he was a cold son of a bitch. The phone
was already ringing in the office as Terry rushed in from the
freeway, turned on the lights, and opened the large picture
window that looked out over a grove of olive trees. Tran-
quility. That was part of the reason Terry had liked working
in this office at first. There was a perfect view of the valley.
It made her feel secure and snug to see the rows of olive
trees withstanding the wind.

"Hello, McClintock Enterprises," she answered effi-
ciently, looking at her calendar, already checking her
Rolodex for the name and number of the flower company to
deliver a hospital bouquet. The sun streamed through the
window. The prism Terry had hung during her first week of
work reflected several large moving rainbows around the

room. She liked rainbows. She believed that there was a pot of gold for everyone to find somewhere in this world. Dale strode through the door as Terry was concluding her phone conversation with the cement contractor who had finished pouring several weeks ago. He was only waiting for his final check from Dale.

"Morning, Sweetie." He winked affectionately at her as she stood up to turn on the stereo and put up the coffee. "I like your new outfit," he complimented Terry on her new beige silk pants suit. "You look like one of the Gish sisters this morning." Terry was nonplussed by his compliments.

"That was Walter DeMain on the phone, Dale. We still owe him $3,500 for his last payment."

"I know, Sweetie. Let's put him off for a couple more weeks. He can live without the money." Dale fiddled with the tuning device on the stereo to find his favorite country music station and avoid eye contact with Terry.

"Dale, that's not the point. We have the money to pay him; let's do it so he will work for us again." She tried to be emphatic. It wasn't her company. It wasn't her money. But she had come to feel sorry for all the people Dale hired that he never fully paid off. He always found reasons not to pay them their final draw. It was unfair. And Terry, not Dale, had to deal with them.

"Look, Kid," he finished, using his most condescending tone of voice, "it's my problem, it's my business, I'll worry about it." And with that, Dale walked into his office and closed the door. Terry sat down and shook her head as Tammy Wynette came on the radio singing the old standard, "Stand By Your Man." In ten minutes Barbara, the busty bleached blond Loni Anderson lookalike secretary would be in to type, take Dale his coffee, and probably give him a quickie in the office. Terry took out the checkbooks. This was her domain. Walter deserved to be paid for a job well done. She made out a check for $3,500 from one of the business accounts that Dale never looked at and signed his name. She had been signing his name for two years. She could forge his signature perfectly, although she didn't consider it forgery.

Barbara came in wearing a low-cut red jumpsuit that revealed much of her silicone-enlarged breasts. Red wasn't her color. Terry said good morning and put Walter's check in a stamped envelope. It was the second check that month she had sent out without Dale's knowledge. The first was to a plumber whose wife had just had twins. Dale had only owed him $875, but the plumber needed the money. It was expensive to have children today. It was just not fair the way contractors ran their business. All profit. Very little auditing of books. As Terry mailed in her voter's registration renewal she wondered if her Chuck had ever conducted his business as illegally as Dale did his. Probably not. Although architects are not notoriously honest, Chuck was as law abiding as Terry. Dale, on the other hand, skimmed and took where he chose. And no one said anything about it. He contributed large amounts of cash to community charities. And no one asked questions. Dale was a man in great power and he knew it. Only little Terry Saunders realized how he cheated his subcontractors. And she was going to make sure his days of cheating honest people were over. She believed in the law and the American justice system. And she was its representative. She felt good in her heart about what she was doing.

Later on in court, when it was proved that Terry paid out over $100,000 to people McClintock owed money to before she took a dime for herself, she had tried to explain her reasoning to the judge who just couldn't fathom that such an upstanding woman, such a fine wife and mother, from such an upper-middle-class background, could have embezzled over $180,000. Terry testified in court that day, wearing the same beige silk pants suit and matching heels that she had worn that day in the office two years before. She had clutched a hand-embroidered handkerchief to her thin lips, and in her melodious voice, she had told the jury her rationalization for her crime.

"I'm on trial for stealing," she had begun, then pointed a finger at Dale, sitting in the courtroom, "but he's the biggest thief there is."

"Money and power put you up there on an ego trip," Terry told me in prison. She had served eleven months of a five-year sentence but would shortly be released, four years early, for good behavior. "I've always believed in a simple life, but money provides a nicer life. Money was not my motivation." She stopped to daintily eat a bite of apple. "I've learned a lot about myself through the crime. I had no background in it. I had no need for money. But the crime built my ego. I was at the point of boredom. The crime liberated me from my husband. Sometimes people do odd things to evade hurt, and in doing so they create more."

Terry sat in the prison interviewing room with her hands folded angelically in her lap. Unlike many of the other inmates she did not wear jeans to our interview, but a neat two-piece pants suit in loden green. Her nails were manicured, her makeup light, but perfect, her hair in place. She was tall and thin, athletic, Californian looking. Today, she works in the prison library to occupy her time. She is one of twenty college-educated women out of five hundred at the prison. In Terry's eyes there is a very determined expression. This is a woman who knows who she is, finally, and is not going to give it up.

Terry was thirty-six years old when she began the embezzling. She wore an aura of responsibility on her shoulders that mitigated any look or gesture of frivolity. She had grown up and lived according to all the proper rules. She had followed them step by step. Her parents raised her in a suburb of Los Angeles. Her father, a wiry, religious, beige man with clean fingernails, had a small drygoods business that, with years of attention and profits reinvested back into the business, flourished into the main department store of the community. Although not wealthy, Terry's family was very well off, and she and her brothers and sisters wanted for nothing and asked for little. As the eldest, Terry felt that everything was always dumped on her; but she handled this with equanimity, never complaining, going to church every Sunday with her parents, never raising her voice, becoming a cheerleader and church speaker, falling in love in her high school sophomore year, and after years of proper courtship and engagement, marrying the star basketball player who would eventually become a successful architect and provide very well for his family. Neither one was outstanding in looks, achievements, or intelligence. They were both superiorally average. They went to a small community college where Terry majored in business and accounting. She and Chuck never had sex until their engagement, and Terry was happy that they had waited so long, because it was worth it. She was not a prude in any way, and enjoyed lovemaking with her husband as much as any young woman does. It was just that she believed in playing by the rules, waiting for the right moment, not jumping into anything too quickly.

Chuck was a proud American husband and businessman. He apprenticed for five years in a major Los Angeles architectural firm before opening his own offices on Wilshire Boulevard. He built his business up slowly but methodically, culling his network of ever growing connections. The only thing Terry did quickly was have children, two in a row, two boys, John and Joel, to whom she devoted her life. She was an excellent mother. She stayed at home with her boys, did not believe in day care, and did not want anyone else to raise her children. Her home was immaculate, her floors shone, she was always smiling. She had a fairly large garden in the backyard of the first modest San Fernando Valley house where they lived. When they moved to the richer area of Santa Monica, and Chuck's business took them into a world of millionaires and Cadillacs, maids and Europe, yachts and Bill Blass, Terry moved easily among the women, sure of herself yet never part of them. She retained her own particular values. She never drank much, she hired only a part-time maid, she refused to spend over $300 on any outfit, and she never even thought to cheat on her husband. She continued to garden in her perfectly landscaped yard, growing her own fruit, and pickling her own vegetables and condiments. She adored being close to the ocean. She and Chuck took long walks every Sunday down the beach. Terry especially liked the feeling of community in Santa Monica. It reminded her of her hometown. Chuck was proud of Terry and their marriage. Her boys never got in trouble, did well in school, and seemed non-neurotic. Every Christmas she had the entire family over for dinner, cooking the turkey and goose herself, baking her own breads, having maybe one glass of wine too much. She never stepped over the line. She listened to everyone's problems, ostensibly the perfect mother, wife, daughter, and citizen. She always voted, she never broke the law, and she always paid her parking tickets right on time. The few that she got. Her bills were sent in punctually, her life was orderly. She went back to work only when she and Chuck decided that the boys' values were well formed and that it was no longer necessary for her to be home every day when they came in from school.

Dale McClintock was one of the most successful industrial contractors in San Fernando Valley, and that was saying something. At first Terry thought herself lucky to have landed such a cushy position. She hadn't worked in twelve years and her administrative skills had only been applied to running her home. Now her salary was high and the job seemed easy. Dale had been to their home for dinner only once, and it had been a great occasion. He had met Chuck through a mutual, residential development deal. Terry had cooked for several days, making Chuck's favorite Swedish food, and baking fresh peach pies. Dale had an easy way with people, especially women. Terry was not interested in Dale's charms; but when he mentioned that he needed someone intelligent, self-starting, and honest to run his giant offices, Terry was flattered when he suggested that if she ever went back to work, she consider the job. She did. And she loved it. So far so good. Everything was going according to plan. The boys were doing very well in school. John might even have a career in basketball, which pleased his father, whose college knee accident had changed the course of his life. Chuck was doing very well, his income over six figures. And Terry was ready to return to work. She was getting a wee bit tired of being so perfect, but she had done it, accepted the role for so long, that to change now would cause too much dissention in the home.

"My husband and I never argued, we always compromised. The boys never saw me cry. We never saw a problem that we couldn't work out together. In a way I wanted this crime to happen. I wanted to come off the pedestal. It was kind of like if Terry does anything wrong, everyone panicked. Maybe I did get the burden off my chest. My husband now looks at me realistically. I was always the pusher in my family with my sisters and brothers, I always kept everything together. Everything was dumped on me. I had to do all the planning. It's been beautiful not to have to do that anymore," Terry explained in our interview, her eyes finally peaceful.

Even today, Terry is not filled with guilt. She wanted to get caught. The crime was a natural part of her evolution. At first she tried to overlook the fact that Dale McClintock never paid the final draw to the people to whom he owed money. She saw how hard these people worked and how insensitive Dale was to their needs.

"It's just the business world and the way it works, Baby," he told her off-handedly. "Women can't possibly understand the way things operate in the big multimillion-dollar world," he caustically tossed off. "Go back to running the office and let me handle the bills." But Terry felt in some way responsible for the people who constantly called the office begging for their money and had to go through her to get to Dale. Not that they conducted their businesses any differently from Dale's, but that was not Terry's problem, or responsibility. Also, Terry never liked the way Dale talked to her; it was so blatantly condescending. As if she was just a dumb old broad who maybe should have stayed in the kitchen.

But the times, they are a changing. "I had a lot of anger at my boss. See, I had his trust. At first I started writing checks to people he owed money to and signing his name. After a while I saw I was getting away with it. The banks and the auditors, nobody caught what I was doing. It was a challenge; it got easier and easier. The amounts got larger and larger, and I couldn't stop. It was like a drug. . . ." Slowly Terry went from writing checks to pay off other people, to embezzling money for herself.

"I knew I would get caught, I always knew it was wrong. I shook for two days after I went to the bank. Many times I thought I'll go in and tell him, but I didn't." She couldn't. She felt as though she was caught up in a force larger than anything she had ever known.

The embezzling began to eat away at Terry. It was something hidden. Something she claimed her husband never knew about, the first thing she ever kept from him. What did she do with the money she didn't need? Her husband was doing very well. The paralegal business was flourishing. "I gave away a lot of money," she begins, trying to explain what happened to the $80,000 she apparently took for herself, "I spent it on other people. I traveled a little. In the grocery stores, I'd see these little old women scratching for change, fifty cents, and I'd lean over and be Miss Big Shit and give them $50, and have them stare at me in complete shock. It made me feel good."

But she does admit that at a certain point she got greedy. Something today she can't explain. "I say I saw what power did to my boss, it put him right up on an ego trip. Then it put me on one, too. It's more difficult for women now. They're no longer needed in the home. They have to work for a living, and it's not easy. With embezzlement I feel maybe women want that image, too, being successful without being successful. Women are no longer the little housewives with the shitty diapers. Women want to take over . . . rule the world. The future of women in crime is vast. Women's role has changed, women are not the same, we are career oriented, most only want good times, most won't put up with the hassles of life."

For two years Terry got away with her crime. She knew it would catch up with her; but from the way she tells it, she almost looked forward to that moment, that moment of liberation from the role of perfect mother, wife, and daughter. That moment of freedom, which would quickly be snatched away from her, that second when she could shout to the world, no, I am not superwoman, yes, I can get caught up in the ways of the world, in the ways of men, too. Terry was doing what she felt her boss and many businessmen had been doing for years and getting away with. But for her, she knew there would be an ending. "It was like falling asleep for two years and waking up in prison."

Terry today claims that she only told her husband that she had been embezzling the night she was arrested and out on bond. "He was a worry wart and I didn't want him to worry," she says protectively. When she envisioned getting caught, Terry never realized just how much of an effect the whole episode of the arrest of the wife of a prominent Los Angeles architect would have on the community and her family.

"The whole time I did it, I felt it would be me, not my family, who would suffer. But my husband has attended more depositions than me, because society couldn't believe that he didn't know anything about it. It was hard on my family in court. . . . After the initial two-week shock wave was over, no one knew how to act. My husband made the comment that he never knew how much he appreciated me, because now he's doing the things he should have been doing all along, attending PTA meetings, going to basketball games, boy scout meetings. Of course he was always working; so was I, but he would come home and his dinner would be on the table. He would read his newspaper, I didn't even realize it was happening until I had the time off in prison. It's really nice to have it all off me."

What does Terry miss the most in prison? She doesn't hesitate for a moment before she answers. "I miss freedom and my boys. I haven't really missed sex. I miss being hugged and loved up. I realize now that I took a lot of things for granted."

What is the future of her marriage to a man who for so long thought he had the perfect wife and mother, the perfect relationship, only to realize he had been fooled by the woman he had shared not only his bed and children with, but his dreams and hopes for the last twenty-two years? Terry momentarily lowers her voice. Her eyes cloud over. For one minute this is not all some kind of righteous punishment for the bad little girl who got caught and has had all the burdens, all the responsibilities and realities of life lifted off of her.

"I'm the one who's pushed for divorce. I thought I'd be here for a while, not knowing I'd get out early. My husband's been here every visiting week. I didn't know how I could go back and have that trust . . . maybe it's just in my mind that the trust will no longer be there. But when we're making love, how can he trust me? To me trust means a lot."

I must admit it is hard to accept this from Terry, knowing how she misused Dale McClintock's trust. "I'm pretty old fashioned in a way. There's that special thing between me and my husband, a lot of love . . . and my community. I've had so much communication with my community, and they don't treat me like I've done anything wrong." That remains to be seen. What happens when Terry returns to Santa Monica to try to get a job again, if she ever will? Will they accept her?

One of Terry's most interesting observations was about the justice system's treatment of women in crime, especially middle-class women. She never approved of the courts' heretofore paternalistic attitude in sentencing females. "Until recently, the system was very lenient on these women and now I'm one of them. I used to preach that some poor man went to prison for twenty years and the woman who committed the same crime got probation; not so much anymore."

The courts are treating women more stringently now, sentencing is harsher. In many ways, perhaps in ways they didn't anticipate, women are becoming equal to men.

Terry seems to have learned a lot about herself and her relationships since she's been incarcerated. Being locked up with five hundred other women has had a very therapeutic effect. Terry wets her dry lips and continues, no longer a self-righteous upper-middle-class model of feminine perfection; but someone, some woman, who has broken out of the mold, and now has to find a new identity, a new role. We both know how difficult it will be.

"When I first came to prison I was in awe. It was like a dream. In prison women can be closer because we have nothing to hide. We all know why we're here. We're more open in prison than I've ever seen on the outside. . . ." But Terry does not have much to do with the other prisoners. She stays fairly remote.

The rough part for Terry—as with most all of the women who had no history in crime, who were not career criminals, but supposedly just good girls gone momentarily haywire—will be how she will act on the outside How will she understand what went crazy, just for a second, what drove her over the edge, just for the moment? What sent her over to the other side? How will she live back in the normal world;

how will she break the patterns of a lifetime? This is where she needs help the most. Reentry into the earth's orbit is not easy.

THE CRIME—Grand larceny, embezzlement
THE SENTENCE—five years, but already out

CHAPTER II

THE OUTLAW

*"The difference between a criminal and an outlaw is that
criminals frequently are victims, outlaws never are . . .
outlaws, however, live beyond the law . . . beyond the
spirit of the law, beyond society . . . outlaws are the can
openers in the supermarket of life."*
TOM ROBBINS
Still Life with Woodpecker

ROSA WAS ALONE in her Miami motel room. It was cold for a
Christmas day in the tropics. There would be no turkey dinner with the family, no presents from Cristo, no elegant dinners at the club. The kind of present Rosa craved was
dangerous, perhaps worth dying for, if you took long enough
to think about it. She had already put on her black pants and
a striped silk shirt.

"Where the hell are my boots?" she screamed at the flashing Ramada Inn sign. She found them and lit a joint of Thai
weed to calm her nerves. It was time to call the others. She
checked her oversized doctor-style satchel for her tools:
hammer, screwdriver, flashlight, masking tape, and hand
towel. Then she dialed, inhaled deeply, and scrutinized herself in the mirror. No one would suspect what she really did.
Her clothes were expensive, her face refined. She looked
the part she needed to play.

"I'm ready," she announced into the phone, her normally
seductive voice taking on a very authoritative tone. "Don't

20

be scared. It's Christmas day. All of Miami will be quiet. Look man, I know the place like the back of my hand. I grew up there, for Christ's sake." She needed more than pot to calm her nerves now. "I said, I'll take care of everything, like usual. You just dress like a gardener and keep your mouth shut. Dig?"

Her motions became more rapid. She was ready to go. She quickly applied mascara, lipstick, and heavy foundation to her neck. She sprayed on her scent, Shalimar, threw everything into the satchel, and pulled on a pair of skin-tight racing gloves. She didn't even glance at the bags of still tagged clothes from Saks scattered across the floor. She opened the door, singing the lyric to a song that had brought her through the fear a hundred times before.

"It's all right, Ma, I'm only dying," Dylan wailed as a blast of thick Miami air hit her in the face.

She drove an anonymous car today; not her usual style, but one that no one would remember. She stopped on a small empty street in Little Haiti and loudly honked the horn.

"Damn!" she chastised the short dark man and the pale wide-eyed woman who climbed into the back seat of her car. Both were dressed in overalls. "You look like they just let you out of the bin."

"Yeah, and your hand is shaking," the man snapped back, unused to taking orders from a woman.

"You still can't drive." She laughed as she drowned out his answer with loud reggae music from one of the Third World stations she liked to listen to these days.

"Aren't you the cool bitch?" she thought as she approached the Rickenbacker Causeway and the road that led to Key Biscayne and assorted wealthy Miami suburbs. The startling Florida sunset was just beginning to spread its fingers over the ocean. And it seemed to Rosa that the rows of palm trees heralded her return to the wealthy suburb where she had first learned her craft.

Rosa drove down the familiar avenue. It was lined with giant tropical estates. She hadn't been on this particular street since she was a teenager.

"We ain't gonna hit one of these mansions, are we?" the man asked softly.

"Just relax and plan what you're gonna do with the money," she cut him off. She needed to concentrate now and let her intuition take over. So much of her success depended on her highly developed instinct on which house to hit. She settled on one that was very large, two stories high, with several Cadillacs in subtle colors parked out front.

"Nobody is home at Christmas." She remembered Donny's old lesson, which she recited like a catechism. "On holidays, people are with their families, at church, or at a party."

She brazenly parked her car in the circular driveway. It was getting fairly chilly. But the air was redolent with the scent of night-blooming jasmine. She grabbed a pair of hedge clippers and threw them at the man. She wondered if Nixon lived on this block as she walked to the front door as naturally as possible and knocked.

"Hello, are you home? It's just me."

There was no answer. The sun was setting quickly now in mauve jagged streaks as Rosa walked toward the rear of the mansion, her three-inch, black spike-heeled boots clicking against the ground like a rock'n'roll metronome beat. She checked the windows for telltale signs of an alarm system: thin silver tape running along the sill or the box itself. There was a second-story terrace beside a royal palm tree that she could scale if she had to. Then she tried the back door. It was unlocked. Biscayne hadn't changed. The people were still smug. They still felt safe from any harm. No intrusions here. No pain, no death, nothing ugly, no divorce, no problems. Just money.

Rosa was amazingly calm when she entered the house. This was her game, and she played it best. She immediately scoped out the set-up. It was quite expensive, worth about six or seven hundred thousand dollars. But it wasn't her style. The decor was too nouveau, upholstered, lots of crystal. No Bacarat or Steuben. There would be jewelry, perhaps furs. But no Russian sable. And no Renoirs.

In the dining room the silver was carefully arranged on the blond lowboy. It was an expensive set: the goblets, a dozen, were inlaid with the semiprecious stone malachite. She walked into the master bedroom on the first floor and removed one of the sham covers. Reentering the dining room, she filled the Bill Blass pillowcase with the entire silver set. Three minutes had passed.

Experience had taught her that jewelry was hidden in either of three places: under the carpet in the closet, in the lingerie drawer, or in with the bathroom towels. This bathroom was lit up like an exotic dancer's dressing room, with floor-to-ceiling light bulbs. The first drawer Rosa opened was filled with peach satin slips and a collection of tiny silk Chinese pouches in primary colors. On top of these lay at least thirty gold chains; herringbone, link, and braided. There was also a lot of beadwork woven with coral, lapis, and amethyst. The largest red pouch opened to reveal four complete sets of important pieces of jewelry: a diamond and gold necklace, ring, brooch, and earrings. There was also a set each of diamond and emerald, diamond and sapphire, and diamond and ruby. Not Cartier, but not bad.

Outside the man honked the horn. Not more than six minutes had passed. Rosa did not tolerate incompetence. He was not supposed to honk unless someone was coming. Her instinct told her that she was safe. But in her fury with her partners she became careless and removed one of her gloves to examine the emeralds. They were not museum quality like her mother's heirlooms. There were veins in these stones. Accidentally, she caught her reflection in the mirror. She saw an emaciated junkie, a tough street broad, an expert cat burglar, with hooded, dead eyes. She hated herself and turned away.

Outside the man honked again.

Rosa snarled. Her goddamn accomplices were too nervous. She didn't even have time to look for the furs. She grabbed the pillowcase, already three-quarters full of silver, and scooped a dozen of the Chinese pouches into it. The bathroom lights were hot. She wiped a rivulet of sweat from between her breasts. Then she walked to the front door and motioned the man to come in. As a rule, she never left the scene of a crime through the same door she entered. It was bad luck. The man held his clippers. The woman, her hair hidden beneath a truck driver's Big Cat Diesel hat, was watering the lawn. It was dark.

"Get the TV's," Rosa ordered. He obeyed. "And never honk the horn again unless it's an emergency, you idiot." The man ached to punch this cocky bitch in the mouth, but he didn't. Without her he probably would have been robbing a dime store in Blacktown, and he knew it.

Rosa checked out the living room. She had to make sure that she hadn't left anything. A tiny vase, illuminated by an overhead spotlight, caught her eye. It was antique, opalescent, and delicate. The colors blended into fantastic swirls of Scheherazade. It reminded her of her aunt's collection of Tiffany glass in Barcelona. She held it up to the light in her naked hand. It was worth money, but somehow it was more a sentimental attachment she felt for it. Just then the woman stuck her veiny neck through the door. "Let's get out of here. We've been here almost nine minutes."

Rosa controlled her fury. She did not like to be rushed. When she hurried, she made mistakes. The man grabbed the woman roughly by the wrist and pulled her out. Rosa put the vase down outside the front door. She walked in measured steps to the car. "Move," she barked at the man who had thought that perhaps he was going to drive. "This is my scene, my job, shut up. Don't say a word."

She pulled the car slowly out of the driveway. The muted street lights were not bright enough to identify her. Then she saw the long silver Lincoln Continental drive up toward the house. She recognized the drivers as the owners of the house. They were friends of the judge who had tried her last case. The wife looked like Helena Rubenstein. Rosa smiled at them, silencing her almost hysterical partners with her hand. She knew the couple's daughter. Her car was almost identical to the one Rosa was driving. The daughter rather looked like Rosa. Counting on their inebriation from the holiday festivities, Rosa waved to them. They waved back to her. It was one of those incredibly lucky breaks.

"I'm going to stash the stuff at your house," she told the slowly recovering partners as she drove along the causeway, the ocean moving like a black suspension net beneath her. "We can sell it off slowly. There's at least a hundred grand here. I have a guy in the Grove, Mafioso, who will fence the goblets for me tomorrow."

"I wanna come with you," the man whined.

"I'm not gonna rip you off. You couldn't get rid of the shit without me, face it. I've already done five jobs this week." She glanced in the rearview mirror. They weren't even listening to her. She would never work with them again. Now all she wanted to do was get high. It was a turn-on to be a woman, alone, in control. Getting over on everyone.

Rosa dropped the woman and most of the jewels off in Little Haiti. She and the man took the goblets and two of the most expensive sets of jewelry to a dealer in Overtown. She had been beaten up before, and was very careful now. A tall black man with a gold earring answered the heavily bolted door. "Hey, Chica, what you got for me tonight?"

Rosa then traded jewelry that would be worth, in a store, at least fifteen thousand dollars for four little bags of heroin plus $3,000 in cash.

She dropped her accomplice off and checked into the Holiday Inn. She had pocketed several credit cards from the robbery. Tomorrow she would spend her way through

Miami's most elegant boutiques in a style befitting Eva
Peron.

Alone in her motel room she took out her works. She
wiped the remaining foundation off her neck with a tissue.
She could only shoot up in the soft part of her neck now. All
her other veins had collapsed. At this point in her twenty-
five-year life, dope got her straight, not high. Without heroin, she had no energy. She found the little rolling vein in
her neck, held it between two fingers, and slid the needle
in. She remembered years ago when Christmas had been a
bright and happy time. When the family had been together
and her illusions had been intact.

She sang a line from a French Christmas carol her nanny
had taught her so many years ago in France. "I'm probably
the only trilingual cat burglar in all of Florida." She laughed
as the heroin hit.

She stumbled over to the bed, alone and lost. Not your
everyday citizen, but not your everyday cat burglar, either.

Rosa got busted for the Key Biscayne heist. It was the first
time she had ever left prints—her pinky impression on the
opalescent vase. The fence who took the silver goblets ratted
her out. Today she claims that she pulled over five hundred
burglaries, and was so efficient as a lady criminal that by the
age of twenty-four she had three part-time men working for
her and was earning at least $200,000 a year. She was one of
Miami's most successful criminals. She was the best in a
town that has come to be identified with not only Third
World leaders, cash and flash, but possibly the largest drug
trade in the world, the "Miami Vice" capital of the United
States. And the fantasy of "Miami Vice" pales in contrast to
the reality of the true crime scene there.

"There is a weird war going on inside me," Rosa explained
in our interview at a Southeastern maximum security prison
for women. "Half of me misses the lifestyle and the other
half of me realizes how really dangerous it is. Specifically in

Miami right now. And how dying is such an easy thing to
have happen to you in Miami today, especially if you're living the kind of lifestyle I did. And in that sense I don't like it
because it is very scary. I never used to lose sleep then;
now, if I lived with somebody like the men I lived with before, I don't think I would sleep. Cause there's the thought
of somebody coming to rip us off. And they just blow everybody away. It happens every day," the lovely redhead who
was one of Broward and Dade counties' most notorious criminals, reflected over her cigarette and weak prison coffee.

Rosa does not look like most of the other incarcerated
women. She is special to look at, slender, well-proportioned,
built. She has refined features, almond-shaped amber eyes
of great intelligence, a chiseled nose, a Spanish heritage
chin, short red Castilian hair, fresh, soft skin that belies the
fact that she has been an on-and-off junkie, and the impe-
rious tone of voice of the wealthy. She is trilingual, wanted
to be an archaeologist, is a vegetarian, has traveled around
the world, wears designer clothes like a socialite, reads compulsively, has the manners of a debutante, and considers
herself apart from the other prisoners. All in all, Rosa gives
the impression that she is from royalty, temporarily deposed
and mistakenly incarcerated.

Rosa's parents are from old and wealthy Spanish families.
Her father was a distinguished international banker and arbitrageur, and her mother comes from an ancient Castilian
dynasty that has controlled a number of businesses, including the fishing industry. It was a privileged life of Catholic
school, private tutors, and prayer. Suzanna often told Rosa
stories of the eager flat-faced fisherman who adored her
grandfather. Before the family lost most of its fortune in the
late 1970s.

Rosa's descent into crime began at a very early age, despite circumstances that promised to give her a life of wealth
and breeding. It is almost as if Rosa was born a natural outlaw, a modern-day fairy-tale princess with the heart of a ren-

egade and the soul of Belle Starr. Fifty years ago she would have been an aberration or have become a legend like Bonnie Parker. Today, she is something less than a legend, more a part of the alarming trend—the staggering rise of crime among middle-class American women, women who turn to crime out of choice, not necessity.

Rosa has lived all over the world and attended an exclusive girls' school in the United States. Yet, by age sixteen, this daughter of European aristocracy was scaling the walls of her neighbors' houses in black tights and gloves, creeping into their plush bedrooms to steal furs, jewels, paintings, and antiques: familiar accoutrements of the lifestyle she had come to reject.

She was arrested seventeen times. She was convicted four times. She has spent eight of her twenty-seven years in prison, serving in county, state, and federal institutions.

Today she is serving a four-and-a-half-year sentence for larceny and grand theft at a maximum security facility. How did this little princess with beauty, brains, and money end up as a career criminal?

Rosa's mother, Suzanna, had grown up thinking that every fish in the world swam past her family's estate beach. Suzanna was educated in England, Paris, and New York. "I went to school with several children of America's elite. We had governesses since we were born. They were English. The nannies were French."

Suzanna looks like visiting royalty, her gray hair is pulled back into a French knot and her arthritic hands are folded demurely in her lap. She conducts herself like Ingrid Bergman in *Anastasia*. But her edge is gone. The woman whom Rosa describes as once having spent her time collecting Louis XV and XVI antiques, going shopping, and getting her hair done has spent too many years of her life involved in her daughter's crimes, attorneys, and newspaper headlines. Her family is very discreet and detests publicity.

"We've always had this obsession not to come out in the newspapers. So the family hates Rosa because of what she did to our name, and they feel that she's destroyed my life."

Ignascio, Rosa's father, was Suzanna's only husband. He came from a middle-class family, considerably beneath his wife's, but he wielded influence. He was always friendly with those in power. As an international banker and arbitrageur specializing in international currency, he was often called to Europe and Asia overnight. For many years, his career kept the family residence in Scandinavia.

"Rosa had a divine life. She was the youngest child of Ignascio and myself. We had an older son who went to live in Jamaica with my brother at an early age. Rosa had a nanny who took her to the zoo, the park, and other wealthy children's parties. In the winter we skiied. Rosa was so determined to excel she skiied at age two, on special skiis made just for her." Suzanna took trips to Paris for couture shows. Rosa accompanied her. Life was a series of lunches, cocktail parties, and balls. There were fine wines, expensive antiques, and family heirlooms. Rosa was very close to her protective father.

In the early 1960s, Rosa's father decided to devote full time to currency arbitrage in the United States. He moved to Manhattan and dealt out of Wall Street and Fifth Avenue pockets of private investment wealth. But his income was temporarily cut in half. There were huge fights in the family because he no longer wanted to spend any of Suzanna's family fortune. Suzanna had many European friends in Manhattan who lived the life of the jet set. The family moved to a large apartment in midtown Manhattan, but it wasn't the Upper East Side and Suzanna was despondent that she couldn't give her daughter all the luxuries she had enjoyed. Rosa hated the arguments between her parents and began to resent the fact that she was being cheated of her rightful heritage. But her father was a proud and stubborn man who had to feel independent in his life.

"Mother couldn't deal with daily realities," Rosa explained in a slightly condescending voice in the freezing interview room at the prison. "Like how to fasten the twenty buttons on my school shoes. Women from her stratum of society weren't prepared." And Ignascio resented what he considered his wife's spoiled attitude. His world more and more revolved around men, figures, travel, and escape from his wife. But Rosa's life, at least on the outside, seemed very normal: roller skating, movies, and museums, where she learned to love art. It was here I learned to tell a Picasso from a fake, to recognize a pre-Columbian pen-and-ink drawing. Most thieves don't know a Woolworth diamond from a Cartier. I do." She and an older cousin from Suzanna's family who came to live with them from Spain attended one of New England's top five private girls' schools, where chaffeurs in limousines picked the children up, and lunches often consisted of caviar pie.

In 1968, at home for Thanksgiving vacation, Rosa overheard a conversation between her cousin and her mother that alluded to some sexual misconduct between her father and cousin. Rosa was shattered. Her father was her idol. She found a bottle of sleeping tablets in the medicine cabinet and swallowed them all. She was eleven.

Her parents separated, her cousin moved to France. Rosa tried to run away from home. It was 1968 and the city was exploding with be-ins, be here nows, gurus, good vibes, rock music, and a sense of brotherhood that made her think everything was going to be all right—no matter what. "Woodstock was a magical time. I don't think I have or will ever experience another era like it. A lot of people saw it as a sick time, full of drugs. But to me the true meaning was that you chose to be, to do, and to love anyone you wanted. I was brought up with such strict class restrictions. I was supposed to be a virgin when I got married. I just rebelled against the whole thing."

She searched for solace with the street people of Central Park. She was someone special to them: rich and important.

She wore a jewel in her navel and Indian saris. She took LSD. The East Village became the mecca for all she wanted out of life. But her parents felt that Rosa needed institutionalization. For almost three years she was sent to a series of chic treatment centers. At the institution in England they gave her mind-altering drugs. She remembers today, angrily pushing a strand of her close-cropt red hair back from her face in a leftover gesture of glamour. "Inside I was all messed up. I was too young to realize that there was any tomorrow. It was only when they cut my hair as punishment that my mother pulled me out."

Rosa never returned to school or any structured environment. She painted. She resented her mother, now being supported by her parents, for keeping Rosa away from her father. The father, for his part, got his young daughter a room at a hotel for women. Although she saw both parents daily for money, she lived alone.

She didn't believe in junkies, the Mafia, money, or bad vibes. She was a provocative-looking teenager with startling red hair and huge kohl-rimmed amber eyes. She had a voluptuous figure, slender ankles, and a tiny waist.

"I realized from an early age that men dug me, and I used that to my advantage. I always had someone to do something for me." This became her pattern.

In the mid-1970's, Rosa's mother decided to move to Florida. Rosa went along just for the summer. Suzanna found a lot of wealthy Europeans living in the Miami area. Especially people she knew from childhood in Catholic school. Rosa was fifteen when she moved. The Florida scene was just beginning to change from retirees and wealthy Republicans to drug dealers, South Americans, new money, and tinted car window transactions. Rosa was very impressionable. And she was a rebel. The high-class condominium where she moved with her mother had too many rules and regulations for her. She met a young man from a wealthy Fort Lauderdale family. His father and mother were both lawyers. His grandparents had beaucoup dollars. He had long hair and was the only freak for miles. She was too young to live with him, so they got married. No one knew that Donny was a junkie and cat burglar, preying on his rich neighbors.

Rosa learned the tricks of her trade from Donny and still maintains that he was the best. "He knew alarm systems, air conditioning ducts, splicing electronic equipment. We had both been raised around exquisite jewelry, and I taught him about antiques. He wore surgical gloves; he never got caught. We'd go riding on bicycles and walk on the seawalls which cross everyone's backyards and do whatever we wanted to those gorgeous houses."

Rosa's parents reunited in 1975, for reasons that have never been clear to her. But at long last she had a semblance of a normal family. Donny adored Rosa. He took care of her, brought her breakfast in bed, paid the bills, and sat around all day reading about his hero, Spiderman. Rosa finally permitted him to shoot her up with heroin. She needed to feel a part of something, someone, and totally share his life. She couldn't do that as long as he was stoned and she was straight.

"At the beginning, the robberies were only for kicks. I got pleasure out of the fact that I knew how to do it, get in there, perform like this, get out, and nobody knew. Part of me felt I was getting back at all those rich people who were so smug, living in those mansions, doing drugs and things that I was condemned for. I wanted to be like them in a way, the way I was raised, but I just couldn't anymore." The turning point for Rosa had come and gone.

Donny was finally arrested for holding up a supermarket. Rosa was left alone with a secret and no one to share it. She had a habit. She had never procured dope for herself. Donny had taken care of all that. Overtown, the black ghetto where the best smack was available, was dangerous. She was scared to death. "I wasn't ready to deal with what I didn't know I had turned into. So I started acting crazy, doing what all junkies do to support themselves—steal," she sadly remembers. "Finally it all became too much for me and I don't know how I did it, but I went cold turkey and kicked. I was lucky I hadn't been shooting that long a time."

She was looking for something to fill the void in her life when she ran into Cristo, an extremely successful Jewish-Cuban organized crime figure. Cristo was a notorious drug dealer who could afford to give Rosa that high gloss, fast rolling, to put it mildly, life of thrill that "Miami Vice" depicts.

"Cristo had bodyguards to protect us from other drug dealers. We lived all over Miami in different townhouses, moving constantly. For months we lived in a thousand-dollar-a-day suite at an exclusive retreat for Florida drug dealers. We'd get up around noon, go out for breakfast to some place like Marshall Majors. I had my own white Cadillac. He even bought me a plant store so I had something to do. Three hundred dollars a day play money was nothing. I had the best stashes of drugs. We'd go shopping every week in the Grove at the I Ching store for oriental rugs, like for ten thousand dollars. He bought me a lot of jewelry. I bought a lot of clothes. I accompanied him on his business trips to Colorado and the islands. It was the whole nine yards." And one can easily see how this little socialite fit right in with the lifestyle, thinking that she had been born to live this way.

Suzanna saw Rosa frequently during this period. "Cristo and Rosa threw money around like mad. They really lived it up. Anything she wanted, he got for her. Her white Cadillac had gold spokes on the wheels."

In a peculiar twist of corrupt morality, Cristo's people, some of the biggest cocaine dealers in the country, didn't accept anyone with a drug habit. So Rosa had to hide her dope in the folds of curtains and rub her track marks with aloe to heal them. "I always tried to take care of myself physically. I used expensive creams, and aloe will take away track

marks almost overnight. I had permanents, I went to the
beauty parlor every week for manicures, and I was always
real big on going out in the sun, swimming, and wearing
body makeup on any tracks that wouldn't disappear overnight. I loved to dress, cream colors, purples—I was really
into purple—spike heels. I was moving in circles where you
had to look good, whether to make money or just to be
there. Cristo was doing a lot of Quaaludes, so he didn't always notice what I was doing . . . and when you do dope,
after a while, you don't nod out. It turns into speed in your
system, or so it seems. If I didn't have it that's when I'd start
yawning; my eyes tear, getting bitchy as hell, and I wouldn't
want to do anything or go anywhere." It was a spectacular
but empty life Rosa chose to live.

"The lifestyle she moved in meant fast circles of drugs,
lots of money, and prostitution," recalls Rosa's federal probation officer today over the phone. And the element of death
was very pervasive.

"If I hadn't been using drugs, the older I got I would have
gotten into the power, doing it myself rather than just being
a girlfriend. I could be in jail today for a capital offense. I
could have ended up a high echelon dealer, which includes
killing people. And that's just part of the lifestyle, whether
you like it or not," Rosa defiantly declares.

Cristo was another man who took care of Rosa, but it
wasn't enough. She wanted her own. She returned to bur-
glarizing. Alone. "I didn't need the money. It was just a
thing to do. I had a hollow place in my heart. At this point
everyone I saw in power was a man, a dope dealer or whatever. The only time I had it together on my own and could
tell everyone to kiss my ass was when I was doing crimes.
Then I became powerful, just like the rest of them." She
pauses a moment, overwhelmed by pride in illegal acts she
forgets were purely destructive to her.

Rosa started pulling B and E's when she and Cristo were
breaking up. She was shooting dope so bad that Cristo's peo-

ple were pressuring him to get rid of her. Rosa decided to get even, to vent all her hostility on unknown victims, in the area where she and Cristo lived. "I was laying at home one day. Everybody, Cristo, body guards, connections, had left the house but me. This was in a real nice neighborhood in South Miami. And I was bored. I had taken a bunch of downs. When I woke up I was groggy and belligerent. So, I didn't have anything else to do, and I was mean, and I just said to myself I'm going next door. Now I was still with Cristo, he was still giving me a lot of pocket money, daily. So I could have had any amount of money that I needed. But instead I went next door, and I saw the backdoor was broken, and I could get in, and I cleaned them out. Jewelry, antiques, which they had a lot of. Normally I wore, if it was a daytime burglary, a three-piece suit, alligator shoes, a bag, a sophisticated hairdo, upswept, decked out, real dressed up. So I'd knock on the door, pick a huge house, whoever wasn't home, I would go around to the back. Now I could have been a realtor, a million things. No woman dressed up real nice is going to be looked at, no one is ever going to think, oh, there's a burglar, you better watch her. So, when I'd actually ascertain that no one was home, usually people are working, the maid is out, I would first check to see if any alarm system was in operation, if any windows were ajar, because if they were that meant the alarm system wouldn't work, I don't even know why most people buy them really. Rich people aren't very careful in their own neighborhood. So, I'd normally take in a pillow case with me, and clean them out. Not the first time I started up again, because I just walked next door, but normally I'd park my car, or the car I was using, right at the front door, and I'd wear gloves, so no one could ever find many prints, although they don't seem to find many prints anyhow." She coughed into her hand lightly, so polite, so mannerly, it was difficult to believe that this was a notorious and cold-blooded burglar. "And if I went at night, I usually wore dark colors and boots. I found I

could get around better in boots. Sometimes I had to scale a
tree, to get into an open window, but in Florida you usually
don't have to do that because most houses are one-story. But
I've scaled trees, roofs. So anyhow, on that first robbery by
myself, long after Donny was gone, I took all the jewelry
and antiques straight to my dope man. I gave a few chains
with diamonds on them to the taxi driver who took me
there. See," she pauses as if to record the dramatic effect
this will have on me, "I didn't need any money, I didn't
care, it was just a thing to do, I really got pleasure out of it.
Later on it was a business to me. I found it amusing. I mean
to the average mind I know it's not amusing," to put it
mildly, "but this is where my head is at. I won't be happy
working at Macy's from nine to five. So I have two pre-
rogatives, one I either do my thing with crime, which I can't
again because I can't face prison again, or I get into something that is so interesting or emotionally satisfying, which
the only thing I can think of now is drug counseling. Or, I've
even thought about working with insurance agencies, because, they came here one time to talk to me and I know
because of all the robberies I've pulled, when people get
robbed, a lot of them fake it for the insurance money, and I
can pretty much tell you what was taken out and what wasn't
by the time span, by how many criminals were supposed to
have perpetrated the crime. I know what's feasible and what
isn't. One lady said I took all of her silver in a five-minute
time span It's ridiculous, I couldn't have done that and have
taken everything else I took." Rosa gazed out the window at
the courtyard in the middle of the prison where all the inmates were taking an after-lunch break. It was chilly that
day, and many of the big, butch dikes with the stereotypic
short haircut and man's walk, their masculine work boots,
their men's pants and tee shirts with the sleeves rolled up to
put their packs of cigarettes into, were holding the hands of
their girlfriends, protecting them from the cold winter wind
with their bodies, and their fierce demeanors.

"I guess I felt I was getting back," Rosa began, unsolicited. "I had messed up my life to a point where all my family kept telling me I'd never be a member of society again. That I'd never be able to get married and wear a white dress, I'd always be what I had become. I'd never be accepted again. And all these schmucks living in these big houses who were probably doing the same thing, snorting coke, or whatever, they were the ones. I wanted to be like them, which is who I was raised to be, but I couldn't be anymore. I feel that maybe I was getting back. Because I got a thrill out of it. Yeah, and another thing, everybody that I ever saw in great power was a man, a dope dealer or whatever. And when I was living with a man I was dependent on him. So the only time I had my own standards is when I was robbing. And the women I've met that have become professional criminals, professional thieves, professional drug dealers, are ten times more cunning, ten times more cold-blooded, more capable, more dangerous than men, and believe it or not, they have more nuts as far as going and doing something. Because men think that because they're men that women are just something to be used sexually. So if you're an intelligent woman, you can use sex to your advantage. Because immediately you have control of that man, and if you know what you're doing in every way, including the burglaries, et cetera, you always have that over the men. It's a mystery to them. And women are not going to go out and blow it on another man or woman. A man will buy a woman trinkets, whatever she wants. I had cars, houses, wardrobes, traveled, and almost all the people who worked for me were men. You see a criminal, a business crime, embezzling, computer ripoffs, that's a whole other lifestyle, somebody you see every day. I was an outlaw, I lived like a man, on the outside." Rosa finished and continued to look outside the window. For a few minutes there was silence, and no eye contact, which she normally made immediately.

Rosa was very frank in our discussion about sex. She

looked so feminine, so alluring, sitting there in the large metal chair as we spoke that it was difficult to believe how far she had journeyed in her head, emotionally, spiritually, and physically.

"I was always bisexual," she began, examining the long nails on her right hand, "that was part of the fact that when I was coming up it was a normal thing to do for me and in my circle of friends. Yeah, it was part of the open-mindedness." Although I never experienced that in the open-minded life-style I lived. "I didn't really ever consider it gay or not. I like women's bodies, not better than men. I've never liked them better than men. But I like them. I realized when I was a kid, about twelve, that I was attracted to them. And I never bucked it, I just went along with it. I just kind of figured that I had the best of both and that I was the one who was normal. I still sort of feel that way. I'm comfortable with it. I know a lot of people aren't. I vehemently deny it with my mother. Only because I know it hurts her. To her it's real sick."

Cristo never considered the female lovers Rosa had as a threat. Usually she shared them with him, so it wasn't any big thing. "You've got to understand, this man wanted to marry me," she boldly announced, as if that was something to be really proud of, a Quaalude junkie, cocaine dealer, Mafioso type, who had lots of money, was not exactly what the private school she attended had in mind for her mate.

"He was completely in love with me. He occasionally fooled around with other women to hurt me, and then he would tell me and I would forgive him, and we would be all right. It was like mommy understood. And when we had another woman with us, after we were done with her, I'd tell her to leave. It wasn't emotional at all. Only one time did I get jealous of him." She begins to laugh. "See. I met this girl who had the shit beat out of her by her husband. Cristo and I were staying in the Grove, we had a suite there, and I was copping dope and I saw this girl, all beat up, she was sick, she didn't have any money to buy drugs, so I said I'll buy you some drugs and take you home and patch you up. I didn't do it sexually at the time, I just felt sorry for her. It was a big mistake, because when she realized where I was living, in the suite and all, it shocked her. I don't think she had ever seen that before. You know, the Mercedes, the whole thing. To go from the street, after being beaten up, to be in the jacuzzi, drinking Dom Perignon, handed dope. I mean, I would get paranoid if it were me. I told her, look, I'm taking you into my home, and I don't mind if we all go to bed together, but don't let me ever catch you fucking my old man behind my back, or we're through.

"And one day I came in and caught them, and I had a complete fit. But I got myself back together, and I said, OK, just make sure it doesn't happen again. I mean normally Cristo would have been upset that I brought someone up to live with us, but this time he liked it, probably because I said, don't worry we can both freak out with her. I conned him like that. As long as I could get high and do what I wanted, nothing bothered me. And she slept with us every night. So one night, remember she was not as pretty as me, she was just passable, one night he was supposed to pick me up at my mother's house and take me out for dinner, and he didn't. When he did arrive, he arrived with her, seems they had gone out to dinner. So I politely went in my room, got my gun—I kept a gun at my mother's house—met them at the front door and told her to get out of my life. My mother freaked out, the gun and all, and he freaked out, and I said, 'I know neither of you are going to try to take this gun out of my hand and be that crazy to try to get between this bitch and me.' I told her to get out of my face and walk to the end of the street and whore her way to wherever she had to go, which was how she would go anyways and that if I saw her again I was going to hurt her. I got jealous. That was the only time. Only because I saw she had a plan to move in on Cristo. I saw her again years later. She was a reborn Chris-

tian and she happened to come to see me in jail. And I said,
'I know you from somewhere, but I don't remember where.'
And then I remembered. She had a child, was remarried.
She looked good then, pretty even. You know that radiance
people have when they're real together. She prayed for me,
we prayed together, which I found amusing at the time."
Rosa uses the word amusing a lot, more than most of us do.
As if life is supposed to be amusing.

Today Rosa says that the total value of all the merchandise
she stole, gross, had to be in the millions of dollars. Sometimes outlaws have a tendency to romanticize their loot, but
burglarize and burglarize well, she did. She had several
rules she followed. She never robbed a friend. She figured
that if she ripped her family off that they would continue to
love her regardless. But if she found a good friend and she
messed with them, that person would be through with her.
She would never rob a black or Cuban's house. "I could tell
Cuban residences because of the way they have their knick-
knacks. Their papers are in Spanish, and they have meticulous gardens, with lots of flowers. They also have voodoo
candles."

But despite her rules her life fell apart after Cristo and
she split. She turned into a total desperado. "I liked the
whole Annie Oakley attitude, living as a desperado, running
with guns, the fastness. It was so completely different from
how I was raised. I never knew what I was going to do from
day to day," says the woman who spent her childhood with
nannies.

After Cristo, she started to use a lot of coke, along with
the heroin. One time, she embarrassedly admits, she even
attacked Cristo's aunt to get her jewelry.

Rosa served a year with several years probation. While
serving her sentence in Dade County jail, she met a girl who
liked her. They shared stories. When Rosa got out of prison,
the girl introduced her to some Cuban dealers, low class,

but dripping in gold and diamonds. "These were real cocaine cowboys, and because I was also Latin, they liked me. They used to pay me to transport guns and money. I got paid sometimes ten grand, sometimes a grand. If the goods were guns, I took them on a train. If it was money, I flew."

In 1980 Rosa met José, a stone-cold junkie, another Cuban drug dealer with skin the color of antique gold, who lived on a farm in Florida with his father and brothers, who headed up the gang of smugglers. Rosa embraced Santeria (Cuban magic), and the spirit life. They shot dope every day. "Heroin made me straight, not stoned at this point," she explained.

Rosa met José at a dope house, sort of a modern-day opium den, a shooting gallery, a place where you pay to go in and get shot up with dope. These homes are disgusting, filled with rats and people literally dying beside you. They are places where you share needles with strangers who carry diseases, and no one cares. José was definitely the love of Rosa's life, she gave up everything she was doing to be his girlfriend. His people practiced magic, Rosa's family totally disapproved. But Rosa began to embrace Santeria as her own. Santeria, originally a religion practiced in Africa, was brought to Cuba by emigrants. The basic difference between voodoo, which is from Haiti, and Santeria is that Santeria states that you can fight evil with goodness and win. Rosa's interpretation is twisted to suit her own purposes—as is much in her life. Since she was on drugs so often, her study of Santeria was superficial, drug-induced and incorrect. Many people who use drugs bend religion to their own purposes, trying to rationalize their crimes as the way of the gods.

"You see I believe that probably because I've studied a lot of anthropology and the religion of the Mexican Yacci Indians, and the American Indians, that it's all the same thing. I believe that there is as much a good force as there is an evil force and you can tap into any one you want. I did some of

the rites then, principally white magic, but through José I
met a lot of the people who practice both . . . and I had
some experiences. I'm shortly expecting some magical neck-
laces in here. I don't know if they'll let me have them or not,
but in any case José's people were really into that."

Compared to Cristo, José was a small-time dealer. He
sold maybe three kilos a month, which to Rosa was nothing.
If he made $75,000 a month, half would go to his father, who
was head of the gang, some would go into the two houses on
the compound they lived in, and a lot would be blown on
drugs. Rosa was now shooting goofballs, or speedballs, a
combination of cocaine and heroin. One night early on in the
relationship she ripped José off. She ripped him off because
they had an argument and Rosa felt like she wanted him
dead, but she wasn't going to kill him. She thought that because the kilo she stole from him was fronted to him by Colombians, that the Colombians would off him when they saw
he couldn't pay them. She took the kilo and split to Woodstock, New York, where she lived like a rock 'n' roll queen,
briefly, dealing the kilo off in ounces. Meanwhile, the Colombians found out that Rosa had stolen the dope and went
to José's house and tied him up, beat the shit out of him,
broke his arm and nose, and took all of his money. Rosa
came rushing back to finish José off, but when she saw him
she couldn't do it because she was still so in love with him.

"Thus began the four worst years of my life, because between his family not accepting me and my family not accepting him, we had to have our love on the run, which costs a
lot of money and is insane. We were drug dealing and meanwhile, doing more and more drugs." Rosa got up in the middle of that day's interview and began pacing back and forth
in proud little high steps, like a thoroughbred's dressage
walk. "We began free-basing. I used to wake up with a pipe
and a syringe, that's how I started my day. Then we started
doing burglaries, which he had never done and I had to
teach him." I wonder how Rosa could have robbed suc-

cessfully, junked out all the time, and as she prances about the room, she explained. "I do my best work on junk, because it makes you feel like you've got the nerve to do it."

Burglaries became a business for the couple. They'd go to sleep at six in the morning, because they had stayed up all night racing into Miami to cop dope. "Instead of having pieces of heroin, which makes sense, we would go out maybe ten times a night to score. I don't know why we got into that, going from the farm all the way back to Miami to see the goddamned niggers and buy dope, but we did. So we would either stay at motels, or at the farm, which was gorgeous. We lived in the house with his dad, who was rarely home. His brother lived in the other house. His dad," she stops to light a cigarette, a smile beginning on her lips at the thought of yet another man, "well, he was just a lady's man. He used to go out a lot. And leave town a lot, for business reasons. But he was down; he was cool. Anyhow, he finally accepted me. So José and I would get up at two or three in the afternoon, shoot up, and go do burglaries. The main areas we hit were Key Biscayne, South Miami, or Coconut Grove. At these times it was hard for me to keep my physical appearance totally together because I was so junked out; you can't go into a shooting gallery in white linen suits and emerge looking the same. And we went to these galleries every day because they were the only places we could get off fast. See, we used to leave the house, do the robbery, from the robbery go to our connections to sell, from there go to the shooting gallery and cop and get off. And then," she sat down, her legs suddenly still, her voice softer, "we'd go out and do it again. Because between the two of us $500 was one sitting of shooting." Then they would party for the whole night, or what they called partying, which was drinking, having sex, and shooting dope.

José was an extraordinary lover; even on drugs his endurance lasted forever. As a matter of fact, having sex several times a day was all that Rosa and José did, in between shooting drugs. And Rosa recalls that José and she became acclimated to the heroin. "For most men it's hard to come, let alone keep a hard on, on heroin; but not for José. I think after a while the heroin got into our system and it didn't affect us any more. Our sex life was the best of my life. He could make me come in several minutes . . . always. I was insatiable as far as José was concerned, I loved the ground he walked on. We even looked like brother and sister. I was so in love with him that it got to a point where I used to do everything. I didn't want him in any trouble. It was only in the last phases of our relationship that I started to turn him out, so to speak. I bought him three-piece suits and sent him into a bank with a huge check and explained how to cash it. He had never done anything like that. I had never seen him in a suit. He was a bum. He was a daddy's boy. The only thing he ever did when his father was alive was deal coke."

At a certain point in the recollection of Rosa's long history of incarceration even she becomes confused about when she went to prison, and for what. She has been incarcerated at various times for refusing to testify against a potential drug dealer, for perjury, and then, when she was living with José, for violation of parole, dirty urine. The Feds knew she wasn't living a clean life. She did six months on this charge, and the day she got out she shot dope at the airport. Her attorney, a public defender, tried to get her jobs, impressed as he was by her intelligence, and her family history. This was no ordinary junkie or thief. But Rosa couldn't handle the real world, she was too smashed on drugs, and she couldn't end her addiction to pulling robberies. While Rosa was gone, José had started ripping off his father's Colombian connections for drugs, kilos. When Rosa found him again he was literally covered with oozing sores, from all the coke, dope, and disgusting life he was living on the street. Rosa took him home immediately, patched him all up, and made body lotions and homemade poltices she concocted out of vitamin E and aloe, and got him back on his feet. In the meantime she was shooting drugs every day. Not as bad as before, but with consistency.

Rosa found José to be an excellent accomplice. She trained him, and he listened to what she said. For her, burglaries produced a big adrenaline rush, gave her a thrill, especially when she got home and examined all the articles she had stolen.

"I would take the objects out of the pillowcase I had put them in, and look through them, and feel good. They were mine now and nobody knew. It was a thing that I had done and got away with. And percentage-wise, I got away with a lot more than I ever got caught with. There was a sexual thrill for me, in a weird macho sense, like I was a big bitch. It was a power trip, sort of being on top, in control, something you usually see men doing and feeling. And then there was an arrogant attitude I got later, I used to have arguments with the men I was with, after I pulled a good robbery, because it was my show, and that's how it was going to go and we were going to do this and things were going to go my way, and they didn't want that. They wanted me, after the fact, to be cool and subservient, and behave and shut up. The only one I used to do that with was José. I'd shut up, sit in the corner, and let him buy the drugs, because I loved him; and if that's what he wanted to believe and if that's what he wanted to feel, that's what I would let him do. Most of the time." Rosa pauses for a moment, and then continues, "Men find women who pull crimes sexual, because they're untouchable in their minds, sort of like a cold woman is harder to get through to than one who is a nice little girl, and I think it turns them on that any woman holds her own, especially if she can handle herself as well or better than a man in a high stress situation."

Because so much of her young life has been lived in high stress, Rosa has turned to a religion outside of herself to give her solace. Today she embraces mysticism as a way of life she feels most comfortable with. She discovered the occult on one of her many forays outside of the country, to the Carribean to visit her older brother who has become completely absorbed in this—never returning to America.

"I'm more comfortable with that than with Catholicism, which is how I was raised. I think Roman Catholicism is total hypocrisy," this career criminal explained, "and I'm not a stiff person. So, after my experience with Santeria I embraced mysticism. I don't eat meat, I feel I have real values now. I'm not materialistic." Rosa's rebellion against her family's values, the lifestyle of the rich and famous, $25,000 coming-out parties, Rolls-Royces, anything materialistic was her way of justifying who she is and what she has become.

In the 1960s it was hip to be a seeker, a religious searcher looking for answers to the creation of the universe, who we are, why are we here. There was a proliferation of Eastern cults and gurus that many celebrities not only followed and made chic, but also supported and brought to this country. In Miami, then and today, there are so many Latins that Santeria has many temples and practitioners who not only perform private rituals, but pray and incant to save the souls of the drug dealers and other criminals who have found so much success. The *brujas* (witches) have been known to cut off chicken heads, drink the blood, beat the men with whips, make potions, cast spells, stick pins in dolls—to save their sons or cousins wanted by the law. To no avail. The Drug Enforcement Agency doesn't recognize voodoo.

José was one such follower, and because Rosa found her identification through men she embraced anything he believed in. Almost as if she couldn't hope for any love or protection from her church, or her people who had borne her, misunderstood her, tried their best, watched her rebel, and finally rejected her and her self-destructive ways that had eventually destroyed them. So Rosa checked into other venues, other possible places to find love.

By the time Rosa finally got busted for her Key Biscayne heist, things had become even more bizarre in her life. She was no longer able to shoot herself up in any place other than her neck or under her tongue because she couldn't find any veins that weren't totally collapsed from the constant barrage of dope.

"I couldn't get myself off so I had a sissy who was the only one I'd let hit me. She was really a guy dressed as a girl, with nails out to here, but I never met a better hitter in my life. I used to pay the shooting gallery to let her go, and pay her to stay with me for the afternoon, and then after she got me off I would paint her nails, it was sick in a fun weird way," (I notice that weird is another one of Rosa's operative words about her life,) "and I'd buy her jogging suits, velveteen ones. His arm was half rotting off, but he never missed. He had a lot of patience actually. José and I offered to take him home with us and get him out of that disgusting place, but he wouldn't go, he said he wanted to die there."

But the effect of shooting speedballs, the combination of cocaine and heroin, was making Rosa highly psychotic. You might have put her in a straitjacket if you hadn't known that she was a coke fiend. She was hiding under chairs, under beds. And she was beginning to think that she was insane. Rosa could not give up shooting. She tried to capture nostalgically that feeling of dope, "If there's anything that can make you feel completely good, shooting drugs would have to be it. I mean completely good where your whole body from your toes to your scalp feels great and your cares have disappeared into thin air. I've come shooting up. I've literally had orgasms where suddenly from feeling really good all over I felt a rush in my pussy that was an orgasm. The feeling is the best."

But the feeling wasn't enough to sustain coherency or maintain sanity. Rosa quickly lost both. Her work was becoming sloppy, and finally she got busted, in a very dramatic way, in front of a large pink deco home in Fort Lauderdale by five cops who had been looking for her for two years. They surrounded the car, and Rosa ran. They threatened to shoot her if she didn't stop, and she didn't; so they beat the shit out of her, as she was slipping out of her clothes, running, and when they finally nailed her she was naked in the searchlights, with a ruptured, pussy abscess from a bad shot on her leg; and José was crying, and her career was over. Rosa made a deal with the police. She gave them the MO's of eight unsolved burglaries in trade for a lesser sentence. She asked two things in return: that José not be called as a co-defendant, and that she not be tried as a career criminal.

Rosa's release date is early 1988. She finds prison life intolerable. The austerity, the regulation garb, and her job as one of the many prison maintenance workers, which entails scrubbing, cleaning, and mopping, is hardly what this little outlaw had in mind for herself.

"The only reason I'm not ripped off every day or intimidated is because I did hang out in the streets before I hit prison. I know how to do my time." Doing time means making life bearable by not thinking about the outside or "free" world and minding your own business. Mostly life behind bars revolves around the mundane: cigarettes, coffee, letters. Rosa reads a good deal: biographies, history, and anything that has to do with Indian culture. She has been off drugs for almost two years, so she tells me.

There is much speculation on the outside about how many female inmates in this country are lesbians. Few of the inmates I interviewed admitted to being bisexual, let alone lesbian. But they all talk about the degree of what they call "homosexing" in the prison. Rosa was the first one to talk about her true sexuality. For her, part of the looseness of the whole Woodstock, sixties, drug-dealer scenario was sexual, and she found herself at a very early age attracted to women, as well as men. I often wondered why she was one of the only ones to openly admit her bisexuality. Perhaps there still exists a double standard even among criminals: you can talk about your crimes, your time, but not who you do. Almost as if they are embarrassed by the stark facts of their libido.

Rosa has had several girlfriends in prison, although it is against all the rules to be caught in the sex act with another inmate. But it happens all the time. She maintains that the women she's with are only temporary substitutes for the real thing until she gets out on the street again and can find a suitable man. Until then, it's stolen kisses by the water heater, the thrill of getting caught adding to the whole stimulation of prison sex. The forbidden. Breaking the rules. And the sex game in prison is big bucks.

"The majority of the women in here aren't really either bi or gay, it's a game they play to get money. The stud, usually a big black, scares the little white girlfriend into giving her bucks to protect her. Only one in a thousand is really bi. And on visiting days you see all these supposed big butch studs holding hands with their husbands and kids. It's just a game," Rosa explains, "a game to get the scared white girl's money."

Rosa cannot forever blame her family and their problems for the ruination of her life. Her father's money was all spent years ago, and her mother, Suzanna, lives in a small house, on a fixed income. Most of her heirlooms were either stolen by Rosa or sold to pay for attorneys' fees. Rosa cannot return to life with José because she has found out that he has become a male prostitute on the streets of Miami, and her fear of contracting AIDS would prevent her from sleeping with a bisexual junkie. What is she to do?

There are important reasons why Rosa can't come home. The lure of fast life and easy money, the profound South Florida corruption and contradictions are too familiar, too easy to fall back on. The romantic dream of being an outlaw too enticing.

"I think that rebelliousness is in my blood, I've never been an average person, and being an outlaw was something I just naturally was. I feel if I really asserted myself and studied archeology I would be one of the best, because I have the capability and intelligence to do it. Now why would

I want to go and get into this life of crime? Well, I liked living like a desperado, running with guns, and the fastness was so completely different from the way I was raised. Outlaws don't have to dress a certain way, they don't have to talk a certain way, they aren't pretentious like the people I was raised with. And with criminals I was someone special. There's not many female cat burglars, there's really not. There's not many women who have the nerve to do what I do, not even in the circle of delinquents I lived with." I wonder if Rosa will ever be straight.

Rosa is emblematic of the new breed of women who are becoming accomplished criminals. "Women are getting more and more to believe that they can do whatever they want to. They're waking up to the fact that they are as good or better than men. And a lot of women who have been messed up or hurt by men get an attitude, and that attitude is cold blooded, and we can use that to our advantage with men and in crime. A woman can make it in this world regardless. Women can use men, put them on front street and have them do things that are essentially too dangerous for us to do." Women don't need men to help them anymore, specifically in crime, they have come into their own, and they can get over on men in power.

The only deterrent to Rosa's returning to a total life in crime will be concrete work that offers some thrill, some excitement, but is legal. Work like the rest of us do. And acceptance that life is the combination of the little day-to-day incidents—it is not always exciting. She has considered working with insurance adjusters, doing drug rehab, but can she face reality?

"I definitely don't see my life as ending now. In this day and age I won't be an outcast forever. My immediate family won't forgive me, but I've forgiven myself. I faced who I was, a slimy, dealing junkie, common thief. But the way the world is now, the way women are, I still have a chance to be somebody," she hopefully concludes.

"She is a very bright girl," her former probation officer told me over the phone. But that is obviously not enough. Most of the women I interviewed were bright women, women who had opportunities to do many things with their lives.

Rosa still has the dream of the rich little princess. "You know, I have a fantasy that a really nice man will come along. He won't be a junkie or an outlaw, he'll be interesting, and he will love me and I'll love him and he'll take care of me forever."

THE CRIME—Grand larceny, grand theft (this time)
THE SENTENCE—Five years

CHAPTER III

MONEY ADDICTION

"I am addicted to money. I am a moneyaholic. I am sick
when it concerns other people's money. Money represents
power, it represents good feelings, it represents reward for
a job well done. Money represents the love that I never had
from parents who were never for me. I was never good
enough for them. I was always the bad girl. Then I just
became a law-abiding person who has a big problem. I am
a moneyaholic."

DEBBIE
Women's Prison, New England
November 16, 1985

SUPPOSEDLY, MONEY CAN'T buy you love. Supposedly, the
best things in life are free. The rich don't live differently
than we do—they just have more money. When you're
really in love, money is irrelevant. People love you for who
you are, not what you have. Money is merely green paper
with words—it won't get you into heaven, or prevent your
descent into hell. Living in the material world is a dilemma.
Just ask any material girl.

But money is who you are. You are the car you drive, the
house you live in, the clothes you wear. In the 1980s, we
even wear clothes with other people's names on them.
Money is complex—you have credit, credit cards, interest
on credit, penalties on the interest on the credit, money
funds, money markets, money lenders, and money counter-
feiters.

When you are a little girl growing up in a middle-class family, money is not usually an issue you discuss. Daddy has money, mommie has access, and you reap the benefits. You get an allowance, you can ask for toys, like radios, computers, horses, vacations. If your parents do withhold money from you, it is usually as a form of punishment. Really, today we never even see a dime of what we make in cash—it goes out to everyone in payments, from our checking account. And we really don't think about it. Unless we don't have it. And then money is everything. But to live broke in this country in the 1980s is to be condemned to a life of wanting—and not having. You can become addicted to the feeling of acquiring money, like taking drugs, or drinking alcohol, or having sex. The money rush gives you a similar and momentary security.

The New England prison for women where Debbie is incarcerated looks pre-Revolutionary, truly American. The structure itself is almost patriotic. It gave me a very eerie feeling as I approached it driving in my rental car along the icy mountainous road. A deserted nineteenth-century cotton mill, the prison sits high atop a snow-capped hill. It was late November when I arrived to do my interviews. Most women's prisons are remote, set apart from society because so-called normal citizens don't want to deal with a prison in their midst. The further away from the community a prison is set, the less likely a prisoner is to escape, and the less likely it is for an escapee to enter someone's home.

The entranceway to this prison is slippery, the large, metal doors frigid to the touch. It is a forbidding Gothic picture, with turrets and winding stairwells, painted a nondescript beige. While the guards checked my tape recorder and purse for contraband or forbidden implements, John Cougar Mellencamp sang on the waiting room radio about America and the plight of the farmers. America seemed distant that day, in the isolated world of guards, officials, inmates, and rules so complex I could barely follow them.

Deborah came to the interview wearing a light jumper of navy wool jersey, a pale yellow turtleneck, no socks, and sandals. I wondered why her legs weren't cold. I was wearing two pair of socks and boots. Perhaps it was because the heat in the prison is steamy when it is on, rising in vaporous mist from the pipes. But in the office where I conducted interviews, the cold lurked in the corners of the dank room like a bad memory. Debbie is large—at least five-ten; her frame is massive, gone to fat. Somewhere in the folds of her double, triple chin, I discern a startling face. Quick, observant gold-flecked green eyes. Beautiful long thick blond hair that she has set in antique combs. Her legs are so heavy that they touch at every juncture, knees, thighs, calves. Prison food is for the most part starchy. Maybe that explains her gross form. But Debbie was quick to tell me that she always had a problem with her weight.

"I remember stealing cookies when I was only four years old. My mother started calling me fat when I was eleven. I had a pot belly. I think if she'd left me alone it would have gone away. But I ate. Mother never held me very much . . . and to this day I'm still bothered when women touch me, because I don't know how to handle it. I was never hugged. To me it was normal to grow up that way. I just figured all my life that I was the bad nasty little kid and it was my fault," she explained as she unconsciously rocked back and forth in the chair, using the kind of rocking movement that mothers do to comfort a young baby, or that mentally disturbed people do when they are taking heavy medication.

Debbie was convicted by a New England court, of eight counts of larceny over $100, scheming or plotting to commit a scheme, one count, and one count of bank embezzlement for a bank employee. Basically, what she did was embezzle almost $250,000 of parking meter money from a wealthy

Connecticut town. This was her second offense. She readily admits her guilt. She will serve two years for each nine counts, but she will serve them concurrently. Restitution is being worked out by the courts.

Debbie is thirty-six years old and was reared by upper-middle-class parents in a wealthy Connecticut town. Her parents followed the usual prescribed route of the young executive couple on the rise. They made good money and the family went to church every Sunday; they were Presbyterian, New England's finest. Debbie's father is a nuclear physicist. He worked over the years for Westinghouse on guidance systems, on the NASA space program, and for a private, satellite manufacturing company. Today he works for the government at a top secret job, and is periodically investigated for secrecy clearance by the FBI. Debbie's mother has a degree in psychology but never worked full time. The couple had two daughters and two sons. Three went on to college, but Debbie did not. Education was a major issue in the household, and Deborah, being the eldest, was expected to set the example. But she had other priorities. Like emotionally surviving.

Debbie's mother got up very early every morning to make the family breakfast before they went to work and school. The large six-bedroom house was located on an acre and a half of land with a pond. It was furnished eclectically. There were pretty antiques from one grandmother, predominantly art deco pieces, mixed with some outstanding colonial furniture, like a Federal desk, and a long mahogany dining room table. The family kitchen was huge and included a pantry where breakfast and most other meals were eaten. But there was not a lot of light in this house. The rooms were painted muted colors, and heavy vermilion velvet drapes hung to the floor covering most of the windows. This dark, large house was the daytime domain of Debbie's mother, who padded barefoot from room to room, alone, every day.

"I guess in the beginning all she did was just take care of

us kids, and now that I'm a mother I can see how with four children she had to put a lot of energy into just keeping us out of trouble. I remember her looking very plain then. She usually dressed in a mu-mu although God knows she had a lot of clothes, and nice, conservative jewelry to wear, like circle pins, and pearls. But she was only about five-four," Debbie recalls. Debbie seems gigantic, her legs the size of two thin women.

"My mother had a simple, almost peasant face, coarse skin. She may have been pretty when she was young, but I never knew her as pretty; she was just my mother." Debbie's mother is barred from visiting or writing letters or communicating in any way with her daughter in prison.

Every afternoon Debbie returned home after school, dropped off by the bus, to find her mother collapsed on the chintz-covered sofa watching soap operas, sometimes asleep. Not so different from millions of other American families. Except that Debbie's mother was abusive. Debbie had to be home precisely twenty minutes after the school bell rang, or she would be punished. She was made to sit at the kitchen table until her homework was done or supper came—whichever was first. Debbie started to do the opposite of what her mother wanted her to do.

"I remember one time I had an accident in my underwear. It wasn't on purpose. But she rubbed it in my face and ever since that day, for the next five years, I would hold my bowel movements until they were so big that the body made me have them. My mother could not understand why. I was seven years old and I would hold them until they were so big that they would plug up the toilet. I was limited to the downstairs bathroom because I would damage the plumbing upstairs. She would feed me raisin bran every morning for breakfast, and more prunes than you can imagine, trying to make me go. And the more she tried to make me, the more I held it in." The story is sickeningly accurate. Debbie combs one side of her hair over and over with her antique hair comb as she recalls each detail.

The neighborhood kids at first tried to play with Debbie and her brothers and sisters, but they finally stopped coming around, and Debbie believes it was because they were afraid of her mother. She had to go to friends' houses to play. And she never went to one slumber party. She became deathly quiet in school. She would sit in a corner and fantasize, daydream about horses and nature, tall oak trees and formal English rose gardens. The images she conjured up were of peaceful scenarios; reality was not the stuff dreams were made of for this child.

Debbie's eyes fill with tears, not of sadness but of anger and pain, when she discusses her mother. The assistant warden, a quiet, demure, but very assertive woman with close-cropped dishwater blond hair, tiptoes into our room to get a paper, and tiptoes out, almost in deference to Debbie's emotions.

"I think my father loved me because I was his oldest daughter. I think he favored me. But there was jealousy. My mother is a very jealous woman." She extracts a piece of crumpled Kleenex from one of the many pockets of her jumper to wipe her eyes.

"She alienated my father from his brother, she alienated my father from most of his family because she was jealous. She alienated my father from me. She would go out of her way to do things to show me that she could do it better than I and eventually she would arrange things so that I would fall into the trap unknowingly. She didn't want my father to like me too much." Debbie now sobs, rocking back and forth in her chair, faster and faster.

Debbie's mother's plan to turn her husband against his daughter worked. Debbie is not sure exactly when her beatings began, whether they coincided with her father's job problems, when he became an alcoholic, or whether he had beaten her from an early age.

"My father took a wooden bed slat to me because I stole a fifty-cent magazine and then when I ran away from home he beat me again. He took everything I owned except clothing and bedding and threw it into a box and took it outside and burned it. He got mad at me one night at the dinner table and hit me with the carving knife. I was fourteen when that happened. He broke my arm twice. You can see where the bone stuck through." She pulled down her jersey to show me.

"It's a long tale of abuse. Emotional abuse is hard to prove. But I was constantly put down. I was never good enough. And it got to a point in my school work where I just gave up. Why bother to bust your butt for a C, which you worked very hard for legitimately, when your father would turn around and say, but you didn't get an A. My brother bore the brunt of the abuse. He had it the worst. He was an epileptic; my parents didn't know about that. He would have a petit mal seizure, usually at the dinner table when the tension was at its highest, and one day my father said, 'I've had enough of you trying to get attention like that at the table,' dragged him upstairs, mid-seizure, and beat him. The next week he had a seizure in school; they took him to the hospital and that's when they found out he had juvenile epilepsy." Debbie's memories are so extreme that they sound unreal. Can I believe everything she says?

One gray rainy day Debbie sneaked out of the house, and from the window saw her parents sitting on the bottle-green velvet love seat in the den. Her mother was crying, and her father said something about not having enough money, and being afraid in the high tech shake-up that took place in the aerospace program in the mid-1960s that he was going to lose his job. "During that period, when I was fourteen, the beatings became the most severe. And the alcoholism accelerated," she admits. Although children never really are sure of the details of their parents' intimate life, Debbie feels that her parents' sex life was quite active until the 1960s, and the advent of her father's job depression and temporary dive into alcoholism.

"One summer we knew that my father had committed adultery. It was like 1965. He broke my mother's nose and beat her a lot. My mother was not an alcoholic, but she lied a lot and she emotionally tormented me because she was being tormented by my father. We were at the family vacation home on the shore, and my sister told me that my father and Mrs. Jones were kissing in the kitchen. The Joneses were part of my parents' group that came every summer to vacation, and they all went out on the weekends. One night Mr. and Mrs. Jones left the usual Friday night party and went home and the next morning Mrs. Jones woke up a widow. Her husband had had a heart attack. It was very upsetting for the whole community that year. Then the next year my parents had marital troubles, he had trouble with the job, the alcoholism. It all seemed to come to a head."

Debbie fell into the role of the bad girl. She didn't get any feedback other than criticism, whether she did her best or not. She began to feel she was a rotten child. The role of the bad girl became a self-fulfilling prophecy. "At least I got some feedback when I acted bad. I got hit. At least they were touching me." She nervously picks at the hem of her dress. "When I was good they would say, 'Oh, that's nice,' and give very little superficial praise. Children are very perceptive and open to the ring of falseness in their parents' voice. I could feel the sort of labored effort it took them to praise me. But when I was bad I got instant reaction," she realized suddenly in the midst of the interview, as if she has never had this thought before. To watch her internalize this realization is too personal. I feel that I should leave the room.

Debbie retreated to a very private world of fantasy, dogs, and horses. "From the age of five on I loved animals. When

I was five years old I was in Bennington, Vermont, and I saw a pony drawing a vegetable cart; the man would go up and down the street selling vegetables. And I begged the man to let me get up on the horse, and my mother said it was OK, so I got to sit on the horse, and from that day on I loved them. When I was six years old I drew my first comic strip— I still have that copy book, and it was an anatomically correct horse. I am very artistic. I was an art major all through high school."

Debbie also had adolescent fantasies about Dr. Kildare. She would sneak out of bed at night, go down to the den, turn on the TV, and watch Richard Chamberlain, her secret boyfriend. Animals and doctors were her dreams. Doctors helped people and animals couldn't hurt her. These were her escapes from the horror of a childhood that she still to this day cannot make sense of, even with years of therapy.

Although her parents' peers probably did not guess that their friends beat their daughter, Debbie claims that the people in her New England school knew.

"The gym teacher made me take a shower after my classmates left because she didn't want the other children to be dismayed by the sight of my body. We were in this community-type shower situation where we all went in and took showers together. The bruises on my body were so bad, some of them the size of at least two hands put together, that the gym teacher didn't want the kids to see those black spots all over my body."

So Debbie lived alone with her beatings, and her fears, like most of the millions of abused children do in this country, whether their parents are middle, upper, or lower class. She began to feel she was a victim. She was rotten. She deserved to be punished. She shoplifted a lipstick from Woolworth when she was eleven. She didn't get caught. She stole some candy. No one found out. She did the opposite of what her mother wanted her to do. Hoping for some feedback. Which was meted out by her father. She became rebellious in school—controversial to be provocative. Her teachers treated her like a bad girl. And Debbie's parents would always agree with the one who was criticizing their daughter. They were always on the teachers' side. Her parents never said, "Doesn't Deborah read well? Doesn't she try hard? Doesn't she deserve more?" So, by rebelling, Debbie got all the attention, however negative, that she never got being a good girl.

"At this point I didn't care anymore. I was tired of being hurt. I didn't understand what was going on, I couldn't get any good out of it. And in my little heart, I felt that I deserved it," she quietly concludes.

Debbie was not allowed to date until she was sixteen, and then she was only permitted to go to church functions. She had no real friends, no one to turn to, but food. So she ate. And ate. And ate. Food made her feel good. Safe. Secure. She could hide in her layers of fat from the world. From her parents. From rejection. From herself. By gaining all this weight, Debbie could become invisible—she could disappear; no one would be able to recognize her in the massive distorted body that she was temporarily using. The hittings and beatings would not be able to touch her. Her essence.

Money became a major tool her parents used against her. She was given a dime allowance a week, in the permissive 1960s, until she became a junior in high school. Then they raised it to fifty cents a week. Enough to buy two bags of M&M's and a Clark Bar once a week. Her father was a miser of sorts. Not exactly Scrooge but very similar. His children never got anything close to what they wanted for Christmas, and confessing that they wanted anything at all was tantamount to an admission of weakness. In her last two years of high school, Debbie's parents decided it was time she learned how to buy her own clothes for high school. They told her she had to do that for herself. They didn't show her how she would be able to afford thick down coats and woolen scarves for the Connecticut winter on fifty cents a week, but they wanted her to learn to budget on what little she had. They wanted her to be self-sufficient. But Debbie had to wear last year's clothes. She couldn't afford to buy anything on her allowance. As she grew to her present height, her knees stuck out of her ill-fitting coat.

Debbie angrily recollects, "My parents took pride in that we could survive by ourselves, but they darned near killed us doing it." At this point in her life money became an issue of survival. There was money all around her, her parents' large house, their summer cottage that only the well-to-do could afford, their two cars, her mother's jewelry, her pearls, her father's miniature airplane collection that he worked on so carefully night after night, weekend after weekend, when he should have been playing football with his sons or reading to his daughters. Their booze bill alone could have bought Debbie and all of her siblings clothes for the next three years. But money was withheld. Like love. Like Debbie's bowel movements. And over the years money was to become the addiction of her life—greater than food— greater than any obsession we could possibly imagine.

By the late 1960s, Debbie's father's industry had recovered from its mini depression. He was making very good, if not excellent, money. In fact, he was extremely well off. Well off enough so that he could afford to put all four of his children through college without feeling the pinch. But in her senior year of high school, Debbie decided not to go to college. She had spent thirteen years of torture, and she was miserable.

"My parents were upset about this," she told me in the now very warm assistant warden's office as one of the prison trustees imperiously announced the noon head count. Debbie and I ignored her. Outside snow was falling in a white thick fury. I was still cold. Debbie was talking nonstop, taking off layer after layer of wool clothing she wore under her thin sweater. She emitted a strange body odor. A disturbing chemical smell. The anxiety of her past warmed her large frame.

"In fact my parents were more than upset about my choice; they were very angry. My father told me that either I stayed home and went to college, or I got out of the house and got a job. He didn't want me around if I didn't want to do what he said. So I did. I got out of the house when I was eighteen. I got out of the house and I got a job with a large life insurance company and my father spent six months begging me to come back home, at which point I told him to stop doing it because I was happy," she finished, looking out the window at the growing snow drifts, perhaps thinking of her own daughter, who is now living with friends, because Debbie refused to subject her to her grandparents.

At the insurance company, Debbie did very well; she worked hard and acquired office expertise and the ability to manage figures. Her hard work was recognized. But her weight had become a major problem. Many businesses do not like extremely overweight people working in an area where clients can see them. Once a year employees were required to have a physical, for their own insurance. The doctor who conducted the examinations offered to counsel Debbie to help her get her extra weight off. She went to see him in his private practice. The doctor, a mild-mannered New Englander, commented on Debbie's overall emotional state.

"You seem to be an emotional and physical wreck," he told her then. She remembers today that it was fall of the year when the exam took place. The New England leaves were turning their burnished best. Debbie felt lousy.

"I had no esteem at all. So when this doctor gave me diuretics and amphetamines to start me off, I agreed to take anything." Most of us listen to our doctors. Well, after a short while, the amphetamines started not to work because Debbie's body had got used to them. She began to steal ex-

tra ones from the doctor's demonstration box that the phar-
maceutical people would leave. For the first time in her
teenage life, Debbie reached her proper weight.

She rhapsodizes about how her body looked then, as if it
were just yesterday, not nineteen years ago. "I was thin as a
rail. I was beautiful. I felt so good; I looked good; I wore
pretty clothes. I mean I still have those clothes. It was so
beautiful not to have to be ashamed of myself. Today I'm not
really a clothes person. Clothes are a problem to me because
I'm so overweight. And shoes are the worst. New shoes hurt
me when I first buy them. My feet get torn up and shredded
for months. I go through hell breaking them in, so I wear
shoes until they are almost completely off my feet. But back
then, I felt so nice. But as I started to take the drugs more
and more, I started not to take care of myself. I didn't eat at
all at that point and then I started buying drugs on the
street, black beauties, things like that. One day somebody
sold me these two little white tablets and I took them and I
almost died. I don't know what happened. I lay on the bed
and felt car sick, like I was floating on water. I had no control over it, and I couldn't even move at all. So I stopped
taking the drugs after that. It was hell to stop, but it scared
me so much. I got fat again, but I used the excuse, which
would you rather be, Debbie, fat or dead? And I chose fat."

Debbie moved to Tennessee in 1972, to get as far away
from her family and the strict Protestant ethic and spirit of
capitalism as she could. She moved to the South—the land
of honeysuckle, red bud trees, magnolia blossoms. The
South offered her a feeling of softness—the air was smooth
and languorous, the people soft-spoken and ostensibly polite. Life seemed slower, the speech mellow. The people
there had no idea about Debbie's background, her history of
being the bad girl, the victim of an abusive family, the victim
of fourth and fifth grade teachers. There she was just another
heavy woman looking for work, alone, from the North, un-
aware of their customs, their music, the Grand Ol' Opry,

their history of secession, their prejudice, their great literature, their pecans, their sheriffs, their prison system.

"I spent two years studying at a Tennessee technical school taking business courses and getting my Registered Emergency Medical Technician's license. I worked as a surgical technician," she remembers today. But when Debbie moved to Tennessee, she thought she was going to get a job right away. She ended up having to work at six different little part-time jobs all through her school term, just to survive at a meager level. She felt discriminated against as a woman in the South.

"When I got the diploma for a Registered Emergency Medical Technician, I applied to three different places for a job as an ambulance attendant. One job offer was from this guy who owned a cab company and an ambulance company. And his driver didn't show up when they got a call and he said, 'Well, I'll let you come along and show me what you can do.' I performed very well on the job, yet I never received a job offer from him and later I found out it was because I was a woman." Debbie feels that women are not really seen as total people yet, and perhaps because of the history of mistrust and abuse with her mother she also believes that women are their own worst enemies. "Women don't help each other to succeed. We're too busy holding onto what little we've got that we get jealous when another woman starts to make it. Women have come a long way, but not far enough," she finishes, half-mocking the Virginia Slim ads. "You've come a long way, Baby."

But it was not her role as a discriminated-against woman, nor was it the influences of another woman's jealousy, that caused Debbie to begin her serious criminal career, petty as the first crime might have been. It was her inability to deal with life without money that stimulated her to act dishonestly. "There was one period when I didn't have any money at all in Tennessee, all I had was the money to pay my tuition and that was it. I was down to two hot dogs in the refrigerator, and when those were gone, I had no food. So I went to a convenience store and I stole food. I felt guilty about it, and later when I got a job I couldn't go back into the store. But it seems whenever life gets stressful, very stressful, it pushes a button in me, I start stealing," she admits, guilty today but desperate then. She could have tried to call her parents for money, difficult as it might have been, or worked at another job. But Debbie found crime suited perfectly her terrible self-image.

Finally, Debbie's need to steal got her arrested for the first time in her life. "I worked for a company that ran self-serve gas stations for Mobil Oil and I used Mobil credit cards to make double charges. In other words, I'd make up two slips instead of one and copy the signature onto the false slip and I'd take the money. I ran up a debt of three thousand dollars, and they put me in prison and made me pay restitution. I was in prison for a year. I served nine months and the last three months of my sentence was served at pre-release in a large Southern city."

The first-time incarceration scare stopped Debbie from participating in crime for six years. She moved back to New England and again became a law-abiding citizen, except once when her boyfriend in Boston was having mental troubles and she began shoplifting again. She went into counseling at the mental health clinic for help. Today she admits that she needs constant therapy to stay away from patterns of the past. "I need peer support groups. I don't necessarily like the idea of group therapy, but it's something that I need, whether I like it or not. I need a psychiatrist. I will probably be in therapy for a long time. I need someone that I can fall back on, a friend that can see and understand when I'm in trouble."

Whether it is attributable to her New England background, the type of education she had, the people she was exposed at the shore, her parents' friends, or her father's job, Debbie the embezzler has a very middle-class attitude toward the law, even today. She considers herself a straight person, someone who did not like breaking the law but couldn't help herself, someone who is addicted to money and the feeling of security it brings, because she has so little internal security. Like an alcoholic who wants to stop drinking and can't, who sees every situation as a temptation to begin drinking again, Debbie sees the forces of life as conspiring to put her in a position to steal. Her three siblings, however, all from the identical background, are law-abiding citizens today. One brother is an attorney in Illinois. Her sister Lea is living in Baltimore and has just finished college. Her other brother Tommy is a school teacher in Ohio, married with 2 children.

Debbie follows the pattern of many abused women. She married a man who would abuse her. Whether women choose these men consciously or unconsciously, they repeat the patterns of their youth. But Debbie chose to marry a man who made her feel worthless, just as daddy had. And by treating her like the dog she secretly had come to believe she was, Debbie's husband triggered off the mechanism in her that pointed her toward stealing. Stealing money replaced the love she couldn't get, understand, or accept.

In the late 1970s, after getting out of prison in the South and returning to New England, Debbie began breeding, training, and showing golden retrievers. She figured that it was safe to deal in the world of animals. Through a friend who had seen an article her future husband John wrote from his mother country of Ireland in the newspaper, *Retriever World*, Debbie began writing to the man who would become her husband. They corresponded for over a year, discussing various breeding techniques, sharing their common love of dogs, discussing different champions they knew of, lineage, winners they raised. Her future husband was a teacher. And somehow, through one of the many mysteries of life, after exchanging daily letters and photographs, Debbie and John fell madly in love through the mail. At least Debbie fell madly in love. When she met John at the airport she couldn't believe her good fortune. Her heart pounding, she gazed at the handsome, continental man who greeted her with a bottle of champagne. He was tall, thin, and fair, dressed impeccably in a tweed jacket. He was educated, erudite, kind, and he loved her. She could not believe it was happening to her.

Even today the mention of his name brings a fine mist of tears to Deborah's green eyes. And the story of his love and betrayal evokes sobs from this child woman. "When John came over here, he tried to get a job as a teacher. In 1980 and 1981 there were no jobs for teachers. I tried to tell him that. I even agreed to go to Ireland with him so that he could keep his job. But he said no, he wanted to stay in the United States. He refused to get any other kind of job, and he went into a depression and things got worse. John was very educated, he was working on his master's degree. At the beginning sex was fantastic, but that tapered off. We had a small wedding and moved to low-cost housing because we couldn't afford much. I kept wondering what a man like him wanted with a woman like me. . . ." Citizenship. Support. A way out of Ireland.

Debbie's parents were at the wedding but didn't pay for it as is customary with parents of the bride. They didn't even offer. Their daughter didn't ask. They did not totally approve of their daughter's choice of mates, but at this point, they had no say in it. And Debbie would not listen to anything anyone said about her new husband. John told her that he had been married before in Ireland, and that Irish divorce laws do not require a reason for separation. Debbie later found out that this was not true. A friend from dog circles told her that the rumor was that he had abused his wife. Debbie stopped seeing the friend. John wanted children immediately. Debbie wanted to get on her feet financially. She had a miscarriage several months into the marriage. She was in the hospital and forgot to call her mother for Mother's

Day. Her mother told her, "Well, I'm glad for you, it's a relief for me you had a miscarriage. You're too poor to have children." Debbie accepted that line of reasoning as typical deprecation from her family.

She quickly became pregnant again. She could not keep her hands off this handsome European who by some miracle became her husband. At this point John became wary of touching her. He was afraid he was going to hurt the baby. But actually it was then that he began a relationship with one of the tellers in the bank where Deborah was now working to support them. John couldn't do anything but teach, he told his adoring wife. And he didn't even try to look for a job. Soon Debbie was onto him and his affair. Things at home were going poorly. She explains:

"At first I paid all the bills. I got a job working in the bank in Connecticut. Then I decided to turn the family books over to him. I told him, I want you to try to pay these bills. I want you to give me an allowance. Well, at first he paid the bills. Then he began using most of the money to buy things for himself. His excuse was, 'Well, I'm from Ireland, I only brought one suitcase full of clothes and I don't have anything.' I only had three suits to wear to work, but that was all right, I was here in America, I was OK. He was from another country and he didn't have anything. That was his excuse. He bought records, magazines, tee shirts with sayings on it. I didn't see one decent pair of shoes, or one business suit in his closet to go out and get a job in."

Why did she stay with him at this point? Well, they were having a child. And Debbie didn't think she'd ever find anyone else to love her again. After all, who was she? So she was prepared when she discovered that he was having his affair. It fit right in with her self-image. She deserved to be deceived.

Two days before her daughter was born, in March, while she was in labor in the front bedroom of their house, John was in the kitchen playing with his girlfriend. And three

days after her daughter was born, her husband was in bed
with the girlfriend. And a week after Debbie had the child,
her husband insisted that she go back to work because they
needed the money. They could not live without her salary.
So she went back to work, and the Wednesday after she
returned, she came home to nurse her daughter at lunch
time and saw her co-worker Elizabeth walking toward her
from her house. Elizabeth lived on the other side of town.
Debbie knew that there was no reason for Elizabeth to be
walking in that direction unless she had something to do in
one of the houses.

The next day Debbie sneaked home and followed Elizabeth to her and John's house, saw Elizabeth go in and get
in bed with her husband. Debbie raced in screaming. That
was when the entire marriage dissolved. There were arguments all the time. John began hitting Debbie, hard, and
often. Debbie took her daughter and left him. She moved
out of the house and waited until he had no money left and
had to leave. He deserted her. He left her with a five-month
baby and over $2,000 in debt. Debbie had no clear way out
of the troubles she was in. She was once more desperate.

Again, she saw herself as a victim. This time a victim of
her marriage. She maintains that she tried to work something out with her husband but couldn't. He didn't want to.
And the bills started to come in. She had to unplug her
phone at night because the creditors never stopped calling.
"My husband told me he had paid the pediatrician; he
hadn't. He left me owing three months' rent. I thought the
rent had been paid. The first phone bill I received after he
left was for four hundred and sixty dollars worth of calls to
Belgium, Holland, friends he was calling, Ireland, calls to
his family, Australia, calls to his sister. I nearly died. I mean,
I was faced with having the heat cut off, the lights cut off,
the phone. I couldn't afford to pay the baby sitter, even
though she knew what I was going through. It was very difficult for a single mother to take care of a child and make

enough money to make ends meet and still be a good mother, and even father, to your child. He never sent any child support. My family turned their back on me and my daughter. They couldn't deal with it. This was before they became religious. I needed money. I did not have enough to pay my bills. It was that simple."

Debbie was hired as a bank teller. They never checked her background. They never knew she had a record from her conviction in Tennessee. They gave her access to a lot of money, first as a teller, and then, when they renovated the bank and her job at the window was gone, they gave her a job as a coin teller. "They knew that I was a strong woman capable of moving heavy objects and things. They asked me if I would object to a job that involved heavy lifting. I said no because I'm quite proud of my strength, and the job was nontraditional. A woman had never worked as a coin teller before. I had mechanical ability, strength, good office skills, and they recognized that. I worked with the person that was training me for one week, and then he left and I was on my own. I was put in a soundproof room with no cameras, just a nice big picture window. We even had our own counter. At this point I didn't even know what was in each box, but I knew I was in desperate straits."

Debbie already knew from past experience that in stressful time she turned to stealing. She was placed near money, a lot of money: the entire take from the town's daily parking meter funds was brought to her to be counted and deposited. This amounted to thousands of dollars each day. The temptation was too much.

The details of the crime go like this. Two police officers had a specific detail. They would take full cans out of a certain string of meters every day and put them into a suitcase with eleven others and put empty boxes back in to replace them. They would take eight of these suitcases into the bank and give them to Debbie and her new part-time partner to count. Debbie's job was to put the boxes in numerical order, pop the seals, take off the lids, and give them to Toye, her partner, who would then take each box, dump its coins in the machine, count it, and put down the correct amount next to the right number. At the end of this they would add up all the figures on paper and that figure had to equal the total amount taken out of the machine. That's how they knew it was balanced. What Debbie did was wait until Toye went home at two o'clock and then alter the figures. If a particular deposit was $21, Debbie would change the one to a zero, and that way she was able to get, in small amounts, enough to pay her bills, and live off her $125 a week salary.

Debbie began paying off her bills. First she paid off the back rent. Then she made a promise to the phone company to slowly pay off her large debt. She did the same with her gas and electricity bills. By June 1982, all the bills had been paid off. Even the pediatrician. It felt so good not to have to look over her shoulder. She didn't care who called, and she didn't have to unplug the phone. She was relieved; it felt like a weight had been taken off her shoulder. Then she started having a problem because there was all this extra money building up. And she couldn't stop taking it. She had paid back her bills, but she wanted more. At that point she had to decide what to do with the extra funds. She stuck them into a bank account. She could buy groceries, she could pay the baby sitter. She couldn't live on her salary, which ended up by then, even after her raise, to amount to $182.75 a week. Why did she have to live on so little? Yet if she saw a crime happening on the street, she was the first to report it.

Her bank account was getting up into the thousands of dollars, and by the fall of 1982 she realized she could make her life a lot easier if she had a car. She had to walk a mile and a quarter to work and back every day, she had all the heavy lifting to do, and by the end of the day she was exhausted. She had to drop the baby off at the baby sitter, walk up three flights of steps, she was going through the pain of a very emotional divorce, and it was then she decided to use some of the money to pay an attorney to finalize her legal situation with John. It cost a thousand dollars. When she decided to buy a car, all of her middle-class values came out. She wanted the best. As an American consumer. She felt entitled to it. She explains today. "If I bought anything with my own money, it was always the best, because the best lasts very long if you take care of it." She bought a brand new Encore Alliance, and she loved it. She deserved it.

The money kept on building up. In the summer of 1984 Debbie took a very expensive vacation with her four-year-old daughter. She stayed at an exclusive inn in Chatham, Massachusetts, and had an absolutely wonderful time. She was living a really nice life. Her daughter was eating the best food. People thought well of her. She felt good.

It was then that Debbie began the Robin Hood phase of her criminal life. She was not worried about getting caught. She was happy. She felt the bank deserved to be cheated because of the stingy salaries they paid their employees. She wanted to share her good fortune with the less fortunate of her friends. She bought a girlfriend a piano. When her friend's dog died, she bought her a registered retriever puppy. She had a tremendous loyalty to her baby sitter who had often worked for nothing. She wrote her a check for five thousand dollars to cover the expense of a new roof on her house. People loved her for her help. She felt accepted for the first time in her life. Money was buying her love.

She told everyone that her grandfather had died and left her money. No one questioned her. She was exhilarated. She was on a high, a roll. The bank deserved to be embezzled. They treated their employees badly. They were cheap and oppressive to work for. Any corner they could cut they did. Granted, they gave her a nontraditional job, but they were stupid. They had never checked her background. Debbie realized that no one's money is safe with the bank. She was a champion of the people. The stingy bank became her stingy father. She not only took its money, she embarrassed it by defrauding its best customer, the town itself. At this point she had embezzled close to a quarter of a million dollars.

Debbie did not know that the bank had been checking waste baskets for a month. They knew something was going on. But they never suspected her. She had four bank accounts all over town. She had invested in a collection of silver dollars. She bought art. She bought over $30,000 worth of furniture from the Ethan Allan Gallery, and on a legal holiday, they opened the showroom just for her. They served her breakfast. The manager, a small, bespeckled man named Mr. Levy, treated her with respect. She was important. A citizen to be reckoned with. She was Somebody.

Meanwhile, back at the police station, the police began to see that there was a drop of more than $100,000 in the take from the municipal parking lots. Some of the boxes that had to be emptied three times a month would yield $4,400. Debbie was going home with $2,200 of it. All she did was alter the sheets, throw the old ones down the toilet, and flush the evidence away. One day she forgot to flush the evidence, and the bank found it. For seven days the police collected the boxes and took them to the basement of the police department. There the detectives opened the seals, counted the money in each individual box, and made a sheet for it. Debbie received the same delivery after they resealed it. She felt that something was wrong. The seals weren't right. But she couldn't stop stealing. And they caught her. She made the news. She was on all local radio and TV stations. They sealed up all of her accounts. It was then that her parents found out about not only this bust but the time she served in Tennessee. She had finally succeeded in self-fulfilling the prophecy of the little bad girl from her childhood. Her parents had been correct. All their accusations were true. She was an embarrassment to them. Debbie sent her daughter to stay with the sister of her best friend in Tennessee.

Today Debbie sees a psychiatrist regularly; or as regularly as she can in prison, because all the other inmates seem to need help. The New England prison does not have a money addiction program. But as more and more women get into white-collar crimes, the system just might recognize what money has come to represent in this country. As Debbie says, "Money represents power; it represents good feelings; it represents love, reward for a job well done, attention from parents who never gave any." And women criminals are different from men criminals. Just ask any of the thousands of women incarcerated around the country. Ask Debbie.

"Women have been raised to feel more. We are allowed to feel more. Therefore we can get it out in less violent ways, we can talk about it; we can act it out; we can get it out without being violent. Men on the other hand have been brought up, big boys don't cry. Hold it in; you're an island of feelings; you should be the rock on which life is built. So when it comes out, when men explode, they explode with weapons and fists. When women explode, they explode with tears." And as there are more single working mothers and fewer and fewer jobs, women, who are usually trusted more by institutions, are hired more frequently without background checks.

Deborah intends to raise her daughter differently from the way her parents raised her.

"When I had my daughter, I made certain decisions. One was that she was going to get the love I never got from my parents. She is very affectionate. A loving child. I can hug her. She is very very good with people; she gets along with everyone; she is happy. As a matter of fact I monitor her television. I don't like her to watch programs where a woman is beaten up or placed in a bad position. I like to keep her away from violence. I also like her to be in touch with what is real. All my childhood I lived in a fantasy world of Dr. Kildare and animals. The biggest loss I feel in prison is my daughter. That's one of the reasons I treat my family as if they're dead. They didn't help with her. As far as pulling the crime off, I'm thankful that it's over. I'm glad I got caught because I stopped and I was glad I got the chance to be put somewhere because I can focus in on my sickness. Get help. But I dream about my daughter. I have a lot to make up to her when I get out. . . ." She never finished the sentence because the security officer came to take her back to her cell. The interview was over.

What is the future for Debbie? She is not a drug addict or an alcoholic. She is money sick. She hopes that with intensive therapy she can stop stealing. She did exactly that for six years after prison in Tennessee. But what happens if she again gets in a stressful situation, one that presses her button? Can she make it with an upper-middle-class taste and lower-class finances? Because Debbie likes nice things. Art. Coins. Needlepoint. Her favorite artists are Van Gogh and Monet. Monet because he's very peaceful. Van Gogh because he's controversial. She thinks today, facing parole in early 1988, that she can make it on the outside with professional help. She can live by the rules. And she had it easy compared with some of her prison mates who were not only emotionally and physically abused, but sexually abused as well.

But she was abused. Her upper-middle-class parents hid their psychoses from their friends. She was viciously beaten until there were bruises the size of two hands on her. You do not wipe a child's excrement in her face. You do not throw out a child's possessions. You do not belittle her in front of other people.

Debbie's final question to me, as she was being led down the long, green hallway of the old cotton mill—her face distorted from memories the interviews had stirred, her hopes high for her release, her future, the future of her daughter— was, "When do you stop being a bad little girl? When?"

THE CRIME—Larceny, bank embezzlement, nine
counts
THE SENTENCE—Two years for each nine counts, to be
served concurrently

CHAPTER IV

THE SCAMS

"I'm not crazy. I'm a woman. I know I can't fight, physically. You never know with what I do when a person might flip over and wake up (realize what is going on). If you handle them right, and are logical, if they keep asking you questions and you answer something back that makes sense, even if you're not sure that it's the truth, if it sounds good enough or you sound like you know what you're talking about strong enough, they're going to listen to you."

THE CONTESSA
Eastern prison for women
November 19, 1985

TODAY, MANY WOMEN have access to funds and business domains once reserved for men. Women have managed to enter professions and positions of trust that enable them to swindle people who still look at them as sweet little homemakers, or professional ladies working hard to achieve equality. Forget poor little anythings. Women have not only achieved equality in crime, they have learned how to use their femininity as an economic weapon, to hone their skills as manhunters, to read the minds of the men who have for so long not expected them to do anything out of the ordinary.

The Grandma

"I'm not sorry I did it, even though I have to sit here for two years. I'm not the least bit sorry because I still have everything; so when I leave prison, I leave here and go back to my home, my cars, my jewelry, my clothes. I haven't lost anything except two years of my life . . . and if I could commit my crime again, I probably would," explained Melissa Sands, a fifty-five-year-old native Wisconsin grandmother who moved to California when she was twenty.

The California penal system is one of the most carefully designed in the country. Its inmates are protective of their rights, and its officials are sensitive to the disenfranchisements their prisoners suffer. The Women's Advisory Council, the prisoners' inmate liaison with the administration, fights hard for and protects personal dignities behind bars, an amenity that convicts in less forward-thinking states despair even to contemplate.

The short, dark-haired inmate, Rosalie, who headed up the Advisory Council at one California penal institution, was so efficient, with her clipboard and glasses, her appointment book and her notes, that one of the guards escorting me around thought she was an attorney. In the California system, everyone talks about Leslie Van Hooten, the leftover Charles Manson conspirator, as if she were their neighbor. Everyone knows everyone else's business, and the women there have a freedom of spirit that makes other prisoners in the nation appear dark and fettered, confined to factories and corridors.

Melissa Sands was a perfect example of a California prisoner. I found that the women were mainly products of their genes and home environment. But Melissa had been conditioned and customized by her locale. She had adopted California style. She came to our interview, a petite, slender, very attractive, gray panther wearing two gold hoops in each ear. Many gold chains, some encrusted with diamonds, hung around her graceful neck, her gray hair was set in an up-dated shag, her fingers were covered with expensive rings, and her long nails were done perfectly, in contemporary style, the white half moons unpainted and exactly outlined in fuchsia. She wore a red sweatshirt that perfectly matched the red of her Reebok sneakers, the tiny heart hanging from her throat was set off with a red ruby. She was not the typical grandmother of Iowa or New York. Her face shone ruddy, as if she had hiked to the interview over a mountain trail. Her eyes flashed.

"My grandson is six and a half years old and while I was in county jail waiting to get sentenced my daughter said she was going to bring him to visit. I said, 'Do you think it's a good idea?' Her answer made me probably the proudest I've ever been. She said, 'You are his grandmother and no matter what you've done, he has the right to be with you and to know you.' Now my kids sort of joke about me being a criminal. My youngest daughter is twenty-four. She said she's going to have a tee shirt made saying 'My mom is a con.' They keep it light."

Melissa was raised in Wisconsin but her family came to California, looking for the gold, over thirty years ago. She has lived in the state most of her adult life. Her family was straight-on middle class. She and her two older brothers all attended Lutheran parochial schools. Her father was an air traffic controller and her mother a housewife who never had to work. Melissa attended the University of Wisconsin, and graduated with a degree in business. She was never rebellious. Today she remembers that when she was growing up and her older brother was drafted into the service and her younger brother became a merchant marine, her life replicated that of an only child. The house was quiet, there were few parties, she received too much attention.

The first indication that Melissa's future was to be slightly unconventional was her marriage, at age seventeen, to a very wealthy young man, whom she thought she loved. She had one child with him. Her parents approved the marriage. The pair were both young; he was only twenty-one and appeared to be a nice person from a good family. Melissa continued to go to college until she graduated. Then she realized she hadn't ever loved her husband. It was a mistake. They divorced and she remained in Orange County.

"I never used drugs, and only drank socially," she recounts today calmly, nonplussed by the constant din of prison noises in the background. "It was really only ten years ago that I broke with the law for the first time. By this time I was married again, and my husband turned out to be an alcoholic. He couldn't support the family and there were things I wanted. I had never wanted for anything when I was growing up. My parents always managed to provide everything I needed. Suddenly I wanted furniture, cars, clothes. When I married him I think I had a naive attitude that I would change him or that things would get better, but they never did. I didn't like being single and dating; no matter what age you are, it's the pits. And you have so many unpleasant circumstances, people you meet. When you have the opportunity to marry someone and it starts out good, you go for it. We bought a house, and then later it became a struggle to make the house payments, and then it was hard to make it at all. I thought I could get away with embezzling from the business I was working for because I'm really good at the books."

Melissa served one year in 1975 for embezzling $30,000 from a small insurance business where she worked. When she got out, her husband appeared to have cleaned up his act and was waiting for her with her two daughters. Life was good. There was money. He worked as an engineer, she stayed home and played housewife for several years until his drinking began again. Finally Melissa took a job at the local lodge—the Californian equivalent to the East Coast Moose Club—a macho gathering of the town's professional men who get together sometimes weekly, sometimes daily, to drink, tell jokes, hang out, and do charity work. For two years she just worked in the office. But they kept offering her the bookkeeper's position. Finally she took it. They never checked to see if she had a record. Who would ever have suspected this quiet grandmother? Implicitly, the men in the club, the judges, the attorneys, the district attorney, the leading men in the small conservative community, trusted Melissa, her warm smile, her friendly maternal attitude, her solid-citizen reputation.

But Melissa began to want things again. Cars. Jewelry. Trips. She began to embezzle small amounts of money from the payroll checks. At this point she was in a great position of trust; besides being the bookkeeper, she was also the office manager. She ran the entire place. She had access to everything there.

"If I wanted to I could have stolen liquor, cash, anything; but I didn't know how to cover those things. Through the books I knew how to cover it and in a multimillion dollar business, two hundred dollars is not hard to cover." Two hundred here, two hundred there, over a two-year period added up to over a quarter of a million dollars. And even today the lodge has never totally been able to compute the exact amount of money Melissa took. Even she can only give a general figure and smile. "I would go out and spend a hundred dollars on dinner and think nothing of it. I was living high. My husband would occasionally ask where the money came from. I never answered him. The money represented pure fun to me. I gave a lot of it away. I would loan people money, or take a trip to Reno or Las Vegas, I never felt that I deserved it. I just felt that I wanted it. It's a definite weakness. I think it's becoming more pronounced in women now. Women want things."

Melissa feels that the incidence of crime among middle-class women will increase drastically. "I think women in crime are slicker than men. They use a little more intelligence. A woman can get dressed up, go into a store, run credit cards, and they don't trip. After a time they do. But women are good con artists," she theorizes, smiling and pulling a tube of lip gloss out of her jeans and reapplying the glossy red to her lips.

Here's how Melissa got caught. On New Year's Eve of 1983 there was some money missing from the club's bar. Melissa maintains today that she doesn't know what happened to it. She never messed with cash because she says she didn't know how to cover it. She feels that either the bartender didn't put it in the safe, or someone else took it. Whatever, the cash loss prompted the club to run a check on everyone who worked there, and they found out that Melissa had a record.

She cheerfully continues in her quiet, soft-timbered voice. "Well, they knew the money was missing because the bartender knew there were more receipts and that there was more money. This went on for a couple of weeks, and the head of the lodge ran the check, because the members were all judges, district attorneys, his staff, attorneys, highway patrolmen . . . it kind of gets to your ego a little bit when you're working in a place and you're in constant charge with all these high-powered executives. My boss had been with the IRS for thirty years, and I got a little bit of self-satisfaction, especially since the lodge is so chauvinistic. You know, it's strictly a men's organization, and I guess I felt good by saying that I, as a woman, got over on them. And that hurt their pride a little." She smiles quietly to herself. Melissa smiles a lot. She enjoys her private life.

The lodge must find it difficult to explain how, with two yearly audits, Melissa Sands still got away with her crime. She would alter checks and deposit the remainder in her accounts. It is easy to alter checks. You just use liquid paper correction fluid the color of the check, or change the payee on the check. If Melissa made out a check to a liquor company, the volume of the payables was so high that when the auditors would do the books (and the lodge used a CPA firm), they never found the changes because they would have had to go through every single item, and this CPA firm would just spot-check. Melissa was just darned lucky that they never spot-checked any of the checks she had altered. So if the lodge owed the liquor company a certain amount of money, she would make out the check and it would be signed. She never forged any signatures, and then she would use liquid paper and white-out the amount and deposit the difference in her account, and the next month she would pick up that payable again. She always did it in small amounts that they'd never check on because they owed such large bills, maybe three or four thousand every month to a particular liquor distributor and they weren't careful. But Melissa was.

She pulled off her little daily embezzlements in a very quiet way, to the tune of at least $250,000. She claims that the lodge never got back one cent of what she took, that it is still in the bank, that she still has her home and her car, and all of her jewelry is in a safety deposit vault. Her closest friend is living in the house, still safeguarding everything. And when Melissa gets out, all her spoils are there for her. She only lost two years of her life and the prison she is in is not that difficult to take. The officials treat her like a human being. She is a secretary, her skills are better than they've ever been in her life, she crochets a lot, she has a TV in her room, a radio, hair dryer, curling irons. The only thing that she has to make sure of is that she stays away from bookkeeping when she gets out, because she could still be tempted by it.

THE CRIME—Embezzlement

THE SENTENCE—Three years

The Hacker

Alexandra Goulaise is thirty-four years old. She was born into a Basque-American family in Scottsdale, Arizona. A true

Southwesterner, her crime is 1986 contemporary: computer fraud. The wave of the future. The undetectable, silent, space-age invasion of the hidden citizen files—files that to-day any talented hacker can tap into. Alexandra attended Catholic girls' school; her father worked for the Department of Forestry in soil conservation and her mother was a super-visor at an electronics company. A solid middle-class Amer-ican family. Her parents had a small replica of the Statue of Liberty in their living room on the mantelpiece, and when their eyes occasionally fell on the little gray plaster statue, they were grateful for the opportunities this country had af-forded them.

Alexandra was the middle child; she had an older brother and two younger sisters. She was always very close to her mother. Alexandra is a serious, almost scholarly-looking, cof-fee-colored woman; she has long graceful hands and ex-tremely pointed, almost grotesquely curved, painted fingernails. She pushed her dark-tinted glasses back on her nose and inhaled deeply on her cigarette as she explained her often tempestuous relationship with her mother.

"When I was younger my mother and I had a lot of prob-lems. She raised us old fashioned, so we didn't have outside friends; we just had family. We had to go to school with our family, we went to the shows with our cousins . . . we couldn't have anyone spend the night at our house, nor could we spend the night at a girlfriend's. Cousins, yes, but that was it." Alexandra briefly stopped her recollections to pick a piece of lint off her obviously expensive brown leather jacket. Then she turned one of her sapphire rings around so that the stone faced front, and continued.

"When I was young, the only thing I ever daydreamed about was getting out of the house, having my own place. I wanted to be a biologist, science and animals and things like that really interested me . . . see, my father worked all week a long way from home, and then on Fridays he'd come home and be home for the weekend. I always did a lot of things with my dad; he was more relaxed. He'd take me out boating, water skiing, riding horses, stuff like that. My mother was strict; she thought girls should stay home and clean house."

Our interview was abruptly interrupted by several inmates, dressed in jeans and work shirts, who were cleaning the floors. Without knocking on the door, they opened it and mopped right in. One smiled at me. She was missing a front tooth.

"I have a story, too," she tells me. Later I find out she is in for Murder One. I have decided not to interview any murderers. Their pathology is an area I do not feel equipped to comment upon. Alexandra waits for her to finish and continues.

She began to rebel when she was about fourteen. It was a rebellion that was to magnify into gigantic proportions.

"When I was about fourteen, I went and stayed out all night long at a friend's house. My mother called the police and they came and picked me up. I couldn't understand her logic, how she thought children should come up, now after I've gotten older, we've become real close. I find myself raising my kids the way my mother did."

But back then, in the early 1960s, Alexandra did everything she could to break her mother's hold, not to mention her heart. While her brother went on to the University of Pennsylvania to become an art historian, Alexandra got pregnant when she was sixteen and had to leave school. Although her parents stuck with her through the whole thing, and more or less raised her infant child, it was a major scandal for the family. The first of many Alexandra was to instigate. And since Alexandra is extremely bright, she knew how to manipulate events to bring total shame and humiliation upon her family.

"I had a lot of medical problems when I was young, I was sort of sickly like. I couldn't do a lot of things that my cousins did. I had asthma, and I couldn't run and play a lot of sports; and although my parents didn't label me a bad girl, my other relatives did. I was the bad one of the whole bunch. You see I had a mind of my own. My family felt a whole lot better than other people above them. They told me I shouldn't talk with black people because they have their own way of life. 'Stick with your family,' they told me. They wanted to more or less choose my friends.

"So since they didn't want me to hang around with black people, I did. I didn't do drugs. But you know, good girls didn't go to the baseball parks and play baseball with the boy cousins. I was labeled bad because I did those things. You know it's not nice to go out and wander around with your boy cousins. I was always being compared to my other cousins, and since they didn't do things I did, I was a ringleader. Then around sixty-nine or seventy, I started hanging around with a real bad group of people, they didn't go to school, they had a car club, my aunts and uncles felt I was just a bad little girl, incorrigible."

By having a car club, Alexandra means they were a gang. This tough Phoenix street gang had knives and guns, satin jackets, gold teeth, and no fear of death. They had monthly gladiatorial battles with Phoenix's Chicano gang, the Low Riders, who cruised the late-night streets of downtown Phoenix in souped-up cars, with madonnas and cruxifixes hanging from their rearview mirror and mini religious shrines on their fur-lined dashboards. Alexandra fell in love with and eventually married, when they were both eighteen, the leader of the pack, Thomas. He accepted her infant daughter from her high-school sweetheart as his own, raised the child with tenderness, when he was there. Thomas was the epitome of the rebel for Alexandra: his father was black, his mother Mexican. Anatypical Southwestern combination of ethnicity. Thomas was into drugs. He beat Alexandra all the time and kept her away from her family. But she adored him, almost worshipped him. He was the leader of a group of postadolescent gangsters, modern-day characters out of

West Side Story. Young punk heartthrobs with no regard for the money they made, the people they killed. They prowled the quiet, dark Phoenix streets, scaring the elderly and taking what they wanted. Warriors without a war.

Thomas was also a forger. He taught Alexandra everything she knew about real crime. She traveled all over the Southwest and West with him to do his deals. They would sit together in a car in the barrios of Albuquerque, or in Tulsa, Oklahoma, waiting for drug transactions to go down, and Thomas would explain patiently to the young, eager-to-learn Alexandra how to forge signatures, how to take forged checks into a store or bank and act confidently enough to get them cashed. Thomas was a pro, and Alexandra a quick study.

It was in Shawnee that Thomas was killed. With Alexandra right by his side. Her parents' dream of a middle-class lifestyle for their daughter was long gone. Their little mantelpiece replica of the Statue of Liberty forgotten. Alexandra and Thomas were standing in the Oklahoma wind, dreaming, the air smelled of the West and fresh corn fields. One of Thomas's so-called friends with a gun came up behind them as they were waiting for the transaction to go through. He just looked at Alexandra—as a gray cloud passed in front of the full, orange harvest moon—and said, "I'm sorry," and shot Thomas through his neck.

Somehow Alexandra got home and managed to stay with her family for a while. The police were there, constantly questioning her. Her relatives were able to reconfirm their opinion of her as a bad girl, and her parents' hopes that finally she would turn toward their way, the straight and narrow, the American path toward success, died with Thomas. Her sister was getting ready to go to NYU and become a broadcast journalist. Her father had been promoted. But Alexandra's course was set that dusky night in Oklahoma. The glamour of fast cars, chrome, and territorial studs had captured her. She could never return to her parents' way of life.

Alexandra's first arrest occurred in 1977. Forgery. Cashing

payroll checks. She was unemployed. She had dropped out of a state college after three years, supported by her parents, but bored. Somebody from the old life, someone who knew her from fast-lane Thomas, came to her and asked if she remembered how to forge. She did. And whether out of boredom or for the excitement, she began to make false ID's and cash stolen payroll checks.

"You just go in there and act like the person that you're supposed to be and you get dressed in the role. If you're being a nurse, or whatever, you get all their ID, hospital card, everything you can about this person; and when you go to cash this check, you are this person for whatever amount of time it takes."

While serving time in a Southwestern institute for women for this crime, out on work furlough, she met someone who worked for a major credit-card company, where they manufactured the cards. They became vague friends. A contact for the future. Their friendship would play a significant part in Alexandra's life.

When Alexandra got out of prison in 1981, she had earned a nursing certificate. She decided to try to make it legitimately. Scottsdale, the middle-class haven of Arizona, is a legitimate city. Alexandra wanted to fit in. She applied and was accepted for a job in a hospital. She worked there for fourteen months.

"I was prepared to do it right this time," she says thoughtfully. "I wasn't planning on doing anything wrong." Only the hospital administrator who hired her knew that she was on parole. He hired her, believing in her; and he assured her that no one else in the hospital would ever know that she had been convicted. Alexandra worked the night shift. After she got off work, her feet aching, her arms stiff, the famous healing Arizona sun just rising above the desert floor, she would go over to her mother's and sleep in the morning. Then she'd go home.

One morning, the hospital called her at her mother's and

told her that she had to come in and pick up her final check, they had let her go. This was after fourteen months. Alexandra really liked working at this hospital. She asked the officials why they were letting her go, and they told her that the hospital had changed hands, and that the administrator who had hired her had spread the word before he left that she had been in prison.

Alexandra had become the fallen administrator's scapegoat. Anything that had been found missing during her shift was now blamed on her. There had been a few stolen items reported when she had been working; but no one had said anything to her about it. The hospital officials had never criticized her work, and they had given her no warning of the end.

Alexandra's feelings were very hurt. "I had been at it a long time and I felt confident now that I could make it without doing anything wrong. So when I went in to pick up my check, I called my ex-parole officer—I was off parole by this time—and we went to a labor board that mediates between the prison and the outside world. I asked them how they could dismiss me, fire me, with no warning, no proof, my work really good. How could they do this to me just because I'd been in prison? I felt that I had paid my debt to society . . . so the parole board checked into it; but I never got my job again, and nothing really came out of it." She spit out the last words: "So here I was on the street with nothing, and instead of going out and trying to find a straight job again, I had had an attitude of, well, I'm just going to do what I do best, and then I started up with computer crime."

There is no way of knowing if Alexandra's dismissal from the hospital reflects the true reason she went back to crime with such ferocity. It is a known fact that ex-cons have a difficult time getting and keeping jobs. But does one mindless rejection justify her return to illegal activities? Could it have hurt her so much that she gave up? Or was she just looking for an excuse to return to easy money? Whatever the real answer, it is difficult not to be taken in by hustlers like Alexandra; it is difficult not to believe some of the pain in the eyes of the women behind bars. The stigma of having an ex-con working at a hospital might definitely have offended some right-wing Scottsdale hospital officials. But all of us face rejection, and unexplained disappointments in life. Most of us don't turn to crime to get even with an unfair society.

Alexandra then decided to call the friend she knew who worked in the credit card manufacturing plant. She called him at his grandmother's house, and although he never came to see her, he just started sending her packets through the mail. Packets of brand-new unused credit cards. Business account cards. Cards with a $250,000 credit line. People would send in applications for credit and before they even knew that they were accepted, Alexandra would get the card first. Thus Alexandra was set up in business. A business that in one year made her personally at least a million dollars.

"Every couple months this friend would send me a package of cards that nobody knew existed, and all the necessary criteria: a copy of the application, the person's past credit history, where they worked, what they did, and I would make ID's for it, a picture ID. And I would become this person and go into a bank and get cash advances, take the card for whatever the limit was and then destroy the card," Alexandra explained very nonchalantly. "I would go out to different banks, if they had in-home banking on their application, I'd get all the criteria I needed for that, and I'd learn everything I had to learn about it.

"For computers, I'd go to computer stores and learn everything I had to learn about how to operate a computer, how to dub in a computer as far as the code goes, and I would sit down at my computer at home and do that." Alexandra became a hacker—a person who spends hours playing with computers, learning how to tap into private computer files around the country.

At first, she worked strictly by herself with the cards and a small personal computer. Then she and a very close girlfriend opened up an in-home business. They went down to city hall and got their business licenses for computer programming and they sat and played with the computers for hours, days, until Alexandra could dub in a business code. Next, she'd make the proper ID, go into a bank and tell them that she'd like to make a withdrawal, say if the company had a $275,000 balance, she'd take out $100,000. And it only took about twenty minutes of her time. The act was simple. The preparation laborious.

Alexandra didn't have withdrawal slips. How did she do it? She gladly explained. "All you need is either a bank statement, or you can dub in on your computer the company's code and it will read back to you the company's bank balance and the account number and you go into the bank and tell them that you need an over-the-counter check to make a withdrawal. They ask you for your number, and I would just write it on a piece of paper, or already have it on a piece of paper, and I'd give them the number, and they'd ask for one picture ID, and then they'd take it to the bank manager, and they would check out the ID, and have the manager sign the papers. They would type on the business check, and on the over-the-counter check, they'd type in the business account number, and I'd fill it out and sign it and they'd give me the money." Very simple so far.

How Alexandra constructed ID's acceptable enough for the bank to accept was unbearably basic and sly. She would use her own driver's license. Leave her own picture on it. Stop off at a store and buy chalk—just ordinary over-the-counter chalk, rub it over all of her statistics. Then she would buy a can of hairspray, spray the license, and let it set. Then she would go to a small typewriter, type in all the needed information, new address, and so forth, that she had compiled from her computer research, and take it into the bank, with her picture on it. It worked perfectly every time.

No one once questioned her ID. And as Alexandra walked out of the bank, she would wet her thumb, run it over the driver's license, and all her original statistics would come back up and everything else was wiped off. She was able to collect $100,000 at a clip with a chalked and hairsprayed driver's license. The simple duplicity of it all was overwhelming.

Alexandra put away $500,000 in six months. Another $250,000 over the next three.

She didn't claim to have felt a huge thrill from pulling off her crimes. Crime didn't make her feel special. Alexandra didn't indulge in any kind of high life. She rented a lot of little cars. She had a small truck. She put a lot of things in storage.

She says today that she always knew she was coming back to prison. She also claims that she pulled off these scams never really knowing until she had been arrested, which was much later, and the statements had started to come in, just how much money she had taken. I am not sure I believe this young woman who was obviously so proficient in math and figures. She knew that she would get caught eventually. But she had an attitude, an attitude that she maintains was affected by getting fired from the hospital.

"It was like society was ultimately down on me because I'd been in prison, and like they always tell you, once you've paid your debt to society, everything is OK. But that's not true, everything isn't OK. They never forget and it always comes back; once a criminal, always a criminal."

She got busted by an uncle who had worked for the sheriff's department for twenty-two years. He and his ex-partner pulled her in. She did not get popped walking into the bank, pulling a credit-card scam. She had applied for and got a credit card of her own, and a friend had needed plane tickets to go visit family. Alexandra charged two tickets to her card. When the men got to the airport, they apparently looked suspicious and the officials stopped them. When they checked the charge for the tickets, they began to investigate. Something didn't look right. They arrested Alexandra and she got out on a two-thousand-dollar bond. And then a lot of reports started coming in, on the phony credit cards she had been using; not on the computer crimes. But slowly things started trickling in, and her bail went up to $100,000. Finally they rearrested her and put her bail up to $250,000.

Her sentence was for five years, but she'll only serve three of these; and like Melissa, when she gets out she will have a load of money waiting for her. Her friend at the credit-card company was never indicted. Alexandra never ratted him out. In the tradition of the true outlaw. Or maybe she is saving this contact for future deals.

Since Alexandra paid her own bond, her family doesn't really even know the severity of her crime. Even after she had been busted, after she had stood trial for one of the cases against her, Alexandra pulled another computer scam. And like a good daughter, she put the money in the bank for her parents, who are by now old and infirm. She put the money away, using her own home computer to hide the accounts, the computer that the police hadn't confiscated, to pull off the crime. Then she put the money into accounts the police still don't know about so it wouldn't be touched. She also bought a lot of furniture and put it away in storage, because very shortly she will be out again.

She has few ties to the free world. She has cut all associations with her boyfriend, whom she claims was a speed junkie. She reads a lot, especially biographies, and she says today that she wouldn't go back into crime at all.

"Any crime isn't worth the time," she says seriously. "I wouldn't advise anybody to go out and do it, because it's time you can't get back. It's time away from your family you can't be with."

Alexandra delicately rips a tag off one of her new shoes. The shoe is dark brown and very stylish, a medium low heel. Her beige sweater is cashmere and falls nicely about her shoulders. She looks subdued, like a successful businesswoman might look, and she carries herself very confidently, head erect, arms controlled.

"I think my crimes exhausted me mentally. It takes a lot out of you to sit and figure. You really have to use up a lot of time and energy; and at the time it's not wasted energy, because you're getting so much money out of it. But it was wasted because I should have been doing something else with my life."

What about all the energy the victims have wasted looking for their money? The police don't even have a clue to where it is.

I left Alexandra's prison after a long week of interviews. The assistant supervisor had been very helpful in arranging my week. I was let into the prison, after a brief search, every day without fail. The guards, male and female, were extremely solicitous. The inmates very forthcoming. The food, cooked by the inmates and served cafeteria-style, was excellent. The women friendly. But I wondered how did so many of us from such middle-class backgrounds end up as criminals? What could Alexandra have done if she had applied herself to a legitimate job? How far could she have come? What could she have achieved? Will there be a place for her in the world when she gets out? As I was leaving, a film crew was setting up to interview one of the most famous inmates whose parole had just been denied. Criminals—even alleged criminals—are becoming the celebrities of the decade. Gary Gilmore. Jean Harris. Now the Ted Bundy murder. The media make crime look glamorous. Television has villainesses like Joan Collins who plot and scheme to cheat and kill wearing expensive gowns, drinking champagne, eating caviar, and getting away with it. But crime is humiliating and ultimately self-defeating. And more and more women are getting into it. Today twice as many women are in prison than were a decade ago.

Will Melissa really enjoy the money she has stashed

away? Will Alexandra, who wanted so desperately to be accepted back into society, go back to crime? I searched for answers to these immense questions as I entered the frenetic freeway traffic and thus committed myself to spend the next hour and a half stuck at a tortoise pace in-between a BMW and a 1969 Mustang. Only the painted cement murals three quarters of the way back to Studio City, where I was staying, distracted me. Outside urban folk art is a new phenomenon. Like the phenomenon of middle-class women in crime. I don't know if there are any answers.

THE CRIME—Computer fraud
THE SENTENCE—Five years

The Contessa's Game

(The Contessa is JoAnn Giorgio; see Chapter V)

The Contessa's game is an East Coast synthesis of the age-old con game, plus the instruction of Venus—the Contessa's mentor, and the Contessa's input, experience, look, gab, garb, and courage. The Contessa is still today, after serving several years in an East Coast prison, a legend on many streets. The Contessa had a reputation for picking out the right vic, hardly ever being turned down, knowing when to split, and in almost twenty years of the con game, being busted only once. Two of the inmates I later interviewed at other women's prisons in the East, who were at least ten years younger than the Contessa, and had never met her, knew of her by reputation.

"Oh, the Contessa," Amber Fairchild, the gorgeous black girl, who was also quite a con woman on the East Coast, exclaimed, "she's the best there is. That ol' girl practically invented the game for us."

Perhaps it was because the Contessa brought a portion of her middle-class sensibilities to her crimes that she was so successful at hitting middle-class people. Perhaps because she was so intimate with the values of those she conned, she knew exactly how far to push them, how to play them, how much they really trusted her, where they really had their money hidden, how much money they really had, and how far their greed would take them. She also understood that what is truly happening in the con game is that most people think they are getting something for nothing; what really goes down is that the victims, in their secret heart of hearts, think that they are conning the con artist. They think that the con artist is dumb enough to give away thousands of dollars to a stranger, that they are smart enough to outsmart anyone.

I laughed at the Contessa's grasp of psychology as I rode the train up to her prison to interview her for the second time. Spring was coming to town when I made this trip. The tight-wrapped little green buds were bursting forth in color; the air smelled sweet; tiny clouds of baby insects flew by, having just emerged from their cocoon or pod. The East Coast town where the Contessa is incarcerated is a very wealthy community. Many business people live here and commute every day to the city, coming back at night to their secure brick fortresses with large tracts of land, their ponds, their stables, their maids, their butlers, their pools, their pagodas, their lawn parties, and their large bank accounts. Some of these people are the types the Contessa might have hit. Some of them probably have been conned. Some are bitter about it. Some just write it off to the crap shoot of life. Some never knew what hit them. Some became so angry about it that they pushed for stricter legislation to enforce criminal prosecution. Some are so rich that it doesn't matter.

The Contessa and I were happy to see each other that fine spring day. She knows I respect her. I know that she was good at what she did. I listen to her insights about people and life, even though at times they sound a little pat. She has much experience on the street. She is a mini philosopher. At this point, I want to call her chapter "The

World According to the Contessa." She looks today as if she has lost some weight. She's an elegant woman of almost forty, and resembles Anna Magnani in her bearing; she seems older than her actual years. She wears virtually no makeup. She doesn't need any. The drama of her own coloring is enough. Her dark eyes are clear.

The Contessa's husband had been there to visit her last weekend. They have plans for the future. She is happy. She will talk freely today. She offers me a cigarette first, because she knows that I never buy a pack. As if to deny that I really smoke.

"The con that I'm associated with is detailed. More than the other one I told you about. It might take me forty-five minutes or so to explain it to you." I assure her that I have nothing but time for her.

"It also might take me an hour to—if you'll excuse the expression—beat you. Sometimes it might take up to three hours, but I'm playing for higher stakes. I'm playing for what it took you all your life to save." The voluptuous Italian beauty with the thick long black hair settles into her chair in the interview room and begins.

"I walk up to somebody, but then I don't look like this when I'm working. I'm in a nice designer suit, or a knit dress, my jewelry's on. I carry a very nice leather briefcase, I wear my leather bag, my leather shoes. I walk up to you and ask if you could help me, please. Then I explain that I'm coming back from an errand, I work in the vicinity for a bank examiner. Our bank is down the street, I name a particular bank, whatever one's in the area I'm in. My boss is currently auditing their books and I'm on an errand for him, and on my way back to work a gentleman drove by in what appeared to be a limousine. He was throwing his suit jacket into the back seat and he dropped a pouch out of his window. I tried to flag him down, I tried to stop him, but he was in such a hurry that he didn't hear me and he kept on going. I want to return the pouch. It will have some kind of crazy address or district number on it."

The Contessa stops and pulls a tiny bit of tobacco off of her perfectly manicured nail. Her hands are lovely, nails painted clear and natural. Very Bergdorf-Goodman looking. She continues, "I usually work with two people. I have worked by myself, but I prefer working with someone else. The person, my accomplice, will say right away, open the pouch. In it there will be a package with a phony thousand-dollar bill on top. There will also be a telegram stating that there's $100,000 there and that the people whose money it is are leaving the country. They're sending it by pouch because they don't want it to be picked up by the IRS. The telegram further states that they are taking the midnight plane to London; they will contact whomever the telegram is going to on arrival. There's a phony name that I make the telegram out to. Then right away I ask the stranger what I should do with this money. This is how I size up my victims. If they tell me to turn it in, and I make a comment like, 'Well, we know what the police are going to do. All they're going to do is keep it.' If my victim quickly agrees with me that the police are corrupt and that they will keep it, I'll never see that pouch or money again, I know I have a likely victim. But if the person is dead set that I should turn it in to the police or the right people and states emphatically that the police are beyond corruption, then I tell them thank you very much, and I get away from there because I see that I can't control them and in the con game, you have to control everything.

"If the vic tells me to keep it, then I ask them very nicely, well, if I give you each (the victim and my accomplice) a thousand dollars, one of the bills each, would you promise me that you won't say anything about it? Let's just say it's a little token of my appreciation. They'll say, yeah, but what are we going to do with a thousand-dollar bill? Where can we take it? Now, depending on how gullible the victim is, I might try right there and then to find out what kind of money they're playing with. I might say, you can cash any size bill as long as you have that much money in your account. Would you be able to cash it? If she says yes, I know she has at least a thousand dollars. If it's early in the day, I usually take a chance, depending on how the victim looks, because that plays an important factor in whom I stop or don't stop. So, if she says, 'Yeah, I can cash it,' I'll say wait a minute. As I said, my bank is down the street, maybe the money's marked, or maybe it's counterfeit. Let me run it through our analyzer to be sure the money is good. If the money is good, I'll be ready to give both of you a little something. Come on, let's go to where I work.

"But now the other person—remember there's one victim and one accomplice I work with, but the accomplice is acting like we're strangers. We'll start walking toward my fake bank. Then the accomplice will stop.

"'Are you accustomed to bringing people on your job with you?' she'll ask me, real innocently.

"'Well,' I answer, 'I didn't even think about that in this excitement.'

"'I'll tell you what, where I used to work, I couldn't bring any strange people with me on my job without some kind of prior announcement. So why don't we wait here for you,' the accomplice says. 'While you check the bill, we'll stay here if you're going to give us both a thousand dollars.'

"Now, I like to hit middle-class people. With some of my accomplices, I play men because I'm very successful with men." And judging from the seductive way the Contessa treats even me, I can see her act with a gullible man who might be flattered that the beautiful woman is even paying attention to him.

"With other accomplices, I play strictly women because they don't know how to control men. I don't like to play a man if he wants to make it into something more than a business relationship. If there are any sexual overtones, I just cut it off. I have no time for that. I see immediately that it is going to be a total waste of time. I'm loyal to my old man." A nice display of middle-class morality by the Contessa. "And my main objective is getting the money. So I leave the two of them, my accomplice and our victim, and I run off for ten or fifteen minutes, long enough for the vic to relax, and for my accomplice to see what his mind is on. When I come back if the person is no good, if it's a waste of time, I just leave him alone, sort of like rush or close, leave it alone or it's no good, I say it's no go. But if my partner doesn't give me the signal, I come right back in and I tell them immediately the pouch contained a hundred thousand dollars in cash plus an undetermined amount of negotiable bonds and we can keep it legally as long as we handle it in a legal business manner.

"Next I say that my employer is going to handle it for us. He's a bank examiner for the Federal Reserve Bank and he says that as long as we pay tax on the money, we're OK. Sometimes I even give out the story I fabricated about President Kennedy passing a finders-keepers law, a luxury tax of ten percent; if you pay it, you can keep whatever you find. I say, in this case, we're going to keep it. I add that my employer saw me running the money through the analyzer and because I was handling money on the job, I had to tell him what was going on, I didn't want him to think that it was the bank's money because I am licensed, I am bonded, I am insured by Lloyd's of London, so my job was in jeopardy, I'm not going to risk my job for this. In other words, I told him everything that has happened. I explained to him about you two. He told me you two did the right thing and he's glad I stopped and talked to you because usually, on my job, I don't stop and talk to anybody because I carry very large sums of money. He said you gave me the right advice, to keep it, not to give it back to the police, because they'd keep it. They'd say come back in sixty days and they'd give me a receipt, when I'd get back, the receipt would be gone and the money, too. So my employer has a friend who works for the IRS who is a judge. He already called him. He said that he'll pay the taxes on the money for us through him. The tax is ten percent. That leaves us $90,000 plus the bonds. Now I don't want anything I have to sign my name to. I prefer cash money. I don't know about you two ladies, but I told my boss he could keep the bonds, he knows somebody on Wall Street where it's negotiable and he can easily cash them.

"Another thing, he's going to invent a legal reason in black and white for us having this money so if somebody asks us, even if it's a couple of years from today, 'Where did you get that sum of money?' we'll have a contract to show where it came from. He also has a friend at Kodak, which is an international corporation, who works in investments. He's going to make it look like we invested X amount of dollars, say five years ago today, and today we decided to liquidate our investment. This is our initial investment plus all the interest we earned. Now I told him I wanted to divide this $90,000 evenly down to the last penny, so each of us would get $30,000 and we'll get it today, say maybe in the next twenty minutes. The only thing he said is when we get this money he wants you to make a deposit of $2,500 into an account. You do have an account, don't you?

"And my partner says, 'Yes, I have a savings and a checking.'

"'Well, if you have both, or if you have more than one account, you should make a deposit in each account.'

"'How about you?' I ask the victim. Then they turn around and I say, 'Do you have a safe place where you're accustomed to keeping your money and valuables? Do you have a safety deposit box or do you keep your stuff at home? Well, you could take this money and put it there.'

"Now I've found out how many accounts the victim has, if they're savings or checking. I've found out if she keeps her money at home; I've also found out if she has a safe deposit box and what she has in that. Then I turn around and send my partner to my bank to get her money out of her checking account or savings because she was coming from my bank when I stopped her and she had a large amount of cash on her, so she can prove herself. I don't use these words—prove—because like I say this is an old game and this is what people use. So I changed it, I've taken what has been around for seventy years and made it to fit myself and the times.

"So then my partner comes back from her supposed foray to get cash and when she does she'll say she met my boss at the bank and he explained to her all about the contracts and showed her what he's using as serial numbers and assured her that there will be no names involved. He's going to take a certain amount of my other monies' serial numbers and make it look like an investment. He'll do it for each one of us. And he'll use those serial numbers in place of the serial numbers on the $30,000. Then my partner says that the boss didn't give her the time to finish her contract, and she asks me (the Contessa) to please take the contract back up to my office and bring hers back with me, too. So I leave then and stay away another twenty minutes, and return with the supposed contracts and give it back to my partner; and I come back also with two packages of money and give one to the victim and one to my partner.

"Now I tell the victim, 'Come here, give me your hand, this is yours,' and I put the supposed money in her hand and most of the time as soon as that money, which in actuality is just real money on the top and the bottom, depending on how I feel and how my luck is running. Sometimes if I feel superstitious, I use all real money, because I'm afraid if I don't put something in I won't get any money out. Sometimes I might be in a good mood and I'll take maybe two or three hundred-dollar bills and get all ones and fives and make that with maybe a fifty or a hundred on top of it, and I'll put it in her hands and this is the time when I know if I'm going to beat them or not, if I'm going to be able to get it all because when you put that package in their hand and they see all the money and you tell them it's theirs, they get a death grip on it, they don't want to let go. And when I see the way they grip it, then I know how to go on from there. But I take the package back immediately, I'll say it's yours, but I can't give it to you right now because you have to make the same kind of arrangement that she did. I point to my partner. You have to have the serial numbers for your contract just like she did.

"Then I ask if she has any money on her at that point, be it five dollars, be it ten thousand dollars, she's going to tell me what she has on her. And she'll go into her purse. 'Well, this is all I have.' And I say, 'Do you have money at the house?' So she might say, 'I have twelve hundred dollars at the house, we can use those serial numbers.' I always find out whose house it is so I don't have to walk in and discover a six foot five son or a husband who's an ex-wrestler. Then we go into the house, we get the money they have in their house, but that's never enough, then I get the bank books out and depending on what they have in the bank, if they've got $50,000 or $100,000 in the bank, no longer can I just give her $30,000.

"That's when I pretend to call my employer and I suddenly discover that the bonds I found are negotiable and they are worth such an incredible amount of money that he would feel guilty keeping it all so he's giving us part of that, which is what you call a raise. Instead of getting $30,000, now the victim is getting $75,000. You want to ask them for an equal amount of cash to what you're supposedly going to give them. Why would somebody give me $70,000 to only get $30,000? But now with their bank book, I tell them I will not touch their bank book. If this is your book it means it is a once-in-a-lifetime deal. Couldn't you go to your bank and get cash out, that is your money, and you did put it there for an emergency. Couldn't you go and, say, take so much out in cash just long enough for my boss to run it through the ma-

chine and take off the serial numbers. Then you will put
your money back into your account, plus what you're getting
today. They go to the bank and it's mine. Once they go to
the bank and come back."

At this point I interrupt the Contessa. I am confused. I
need some air. I need a cup of coffee from the vending machine out in the hall. The room is slowly starting to fill up
with visitors. Many incongruous couples are seated together
in the visiting room. Back in the children's room, mothers
and their infants play together. I find the scam a little difficult to follow at this point. There is more energy than logic
in it. How could people fall for this?

"Don't the people ever check the money you give them?"
I ask the Contessa, who is eating a pear I bought from the
food machine. She munches carefully, mindful of her recently bonded teeth and tells me that she must continually
diet so that when she is released she will look good for her
husband. I feel what she really means is so she can look good
to go back on the street into the con game again.

"They never keep it long enough, Honey. I take the package right back from them. See, I tell them the money is
yours. Give me your hand; it's yours and I put it in their
hand and after they feel it and like the way it feels and I see
the gleam in their eyes I take it right back out of their hands
and add that I can't give it to them until they put their
money in the bank. Then when they come back from the
bank, most of the time I go right with them to the bank, to
make sure they get the money in the correct way. When
they come back out of the bank, then they'll turn around and
depending on the part I'm playing if I'm not in the banker
role but acting as the accomplice, I'll say to my partner, listen, this lady has been so nice to us I hate to ask her, but
why don't you ask her one more favor. Let her take care of
the business for you like she did for me. Usually you get
your partner to go. But in that case my partner will come
back from the bank, if I'm not the one to go, and she'll say to

me, 'Can't you take care of this business for me like you did
for her? Can't you take my numbers up there, run them
through the machine and bring back my money?' At this
point I'll act like, oh, that's what you want me to do. You
have to be very dramatic now, tragic even, and you have to
remember I left my partner up there. So when I come back,
I act like I ran all the way, I'm all out of breath, very excited,
because I'm going to say that my boss is in a conference."

The Contessa could win an Emmy at this point. She
stands up to illustrate her story. She is short, only five-three,
but her looks are so dramatic, her skin so white in contrast to
her hair, her aquiline nose so regal, it would be difficult not
to fall for her.

"That's why I've been transacting all the business. 'Listen,' I say, my boss just stepped out of the office and said if
you think he's going to finish transacting this without at least
shaking your hand, you're crazy. Go ahead, he's waiting for
you.' And I'll write down on a piece of paper an address and
a name and I'll tell her to sit down and don't say anything to
anybody. He will approach her. By that time I'm gone. I'm
home with whatever they had," the Contessa finishes. She
lights up a Kool. She is breathing rapidly. The story, the
remembered action, excited her.

"So, how did you get caught this time?" I ask.

The Contessa doesn't miss a beat. "They caught me in the
bank. The bank manager was aware of what I was doing. The
woman I hit this time was eighty-three years old, but she
didn't look it. The most she had ever taken out of the bank at
a time was three or four grand. She had almost $40,000 in
banks around the city. I had planned on taking eight from
there, and then going to three other branches and taking
eight from each. The bank I went into was in Queens, New
York, and the teller was delicious. Oh, just as sweet as she
could be. She was going to give me $8,000 in twenties. Then
the manager came out and she was a black woman and she
kept telling my victim come here, come here, and every

time the old woman would walk, I would walk with her. The bank manager finally took my victim in back behind the tellers' cages where I could not go and she called the police." The Contessa sounds offended by the manager's protective attitude toward her victim.

"I left, but I guess the greed this time got me because instead of just walking right out of the bank, I went over to the door of the bank, it was a large bank and I knew the area. I went over by the door and I started shucking, you know, acting like I was doing this and that. Watching, but at the same time able to watch the door, too. Then the manager came back and the old woman still seemed like she was all right, but I left because I got a funny feeling. Then I came back. I left and went and talked to my partner and she had the same funny feeling, but neither one of us wanted to be the one to say we had that feeling and then when I rolled past the bank and I saw the woman standing in front of the bank door with the envelope in her hand, the greed took over.

"All told, when they got done, they had me in a lineup. When they had arrested me, it said in the paper they had me for thirty-three cases, totaling a half million dollars. They could only get thirty-three complaints, and then they could only get twenty people to identify me, and they had me plea to only seven cases. My partner got time, but not as much as me. I got three to nine years."

This sentence doesn't sound so severe to me, especially knowing that the Contessa was out on the street taking little eighty-three-year-old women for their life savings. The Contessa is so bright, her cons are so complex, she probably could have been a writer, she could have been a detective. All the energy she put into crime was wasted, and although she might know this in her heart, she will never admit it to me. She still wants to view crime as glamorous.

The Contessa never felt remorse for the people she beat. She admitted to me that only one time did she ever feel bad.

"I never take all of anyone's money, Susan. Only one time did I ever feel badly. It was years ago. I was like twenty-two. I'll never forget it. I was visiting New York City taking a break from D.C. I had a partner named Venus, a black woman who taught me the game and we were playing an old woman. This old woman told us in the course of the con that if she ever lost all of her money or her jewelry she would kill herself. I never paid that much attention to it because people use that expression very loosely. Then about three weeks after I'd taken her money I was driving over 96th Street, FDR Drive, and I happened to pass her apartment and there was no life in her window. It was bare. And I went back past there a couple of other times that same week. I kept going past because I was waiting to see a sign of life in her window, the sign that would tell me she was still there. And I said to Venus, 'I think she really killed herself.' And Venus said to me, 'Well, look at it this way; it's one less case you have to worry about.' I hated her at that point. That was Venus and I hated her."

But it didn't stop the Contessa from continuing to work. Nothing did. Her favorite sting took place on a Sunday afternoon. The Contessa had moved to New York by then. She preferred not to work on Sunday; it's the Lord's Day of rest. But the girl she was working with, her partner, Louise, was a drug addict; she was desperate, she needed the money, and she begged JoAnn to go with her, they were always very lucky working together. JoAnn consented. They were walking down the late November street in New York City, Lexington Avenue, and Louise saw this lady. To JoAnn she looked like a bag lady; she had little pins holding together her old gray coat. The coat was thin, not enough protection from the cold. But Louise was so insistent that the Contessa stopped the woman, and this vic took the lick. This little old lady, with gray stringy hair and bobby pins holding her slip up, transparent eyes and colorless lips, she began talking about how the bank had recently taken $32,000 from her.

JoAnn thought that she was crazy. But then she looked at the rings on the woman's veinyblue hands, rings that they later wound up taking. One was a two-carat solitaire, the other a 1.5 carat cluster. So JoAnn started to think that maybe this woman had some money.

The old woman took the girls back to her apartment, and the front door wasn't even locked. JoAnn chortled when she began the description of the apartment. "I thought I would die. This broad had never been married; her mother had left all the money to her. Her aunts had never married; they died and left all the money to her. The apartment building was in the Village, on Charles Street, right across from a police station, and the division that handled my case. There were no drapes on the windows, no blinds, no shades, no nothing. She had clothes stacked up to the ceiling in cardboard boxes. Her bedspread was made out of white napkins. Her walls were gray, she hadn't painted them in thirty-five years. Her windows were black; she hadn't washed them in twenty-five years. The kitchen was covered in grease. The sink wasn't even hooked up, the water emptied into an old bucket. She had a back room where she kept the clothes piled up. I went in. At this time I was using the scam that we had found $100,000 on the street that Moslems were sending to Iran to buy guns and ammunition to help them in a war against the United States and that we would keep the money legally before we saw it go into arms, and that we were getting $30,000 apiece. So she told me she had a suitcase full of money in this back room, and she went to look for it. She went to a drawer and she pulled out like only $300 and change.

"So I said to my partner, look, let me look for the money. So I go back to the front room and I go sit at the table and she's got honey spilled everywhere, with roaches crawling all over. I got sick. Then I hear this 'eee-eee, eee-eee,' and I look at her and she just keeps on doing what she was doing. I asked her, 'What is that?'

"She said, 'Oh, don't worry about that, Dear, it's just the mouse.'

"Now I'm sitting with my hands up in the air because of the roaches—I am very clean; I hate dirt—and now I put my feet up in the air because of the mouse.

"My partner comes in from the other room, shaking. She can't talk. She found this giant sweater bag full of Social Security envelopes stuffed with money. We didn't even know what we had, but we took it, put it in my suitcase, locked it in the trunk of my car, went back, took her money out of the drawer. She didn't even see us do that, and I said, 'Let's let this old lady go. We got enough.' But my partner wanted the rings. We took the rings. Then we told her that the bank examiner wanted to shake her hand. We gave her the fake address of the bank and a fake name. We dropped her off on the Lower East Side, shot up Houston Street to FDR Drive, and we were gone.

"Now here comes the thrill, am I gonna get all the way home? Am I gonna make it away from the scene of the crime? It's like my heart was beating, my adrenaline rushing. If I had my trenchcoat on, I'd start coming out of it; if I have a suit on, I'll take it off. So that if the victim does go to the police, I can change, put my glasses on, cover up my hair.

"We quickly go to—I've always lived in the suburbs, but I had a place on Riverside Drive; I never took the kids there. Just a little one-bedroom apartment—and my partner and I went in, dumped the money on the bed. And when we counted it all, we made about $12,000 apiece, all on a Sunday night. A surprise. Then I split the take with my partner, jumped back into my car, and the thrill was on again.

"I've run across the Triborough Bridge so many times, I know all the toll takers, and they go crazy as I drive through just throwing my change in. And it's real. I'm getting away with it. I got over again. I outsmarted the mother, the aunt, and everybody else. Most of all, it's like I'm showing you that I'm going to do what I want to make money. But I'm going to live according to your values, to keep the same life-style."

And stick it up yours, as she goes through life cheating us out of our hard-earned money just for the thrill of the win. Just to prove over and over again, I am, I am, I am.

THE CRIME—Grand larceny, second degree

THE SENTENCE—Three to nine years.

CHAPTER V

THE CONTESSA

"There's a part of me that's square . . . you know, most people call us hustlers . . . well, if one of us gets sick, we usually go into the city hospital, or to see some quack doctor . . . but I kept life insurance, Blue Cross. It's strange, even though I was hustling. I still kept those middle-class values, a safe deposit box, the bank account, the home, the good school for my kids, the real safe in my house for valuables. . . ."
JoAnn Giorgio (The Contessa)
Eastern prison for women
November 19, 1985

A BAD WEEK for JoAnn was three grand. She was pulling at least three stings a week for fifteen years, constantly on the go. She put some money aside; she put some in the bank, but there was a continuous drive in her to scam. If she didn't take two stings in a week, she thought she'd die of a heart attack.

JoAnn made up to a quarter of a million dollars in a year, but her basic problem was easy come, easy go. Her attitude all her life was, "If I don't have the money, mom or grand-mom will give it to me." Ever since she's been in the con-fidence game, she has known that even if she spent her last dime, she could get more . . . tomorrow. Sort of the Scarlett O'Hara of the middle-class con women.

JoAnn's daddy was a master union electrician whose side

business was installing televisions in private homes. His father had owned a company that supplied Washington, D.C., stores with blocks of ice.

When JoAnn's mother, Francesca, met her future husband, he was a handsome sailor wearing a uniform. Francesca went crazy over him and they quickly got married. But when JoAnn was two and a half, her parents separated. They were part of the first wave of middle-class American divorces that began shortly after World War II, when things really started to change in this country. JoAnn and her mother went to live with Francesca's parents in Washington, D.C., home of the Lincoln Memorial and resting place of the Constitution of the United States. They lived in the middle-class Northwestern section, right around the corner from Mount Vernon College. The houses there cost $29,000 back in the 1950s, and the streets were lined with tall shade trees. Not too far away, in Wesley Heights, were some of the most elegant houses in all of Washington.

JoAnn was the only child in an Italian-American family. Her grandparents had come from Tuscany in the early 1900s. They were sticklers for education. They built their lives up by working hard, becoming homeowners, and moving up the ladder. And they brought old country traditional values with them, especially the importance of family.

JoAnn was the hope of the clan. She would always have everything she wanted, plus. Her mother worked all day as a registered nurse in an exclusive Washington sanitarium. She has been with the hospital for years. JoAnn was kept after school by her grandparents, who loved their little grandchild so much they gave the bright-eyed darling everything that money could buy. But they couldn't replace her daddy.

"That's the nitty gritty, Kiddo. Everyone else had one, but me. I started to wonder what was wrong with me." JoAnn remembers today, her irregularly shaped black eyes welling up with tears, this hustler supreme, who can beat little old women out of their life savings. She felt cheated in life from the beginning.

JoAnn's uncle, her mother's brother, lived in the same house with the family. He especially spoiled the little girl, maybe trying to fill the role of the lost daddy. He was an elementary school teacher. When JoAnn was only in second or third grade, he started buying her genuine leather bags, large snakeskin and alligator ones from exclusive women's haberdasheries for her to use as book bags.

JoAnn was an excellent student. She went to a semiprivate school at first, but when it turned public, her mother practically exploded and enrolled her right away in a Catholic high school. JoAnn consistently finished in the first track, which meant she earned the highest grades she could get. In the morning, her Italian grandmother would cook specials for the beloved. "She knew I didn't like eggs, so before I would go to school, grandmother would go downstairs every morning and cook me a hamburger in its natural juices, cause that's how I liked it, on a slice of rye bread, only the heart—the crusts cut off, medium rare, because if it wasn't medium rare, she'd make me another." JoAnn laughs in astonishment even today at how spoiled she really was. Especially in comparison to her life at prison.

For hot lunch, she'd get open-faced grilled cheese sandwiches that her grandmother would make after she picked her up from school. Or homemade pasta, whatever the child wanted. Then she'd be driven back to her red brick private Catholic academy. She was never alone; she never knew what a baby sitter was. When she came home after school, the whole family did her homework together. Every Saturday they'd go shopping to one of those Italian markets that smell of olive oil and fennel, where salamis hang long and fat from the ceiling, and provolone and mozzarella cheese sit together like buttery cousins behind an immaculate glass counter. Everything would be fresh sliced, and then they'd go to the bakery and buy the small Italian rolls that JoAnn loved so. Meanwhile, grandfather would go and buy Italian candy for the child: candy-coated almonds and tortoni that he kept in a hidden spot in an antique blue-tinted jar from Tuscany—just for JoAnn, whom he called Chi-Chi. Chi-Chi had her own wine glass from the time she was four, because, "grandfather came from the old country and they were raised on wine, so when I was little it was wine and water and as I got older, it turned into just wine," she concludes, gazing at her reflection in the glass door of the interview room. JoAnn is mature, refined looking. There's more than a suggestion of temper in her controlled expression.

When JoAnn was nine Francesca would ask her daughter where she wanted to go for vacation. It was always what JoAnn wanted to do. JoAnn wanted to go to Disneyland. So they went, the entire family. They took her to see Mickey Mouse, the Pacific, and the snow-covered peaks. As JoAnn grew older, she started to ask to go to Atlantic City. Her mother rented an apartment there every summer for a month, and when JoAnn saw, even as a young girl, that there was more action on the boardwalk at Wildwood and requested a summer there, that's where the family went, no questions asked.

"See, when you're in the middle class, money becomes the thing people can give you the most easily, because they are so busy working. It is, what can I give you, in terms of the dollar sign." I feel JoAnn is categorizing too many people in the middle class. She is not an economist. "But when you grow up in the lower class, they don't have any money, they're lucky if they can put a pound of rice and beans on the stove, so the only things they can give to their families are emotional, the love, the caring, the sharing." She pauses for a minute to light one of her many cigarettes. "Really, when I look back on it now, my life, I wanted someone to say no to me, but they never did. It was always, what does JoAnn want. But, see, it was a double-edged sword, because in really important issues, they just assumed that they knew best, as far as values went, and they never let me make my own decision. I started rebelling at a very early age." She pauses.

JoAnn's explanation for her entry into crime seems very rehearsed to me. She has all the rhetoric, all the psychological excuses, she had no daddy, the middle-class values of her family seemed false, she was looking for truth. But she is too glib. Somewhere, there is another reason JoAnn was attracted to crime. I begin to feel it was the action on the street that really interested her. The guard tells everyone in the visiting room to stay put, the noon time head count is taking place. A tall black correctional officer looks in at JoAnn and me, noting her presence in the room. I half expect him to yell, "Twelve o'clock, and all is well."

When JoAnn was eleven, all her rings were specially made of fourteen-karat gold, heart shaped, and all of them had either diamonds on the side or a diamond in the middle. She would go into a store and see a Crackerjack box, hoping there was a little plastic ring in it, but her mother never thought anything was good enough for her daughter but the best, certainly not a dollar ring made from pink plastic. JoAnn wanted to fit with the other kids, she wanted to be in—partake of the fads. It was not permitted.

"At the time I wanted to be like everybody else. The school I went to, St. Patrick's on Foxhall Road right around the corner from my house, was very strict, but you had the run from the very wealthy, even politicians', statesmen's children, to your upper middle class to your poor, because the area where the school was is in the center of Washington, and less than a mile from school you were right in the middle of a black neighborhood. So all these kids were going to the same school. The middle-class ones always made me sick. Oh, we're too good to talk to the poor kids, I wanted to talk to everyone. Why should I ignore her because her clothes came from John's basement bargain and mine from John Wanamakers?" Later when JoAnn came into crime, most of the people that were doing what she was doing, the poor ones that is, seemed to want what she had, but didn't want. JoAnn found herself wanting the same things all over again, all the accoutrements of middle-class success. But that was later on. . . after the drugs, and after Venus.

JoAnn wanted to be a historian for a long time. Then her mother wanted her to be a teacher. But her grandmother thought she should become a nurse. At age fourteen she briefly considered a career as a doctor. She was always fascinated with people and their minds, what made them tick, what were their weaknesses, their strong points. What could she do to them, how far could she go? But deep in her heart JoAnn knew that her predestined role in the family was to fulfill the dreams her mother had never realized.

We were interrupted a second time by the uniformed correctional officer, tapping on the door of the conference room usually reserved for attorney-inmate meetings. He insisted that I open the door, so he could ask me how many more women I wanted to see that day. Prison life is a series of interruptions, there is no privacy, only rules. JoAnn shook her head at our interruption and continued.

"It was always like I was supposed to be the one to go to college, being that my mother only went to nursing school. JoAnn's going to go, JoAnn has the honors, JoAnn is the star. It wasn't whether I wanted to go or not; it was just something that was automatically assumed. The family had the money, and then they started arguing amongst themselves about what I would become. What was acceptable to the family." And what she became was a rebel, perhaps with a cause, but hardly the citizen of substance that her family not only wanted but expected her to be.

JoAnn came out for anything that was against the societal norm. She loved beatniks. Then she loved the hippies. And in her senior year in high school this hope of her family started along with the rest of the middle-class kids, seriously rejecting everything that the middle class had worked for, telling them to kiss off, we don't want yours, I'm gonna get my own, what good has yours done you, if I make mistakes, I make them. Back then it was the anti-establishment chant: I hate the government; I hate this; I hate that craze.

"But if you think back to it, the sixties, the SDS, the Weathermen, the hippies, the people that initiated it had all the money that they wanted. If a mistake was made," JoAnn smiles slyly, "all you did was pick up the phone and say, 'Mom, I'm in trouble, I need more money', and it still came. So we were really lying to ourselves." But this fact did not stop anyone from anything, except pursuing the conventional course that included college, and the Protestant ethic and spirit of capitalism vision of success. The values of the Eisenhower era, the straight 1950s—values that had always been the implicit backbone of the middle class since its formation—were squashed.

Drugs became the in thing, the cool differential between squares and hipsters, the release from the dull into the extraordinary. Even for little Catholic high school girls in parochial uniforms. JoAnn got a part-time job as a girl Friday in a small office, she was paid to do payroll, expense accounts. She quickly figured out a way so that she had access to the cash. She altered the records to show that the money was safe in the office. She carried at least $1200 in her leather bag in petty cash at all times. But she used to pay herself twice a week and use the extra money to buy amphetamine and resell it on the street.

She didn't need the money, but she wanted it. Money was action. And JoAnn loved action. JoAnn began her criminal career as a natural outgrowth of her rebellion against the cloying, overprotective love of her family. She had no intention of ever going to college. Or ever, ever coming back to the fold of society that lay on the other side of the wall that the outlaws call "the straight line."

The last brush JoAnn had with respectable society was when she was nineteen. Even today, at thirty-eight, the

memory of the story affects her as she looks out at the wait-
ing-visiting room and sees young, desperate couples, often
disheveled, holding hands.

"I was engaged when I was nineteen to a nice Italian-Irish
boy, Kevin, whose aunt is today a famous D.C. judge. You
know a very good family." But the respectability was merely
a front, because it was Kevin who taught JoAnn how to shoot
heroin. She knew nothing about it until they met. He was
going to the Corcoran School of Art affiliated with the prestigious Corcoran Art Gallery. JoAnn was working, and neither one of them wanted their families to support them,
even though the door swung open into either home.

"At Kevin's school the kids were all middle to upper class,
and you know mommy pacifies them by letting them go, oh
yeah they think they want to be an artist, we'll let them get
out of mommy's hair to a school where they can still tell all
their friends that they're in college. And all he had to do was
pick up the phone and call home. Nobody was crucially in
need of anything. And then drugs became so dominant. Everyone was doing them; it was our way of saying we don't
like your set of values for real. I guess I was mad at my
mother because she was trying to make me do what she
didn't, and I didn't have a clue as to who I was," she says
with her eyes. JoAnn and Kevin were an item, but one day
JoAnn found out that Kevin had a little hidden secret. Close
to Thanksgiving, she overheard a phone conversation between him and a male friend—a conversation about oral sex
between those two. JoAnn, who was still fairly innocent at
this point, realized that her beloved was a bisexual. It threw
her for a loop, because this was way before the gay liberation. And the knowledge that her accomplice in the drug
rebellion was actually keeping important facts from her blew
her mind. "I couldn't take it. I broke all contacts with my
mother, who still thought Kevin was a nice boy and wanted
us to reconcile." But JoAnn would never rat out anyone, she
wouldn't tell her mother about Kevin, it was probably too

much for anyone in her family to handle. So JoAnn just got mad, mad at the world that seemed to constantly betray her.

She journeyed physically and spiritually into the strictly black Northeastern area of D.C., 14th Street, the supremely hip Washington strip where everything was available. There she met James, who introduced her to Venus. It was then JoAnn's education on the streets began; it was there she trained herself in the art of commodity exchange. . .drugs. Then in the art of thievery . . . fast talking style . . . the con game. She never looked back. She never had remorse.

JoAnn met James in a 14th Street bar in D.C. She never told him what kind of family she was from, but the expensive way she dressed, the quality of her fourteen-karat gold jewelry and her heart-shaped rings, the pain she was feeling, the hostility she projected, the rejection from Kevin, the fact that she had no identity, this must have been apparent to street hustler, James. And JoAnn instinctively was drawn to the area most frequented by the entire criminal subculture of con people. The upper echelon, of course, who met, exchanged stories, partners, tips, complaints, and ran around together to the seemingly mysterious bars.

She elucidates: "When you go into a strange town, and you're looking for a contact, you should go to the black area because most hustlers use some form of drugs, be it reefer, cocaine, crack, liquor, heroin. Maybe it's a way of proving to everybody else that they have money; but they go in and buy a blow, some people call it flashin', letting people know they have money. And usually you run into somebody and you start talkin', there's a certain look that you can tell, you know if you go into Harlem and you see somebody standing there with a nice diamond ring, and jewelry, and a good wool coat, maybe a designer bag, and you always check out their shoes, and they're good shoes, the way they carry themselves, they don't fit in the neighborhood, be it Boston, New York, LA, Pittsburgh, you know they don't belong there, so automatically you know they're doing something.

What, you don't know, maybe playing the con game, maybe working credit cards, checks, but usually anybody that's in the game is also articulate, and bright. You start a conversation, she might know somebody you know, you might have met somebody else, and the next thing, you know everything that's going on in the town. In Boston, there's an area called Roxbury, in Harlem, it's Sugar Hill, on 7th Avenue, like from 145th Street up Broadway and Amsterdam, the Capitol Bar, on 124th and 7th, Marcell's on Lenox, the Blue Book on Amsterdam, the Oasis on Broadway. That's where I met my husband, but that was much later on. Anyhow," she stops for a moment drifting off into the noise of the prison, the guards sweeping the floor, the crying children who are visiting with their mothers. JoAnn is thinking of her own husband and children. "In a new town you go to where the prostitutes are, some of them will tell you everything, 'Oh, you new in town, Honey?' Prostitutes are still hustlers, even though they're the lowest, but she'll know where everyone goes. And if you really want to be honest about it, most white women who are in the con game I'm into come from a middle-class family. Sometimes it's due to their pimp who can give them the love that mommy and daddy never did."

James paid attention to the twenty-two-year-old voluptuous Italian girl called JoAnn. She was a potential knockout, with her high-placed breasts, her long wavy black hair flowing down her back, and her poreless complexion. Even then she walked into a room like she owned it. James listened to JoAnn's story, watched her desperation trying to cop drugs for her newly acquired habit that was the only thing left over from her relationship with Kevin. He listened to her vocabulary; he noticed her expensive lizard bags and shoes, and suddenly he realized that this woman who looked so innocent had the look all crooks seek out in an apprentice—the upper middle-class trustworthy look.

James asked JoAnn some questions, questions that today make her laugh at her own naivity, like "What would you do

if you had X amount of dollars and you could do anything
you wanted to? How would you feel if you knew you could
talk people out of their life savings?" JoAnn, who had nothing else to do, and loved the challenge of thinking, played
his little con game with him, answering with the answers she
thought he wanted to hear, thinking in her young head that
she had found a man who was going to give her everything.
Then James got bolder and started telling her that she too
could be a player in the game. JoAnn just couldn't believe it;
but she got the wide-eyed curious look of the definitely interested, and it was then James arranged for her to meet
Venus.

Venus was a star in the game played on 14th Street and
Northeast Washington. JoAnn learned everything she knew
about the confidence game from Venus. She trained right in
her hometown of D.C. JoAnn credits Venus with turning her
out, teaching her how to make the most of who she was.
When James introduced them in one of the hip subculture
network bars of Washington, Venus checked her out, ap-
praising her potential. James had told Venus that JoAnn was
the perfect white girl whom they could probably talk into
doing anything. Venus was tall and thin and black. She told
JoAnn she had just come out of prison in New York where
she was originally born. Now she lived permanently in D.C.
with her pimp, mentor eventual husband, old man. Venus
comes from what JoAnn describes as a middle-class black
family. Venus's family had a lot of children and a lot of love.
As they sat in the bar, in the late thin pale fall sunlight,
Venus began questioning JoAnn, all the time trying to decide if JoAnn was a stand-up person, suited for their kind of
work, one who would never break the code. For JoAnn,
Venus was like the dean of the college she never went to.

"What would you do if a complete stranger walked up to
you on the street and told you that all her money had been
stolen, and don't answer me too quick, sugar, you think it

over," Venus asked in her low husky voice as her vodka, straight up, arrived.

JoAnn hesitated to answer. Everything she wanted in life was resting on the way she answered these questions.

"I would be suspicious of anyone who tried to pull any scam off on me," she answered proudly.

"But how would you know it was a scam, Sweetheart?" Venus's voice became a little firmer. JoAnn lit up a Kool to hide her nervousness. You can hustle a hustler, she knew from her limited days on the street selling drugs, but you can't con them in their areas of expertise.

"See, the way the pros work," JoAnn recalls today leaning back in her metal chair in a rather masculine gesture, "they tell you all about their gig. James had set me up for that part. Me, I was curious, but I didn't believe it could happen; so I wanted to act cool. I can go up to a total stranger I've never met and tell them this bullshit story about me finding a packet. Well, back then it was an envelope with money in it, and I'm trying to return it—it just didn't sound feasible to me. But Venus kept saying, it works. Another thing, I was a drug user, and it was an easy way for me to get money to support my habit."

Venus looked at the young girl and sensed all her anger at society, at the world, and all the love she had to give.

"What would you do if you did the game and got caught by the police, Honey?" Venus purred, "cause if you did get caught you know we're together and you don't have to tell them, we'll get you out."

JoAnn thought it over. "I wouldn't tell anyone anything," she reassured the tall black woman with the hawk nose and the soft heart.

"You see, we blacks, we know how hard society is, how they discriminate against everyone, Honey. We've all been hurt; society and the establishment suck. We operate outside of the law but we have our own code, JoAnn." Venus finished, softly touching the top of the girl's head.

Con people know how to run a conversation on anybody, they know how to switch the subject to ease the tension, they use a lot of finesse and tact, they subtly fit in the questions they want answers to, testing how the innocent feels about certain things. Venus knew how to find JoAnn's weak spot, and she played on it. That's how she trapped her. They were all in this life together, the SDS, the hippies, the potheads, the blacks, the brokenhearted, the criminals. They were all fighting the unseen government, and they would all help each other forever.

JoAnn was just hurt enough, just angry enough, just stoned enough that she went for it. After a day or two of questioning and rehearsals, she and Venus went out together to a white D.C. neighborhood and pulled the first hit—for $1200. That was $600 apiece. Venus used an old scam first, a tried and true one most con artists begin with.

There are many variations of the con. But basically there is only one con. Each con person evolves the ideal scam for themselves. JoAnn learned the basics from Venus. With Venus you worked with a partner. Later on, JoAnn took this game and perfected it. She became a legend on the streets. Her con became known as the Contessa's game. (See Chapter IV.) But the basic game she learned from Venus sixteen years ago still holds true, and is still practiced on street corners all around the world. She talked about her art proudly like Jane Fonda might discuss acting, or Georgia O'Keefe discussed her painting. It was amazing to watch the transformation come over this convict when she described her art— behind bars, but never far away from the thrill, the rush, the power. She became even more beautiful when she talked about her con. Her normally pale cheeks colored. I could see how irresistible she could be in action. "The con game has been around longer than I am old, all right? It has many subtleties. The first one I'll run by you is called the Wesen-

dia, where you walk up to a complete stranger with a piece of paper that says you just got off the boat, you're lost, and you gave the man at the bus terminal two hundred dollars to hold seven thousand dollars of your money, so that he would put it in a locker and he would hold the key. And now you're looking for a place to stay." We momentarily pause so I can go get a cup of coffee, two creams, two sugars. "And you tell this to a stranger and they think they're dealing with an idiot—right away they think this. All right, you ask them to hold your money while you go to the bus station to get the rest. In other words, you want them, the stranger, to hold your money because they're the first one you meet and you trust them. But then, as you hand them, well, it's not really money, first of all, it's a bunch of play money or paper cut up like dollars with a real bill on top and a real bill on the bottom, which somebody who is greedy sees, and thinks you've got money, but you give it to them and they put it in their purse, and you say to them, 'Where's your money?' And they show you that it's someplace else and you ask them, are they more protective of their money than yours? They're supposed to be a friend of yours. Would they hold their money like this? And then the game gets good, you take their money and your fake money and wrap it in a hand- kerchief and show them how you want them to hold it down in their bosom. But when you do reach down in your bosom with it, you have another package there already made up, and this one's full of nothing but play money, and that's the one you pull out. And that's the one you give to them. The whole thing is based on trust. Like me trusting Venus. So if you trust a person, you don't open the handkerchief up in front of them to check it. That would be embarrassing. So in the meantime, they think they're dealing with an idiot, they're getting their money back anyhow, so they put it in their purse or bosom or briefcase the way you tell them to. And you walk off and leave them and you have their money."

JoAnn chuckles. "That's one variation of it. I don't myself

indulge in that one because it's not enough money. It's good
if you're out for a little hit, because it's only what the person
has on them at the time. I play for higher stakes. I wear very
expensive clothes, excellent jewelry, leather bag and shoes, I
size up my victims, because in the con game you have to
control the vic, or the lame," she finishes proudly.

After Venus initiated JoAnn into the life, JoAnn gave up
heroin. No one told her to, she felt she had to. Venus was
not a heroin user, James wasn't either. It turned into the
kind of thing where she wondered how she was goin' to talk
people out of their money when her arms looked like rail-
road tracks. Who would believe her? Then it turned into a
game for her. It was like, let me see if I can talk you out of
whatever you spent your whole life saving. To think that she
could trick someone, in a couple of hours, out of a lot of
money, is to say she's stronger than they are mentally, and
that's a thrill. A bigger thrill for an intelligent person than
drugs, which lead nowhere.

By the time the police caught up with JoAnn—fifteen
years later, they had been looking for her for four or five
years. It was the division of police devoted to "Career Criminals" that found her; career criminals being those who make
a profession out of their crime lifestyle. JoAnn was on the
news, on the radio, a suspect in over thirty crimes, with an
estimated take of over $500,000. That they knew of. The lit-
tle Italian girl from the religious family, with no daddy, had
become a success. In the life. On the street.

"Maybe I got to be the best because I wanted to prove to
daddy that I was good, I can accomplish, I could go far. And
since I didn't do it in the legitimate world, the only alternative I had was to go illegal and be the best there was. All
right, so daddy didn't recognize me when I was a medical
secretary, or a girl Friday, or payroll clerk, or daughter,
maybe daddy will recognize me now that I'm a thief and a
damn good one." JoAnn sighs as our interview concludes for
the day.

And as the years wore on, she brought a portion of what she considered middle-class values to her business. Never rat out a comrade, have insurance, buy the best for your kids, import a maid from Jamaica for true respectability.

JoAnn never bought anything on sale. She and her husband, who is black, moved to New York because there is a larger white population of potential victims. They lived in a middle-class suburban neighborhood, among the straights. No one ever knew what she did for a living. She bought jewelry, tending toward diamonds and opals, platinum settings, Rolex watches, and station wagons with the wood side paneling, although she debated over a sleek Mercedes, black, if you please, for a long time. She bought her husband a Kelly-green mustang convertible. He can't even drive. They got a driver. She purchased only the best cuts of meat for her family.

Even behind bars JoAnn maintains this middle-class snobbery: "Last week-end, Easter Sunday, my kids came up to visit. My daughter had her first pair of shoes, without a strap. She'd been wearing Capezios, Mary Jane style, since she was little, that's all I would buy her. But a friend of my husband took her to get shoes for Easter. She came in here with no straps. I had to take the shoes off and examine them and look inside to see what brand they were. When I saw they were Stride Rite shoes, the best, I was satisfied."

Joann certainly doesn't live by the middle-class values of the 1950s that stated we would all go to high school, eat peanut butter and jelly sandwiches, get high-scoring SAT tests, go to an Ivy League college, get out, find a great job, get married, work nine to five, save, have a little family, pray, support the church, be honest, never lie, pay taxes, celebrate Christmas with Bishop Sheen on TV, grow old looking like Robert Young, honor our father and our mother, obey the Ten Commandments, be kind to the needy, vote regularly, never indulge in kinky sex, except for procreation or with a high-paid hooker who would never be found out by the wonderful wife, who looked and talked a lot like Donna Reed.

All these dreams ended with the influx of Third World drug dealers who made more in a year than most of the middle class made in a lifetime, had no values we could recognize, shot each other in the street, but had the best of everything for their children including nannies from Nicaragua, silver Rolls-Royces, and Neiman-Marcus charge cards with unlimited credit.

JoAnn's husband is an older man. She chose a black man as part of her rebellion against her family—specifically against her father's family. "Maybe I was trying to get even with him because the last time I saw his family I was eighteen. They were Anglo-Saxon, very straightlaced, very middle class. Maybe I got back at them by going with a black man," she realized today in our interview.

Her husband, Leroy, is a retired veteran from World War II. He gets a pension every month, a veteran's pension. "And the only reason he's getting that is because in the 1940s the judge gave him the choice, prison or service. And he took service." Leroy, however, never went overseas. "He spent his whole time in the states because just as his battalion was shipping out to go to Europe, he managed to slip one of the MP's at the dock a few hundred dollars, which in the 1940s was nice money, and this MP turned his head when Leroy went AWOL. His battalion was killed overseas."

JoAnn met Leroy years ago in one of the network bars in Washington. JoAnn's been playing the game for fifteen years, Leroy's been playing about thirty-five years. They call him the Grand Daddy. He began his relationship with JoAnn telling her stories about how she could get money, claiming that he was going to teach her the bank examiner game, explaining how he took money in one state and flew to another state to get to the bank, and somewhere he slipped in "Would she be his woman," and she was just so enthralled by him and his stories, she fell smack dab in love. Even if he

thrill in the humdrum of married sex life in this era of death through sex.

JoAnn and her husband are so into sex that when, several years ago, a friend gave them an article in a magazine about an operation that a legendary billionaire had, Leroy thought about it and decided he wanted the same operation. So they got him into a New York hospital, and he had the operation, microsurgery; a penile implant, so he can get as hard today as he could at nineteen. These criminals are into some serious love and affection between themselves.

They also have some very opinionated views about women in crime in the 1980s. "I know that this is no longer a male-dominated world. There's too many single parents, too many bastards running around. And the courts now look at you, if you're a woman, and from the middle class, to hang you. Like all these years," JoAnn drags heavily on her cigarette during our last day of interviewing, "men put women upon a pedestal, the old madonna-whore dichotomy, and men are going to have to start seeing women for what they are, human beings, just like men, thinking, breathing, reacting. Right now out there in the streets, women are becoming more assertive. Men may be more aggressive, they have the physical strength, but women are more assertive," this jail-house philosopher asserts. And women have more finesse in their crimes. Women are better at details. A good female thief does a lot of little things a man wouldn't. A man will go strong arm. A woman has only her mind, her cunning, her wiles that she's developed over the centuries to trap her husband with, to rely on. And these wiles are what men don't expect from female criminals.

But the prospects for social security and pension funds for an old criminal are not what even a payroll clerk or secretary from the middle class can look forward to. There is no con person union. No society to protect the rights of thieves. JoAnnn knew one old con man, Fingers, who was in his nineties. He was playing until the day he died. And they had to take up a collection to bury him. No one came to the funeral, and no one cared about Fingers passing, except a few of his students who had learned the art from him. So what is the future for JoAnn?

JoAnn's mother told her that she feels that if her daughter had had her choice, she would have become a professional student all of her life. She would have chosen the ivory tower existence and never faced reality. Francesca told JoAnn that she didn't feel her daughter could make it on $250 or $300 a week. A true vote of confidence. Even though Francesca and JoAnn are closer now than ever. The straight life for JoAnn means no big payoffs, no jewelry, bought or stolen from the lames, no Mercedes, no vacations to the islands.

JoAnn runs her fingers through her hair slowly. She purses her pouty lower lip. "My husband's theory is that when I come home I'm to do absolutely nothing. Be a mother to our kids. But I believe in a dual-career marriage." A liberated woman in the criminal game. "Why should he be able to go out and work, and I can't? Maybe not an illegal job. I'm taking psychology courses here, I'd like to work with adolescents, offer alternatives to the life for them so that they don't get in here in September, and get out in November, and by January they're back." Another criminal who wants to work with ex-cons, another criminal afraid to go back to the street again.

"I work as a teacher's aide, I go to college at night, I'm vice-president of the inmate liaison committee, I'm on Weight Watchers, money addiction. I try to stay busy because my day is unending. There's no violence here because whereas in a men's facility, they don't think anything about throwing somebody off a tier, here the women try to get along. This is a cooking facility, you can have smoked meat, vegetables brought in, you don't have to eat in the mess here if you don't want to. We're lucky. This is one jail where you can survive and still be healthy. Maybe I could help open a halfway house for kids, I love kids," she concludes pensively.

Other inmates told me that they think JoAnn is majoring in sociology and psychology to be a better con artist when she gets out. Run a tighter organization. Avoid any slipups. It would be extremely difficult to duplicate the rush of crime working in an office. The thrill. The feeling of power. Especially for JoAnn, a.k.a. the Contessa, supposedly the best white woman out there playing the game. The Contessa had, over the years, people calling her from Texas, California, Frisco, LA., Chicago, asking her to come to their state, offering to fly her there, if she would just help them with their work. They'd rent the car, bring their VISA or MasterCards, whether they were real, stolen, or forged, finance the whole deal. And there's no way she could see herself as one of the have-nots. "A $20,000 job a year, that's not bad, but consider I go through maybe $20,000 in two weeks." She smiles.

JoAnn's immediate plan when she gets out is to go home, lie down in her living room in her soft chair, and relax. She might walk to the refrigerator four or five times to look in there, take a bath, walk to the store, make love to her husband, pick up a glass of fresh juice, because she's a juice drinker, lie on the carpet and have the dog walk all over her, make some lasagna, put some attainable goals on herself that she can reach and feel good about. The difficult goals, if you fail, you wind right back where you started from. She's a beautiful, exotic woman, her husband loves her, her kids too.

What failed JoAnn, this articulate, pretty woman with everything going for her?

"A psychologist would tell me I loved my mother and thought she failed me, being that she left my father. That's the whole route right there. But sometimes I wonder if it's me that I failed, I failed myself. Cause I really didn't do when I was young what I wanted to, and that was going to medical school, not to be a nurse like they wanted me to. But be a doctor, cut somebody open, see what really makes the human body work. Maybe I'm into the mind now. Maybe I'm looking for the answer to what made me do what I did. Maybe that's why I'm into psychology courses, juvenile delinquents, abnormal psych. I failed myself. I never had the children I wanted to, but when I was younger I really didn't want them because I felt they were a hold-up. Maybe I needed to feel needed all my life and I never felt like I was. Maybe that's why I want to work with children. They need me. Maybe when I find out the answer, Susan, I'll let you know, what failed. . . ." And then the guard escorted JoAnn down the brightly lit neon corrider back to her cell.

THE CRIME—Grand larceny (2nd degree)
THE SENTENCE—Three to nine years

CHAPTER VI

OBSESSION

"When the judge sentenced me, he said, I want to make this sentence harsh so that I can show that good girls do go bad, and maybe stop more from pursuing a similar course."
LINDA WILLIAMS
A Western prison for women
December 3, 1985

LINDA WAS A Rainbow Girl growing up in Nebraska. Rainbow Girls is a social organization affiliated with the Masons, based on Bible principles and dedicated to social-service work. Linda would go to her meeting after school in her white uniform and learn about helping others. She was very involved with her youth group at church. She loved school. When the bus picked her up in the morning and drove her past the fields of wheat bending in the Midwestern springtime breeze, she was just plain happy to be alive, to be a part of America.

Linda was a self-admitted Goody Two Shoes. She loved to read, got straight A's, and was the editor of her school newspaper. But everything in her life seemed to revolve around her church, the Rainbow Girls, and doing good for others.

"My parents were very Christian, very WASPish," she remembers today, a high-energy blond in a West Coast style hand-painted sweatshirt, with long mauve fingernails. "I would say my family was very religious, even spiritual."

135

Linda was very much her daddy's girl. Her parents had had problems having children, so when she came along, the first, she was very special, particularly to her father. Her younger sister by four years, Eileen, had all she could do in school to avoid constant comparison to her over-achieving older sibling.

"All Eileen's teachers did was ram down her throat, 'Why can't you get grades like your sister, Linda? Why can't you be more like her?' to a point where Eileen and I were really in conflict. She couldn't stand it."

Linda ended up going into an area of extracurricular activities that was completly opposite from Eileen just so Eileen would have something that was all her own. Even as a teenager, Linda made these decisions consciously—altruistically. Anything to avoid conflict.

This memory is unpleasant to Linda. She grimaces and pulls at her left hoop earring as she relives the pain of her childhood. Today this same sister, Eileen, runs a non-denominational retreat program in Utah. She has never been in trouble for one second.

Linda's parents believed that men and women are completely equal. Both were doctors—her father a psychiatrist, her mother one of the first female gynecologists to graduate from her medical school.

The Williams family moved to Texas during Linda's junior year in high school. Her father had received an offer from a Houston hospital, and the warm weather was better for his arthritis. Her mother quickly developed a wealthy private practice and wrote several books on sex education.

On the outside, her parents seemed to be the ideal couple. They were best friends, and that was the type of marital relationship that Linda would look for. She and her younger sister were encouraged to excel and be whatever they wanted to be. As long as they were the best.

But all was not as it appeared. The Williams version of

Midwestern holiday dinners were Norman Rockwellian feasts, held at a long table covered with white linen and rows of china bowls emanating odors of turkey security and yam Noel. But Linda can't remember one Thanksgiving or Christmas dinner when there was not a giant conflagration.

"Just at the point Mom got dinner done, she was stewed, gone. And she and my sister were at constant odds. So my sister finally got to the point where she just left," Linda explains in her well-controlled voice, a voice that sounds as if it has spoken at many corporate board meetings. Linda's mother was an alcoholic. And her daughter Linda fell into the family role that Alanon calls the Hero. Linda's purpose in life—on a very subconscious level—was to cause no problems whatsoever, because there was so much turmoil at home.

Linda's life revolved around attaining perfection. She became the perfect student, the perfect Rainbow Girl, the best reader, the neatest seamstress, the finest baker in home ec class, the high school spelling champion, the daughter who never forgot a holiday or a birthday, the most conscientious friend, the kindest enemy, the exemplary American teenager, the one who forgot who she really was in her quest to disappear into the perfect. Linda became obsession personified: she was obsessed with excelling, achieving, going on, omitting, ignoring her mother's drinking, and obsessively ignoring her father's pain and avoidance. Linda was for all intents and purposes a square. An egghead. She didn't drink. She didn't do anything that any of her peers were doing in the 1960s. But eat.

"A lot of my past I blocked out. I had a very poor self-image growing up. Now I'm aware of it; but at the time, it just didn't come across that way. But I was fat. And my mother, who was a rail, never said a word about it," this now slim, stylish woman of forty muses. You wouldn't think it to look at her today: five-five, 115 pounds, her arms perfectly shaped from years of playing tennis at courts around the country, but in her junior year of high school, Linda weighed two hundred pounds. She wore a size 20 ½ dress. She lost it all, of course. Because being fat did not fit in with being perfect. And she lost it all before her senior year at the new high school began. She accomplished this feat by employing the same type of obsessive control over her eating that she used in every other area of her life. She put herself on a very strict diet and got involved in a rigorous exercise program. Alone. With no doctor's guidance. She lost eighty pounds in eight months. And she's never gained an ounce back. Being thin is very important in the world of corporate success. And corporate success became the goal to which Linda channeled her obsessive need to excel.

In her senior year at the new high school, Linda was very popular. Her family had moved to Houston's upper-middle-class neighborhood of West University. Linda was once again the editor of her school newspaper, the head of her church youth group, the captain of her cheerleading squad. She had the perfectly acceptable boyfriend, the captain of the debate team, the senior class vice-president. Linda thought she might actually love Chad. He treated her like a lady and never swore in front of her; he never tried to do more than get to first base. They never had fighting groping scenes in the back of his father's silver Cadillac. She even kept a bottle of his cologne, Mennen Skin Bracer, on her dresser to smell at night before she fell asleep, to remind her that she was desirable, and good looking, and that somewhere, in the new, rapidly growing, sprawling glass-and-chrome city of Houston, a boy named Chad was thinking about her.

But Linda could never bring Chad over to the house for dinner. As much as her mother encouraged her to. Because Linda knew that especially around company, Mrs. Williams would knock down one too many and get sloppy drunk and say things she never remembered the next day. But Chad would. So Linda and her father formed a little team, hiding their secret, living in denial, never admitting that his wife and her mother, the well esteemed gynecologist, the great cook, and one of the leaders of Houston's PTA, was an alcoholic. Denial became a way of life for Linda, a subliminal, but real method she would use to cope with problems throughout her adult years. She would deny any accusation or insinuation of imperfection.

By the time Linda received her master's degree in education in 1976 from Rice University, she was working after school selling shoes, learning about retail, and had received a prestigious scholarship to finish her thesis. She was a high achiever. She bleached her hair blond, grew her nails long, and began to dress stylishly. The wealthy Houston life suited her well. She missed Nebraska and the security of her Midwestern small home town and neighborhood; but she felt at home in Texas where anything and everything was possible, where dreams of success belong to everyone, and no one knew about her mother.

Her father loved the new hospital where he was on staff; his arthritis had improved; her mother was working well; and it looked as if life was going to be normal. But it wasn't. Her mother never stopped drinking, and Linda moved out of the house, on her own, to find success and fortune in the freest of American societies.

Linda taught school at St. Thomas University for a year, but it was an era when teachers were a dime a dozen, and many middle-class girls looking for a husband thought they'd stand a better chance in education. Teaching did not prove to be what Linda wanted. It was not competitive enough. So she decided to go back to what she had done all through high school and college.

Linda reentered the retail field, specializing in shoe merchandising. Footwear was a quickly growing market that was expanding in sophistication, and worldwide suppliers were supplying the market. Suddenly shoes could be imported from Brazil, Uruguay, Asia, the Middle East, India. Every continent had different quality leather, design, and durability; and Linda learned every detail. She studied pages of statistics. She decided to specialize in mid-range priced shoes accessible to the general population. In six months' time she was promoted to the buying office and from there, with Linda's obsessive drive to succeed, it was only a three-year hike until she became a divisional merchandise manager for a major shoe firm based in Houston. It was as if she could do no wrong. Her area of emphasis was personnel training, working with people. Linda used every bit of psychology she had studied, took every available course she could, including Dale Carnegie's, "How to Win Friends and Influence People." She focused every bit of energy she had to become the perfect manager, and it worked.

Whenever her company would take over a major lease, they would call Linda to fly in, get rid of everything old, do a detailed inventory of the stock, check out the construction of the store, do a demographic study of the buying population of the area, select and train her own people, work the floors with them, set up the retail approach her firm specialized in, and open the new store. This might take all of five months. Almost half a year. Then she'd be called to a new region of the country. And then another. She would spend five months in one location, becoming close with the team of workers she had assembled, hiring local help, learning about the retail plans of her competition, finding living quarters for her employees, devising a radio and print ad campaign, deciding the best shoes to sell in the area, depending on the economic status of her target market and the weather conditions of the state and city, and setting up the various departments so that they ran smoothly. She'd drag herself out of her anonymous hotel bed and suitcase lifestyle at six o'clock in the morning, gulp down gallons of coffee, and be at the new site by seven, work all day with the staff and her figures, order in lunch, send out for dinner, and not leave until eleven o'clock at night. Then she would go out until two or three in the morning with the management and various executives who would fly in to check on Linda.

They would brainstorm every point minutely and dissect her last two weeks' progress. Everything was discussed over cocktails. There were fast figures over scotch, projections for the next year's budgets over gin, raises and salaries over vodka, and plans of where to go next over bourbon. Linda was developing quite a reputation for excellence in her field. She was needed and wanted everywhere. There was a corporate jet at her disposal that often flew her to hurriedly called meetings at five in the morning that began with early, early, bloody marys.

For the girl from Nebraska, it was the jet set lifestyle. No one questioned the hours, the groggy meetings over scotch and soda, and the bosses who were smashed every night. Least of all Linda, who was honored to be moving in these fast, successful circles. It was high times, big business, stock market shakeups, corporate mergers. And then on to the next store. A new locale. New friends. New figures and demographics. New management. New clothes. Different ad campaigns. But the same routine. And the same cocktails. The same hangovers. The same world of being alone and single. But it was exciting, wasn't it?

Then Linda's old Rainbow Girl training came back to haunt her. She felt that she wasn't doing any good for the world. Her conscience drove her back to Rice, where she received another master's degree in vocational education. Maybe now she could save humanity and extricate herself from the roller-coaster life she was living. But the theory Linda studied in her master's program had no real practical application in the current educational realm, and Linda soon found the job and the lifestyle tedious. She couldn't do what she wanted to. She couldn't make nearly as much money as she had been, and she soon realized that the only person she could save was herself. Linda began sniffing out real estate, which was booming in Houston in the late 1970s. Then she started selling it. Her life again began revolving around the same type of corporate people she had worked with in merchandising. A facile and slippery lifestyle.

She had a new boyfriend every six months. There were late night-early morning declarations of love at three A.M. over a last brandy alexander. A succession of successful corporate types filled Linda's bed, one after the other. A banker. A developer. A stockbroker. She was flying to Florida every other weekend to visit a man. And during all this, while she sat in on her boyfriend's weekend meetings, she witnessed a lot of so-called acceptable white-collar crime, like "kiting checks," which is the process of stealing from one corporate account, depositing the money into another, just to keep the business going. In the old days it was called borrowing from Peter to pay Paul. And no one thought anything was wrong. Famous West Coast multimillion-dollar developers whose fingers were on the pulse of the nation's economy had dinner with her. Designer fountain pens, tennis, country clubs, drinking, driving, cocaine: these were the totems of the life Linda lived. And success, of course, success. Lots of money, money to burn, and all the conveniences that power brings.

Finally in 1978 Linda fell in love with Charles, who was the corporate president of a Houston industrial film company, with offices in Los Angeles, San Francisco, and Portland, Oregon. His job was to travel all over the Western states to find major industries that wanted to make films to advertise their products. Ancillary to this job was his role as executive trainer of the sales force. Charles had worked for this company for four years when he met Linda. Like her, he spent a major part of his job traveling and training executives. Like her, much of his business revolved around cocktails.

"His life was the same type of thing as mine," Linda recalled for me in our interview, filing one of her extremely long nails with an emery board she had borrowed from me. It was amazing how relaxed most of the women felt with me. Maybe it was because they sensed the fact that I came from the same type of middle-class background that they came from; maybe they hoped that because I was interviewing so many criminals, I would realize that they were different from the others; maybe they thought I wasn't bright enough to get who they were and what they had done. But most of the women told me very frank details about their lives, felt totally free to borrow my nail file or hairbrush and never asked me about my background.

Linda became melancholy talking about her then boyfriend, now husband, Charles. She is very protective of him, and his invovlement in her business life, which she says was limited to emotional support.

"Charles's routine included the drinking, the traveling, the whole mess, and I think that's part of it," she explained. Charles and Linda fell in love, predictably, over martinis one late night at a downtown Houston cowboy-theme singles bar. They were both highly tense people whose life did not entail the security of a stable home but did include the perks of business, such as large expense accounts, paid vacations, company cars, and the opportunity to see much of this country. According to Linda, they never had a sober moment together until she was busted and became involved in a prison Alcoholics Anonymous group. They had to constantly reschedule their lives to see each other at all; and by the time they could meet up, they were both so exhausted from traveling and talking and working with so many people, that all they wanted to do was have a drink and relax together. And relax and relax and relax.

A typical day when both Linda and Charles were in town together began when either one, normally Linda, raced in from the airport. There was no telling who would get in first; but Linda, feeling guiltier, made more of an effort. During the times when they were separated, their long-distance phone bills were enormous.

If Linda got home early, she would run in the front door after collecting the mail, attempt to super-speed-clean the huge house, which was normally strewn with papers and graph sheets, dry cleaning bags and boxes, airplane tickets, expense account receipts, merchandising and film magazines, and many empty glasses. Their home was one of the smaller mansions in River Oaks, the most prestigious and comfortable section of Houston. The house was colonial, with four tall antebellum columns out front, flanked by azalea bushes and pine and magnolia trees. The ceilings were high, and their patio faced a perfectly manicured backyard and pool with cabana. Every modern electrical appliance that could be had, was. There were built-in stereos, large television screens, VCR's, personal computers, jacuzzis in the immense pale bedroom, a sauna in the wood-paneled bathroom, built-in stereo speakers everywhere. In the tiled kitchen were cuisinarts, juicers, blenders, microwaves, rotating cabinets—and a full-length bar.

Linda would virtually fly in and out of the rooms, grab all the dirty glasses, quickly try to organize her current files in her private office, while simultaneously filing Charles's accumulated papers. Meanwhile, she would make herself a drink, no matter what time it was, because she was home, and it was time to unwind. She had a part-time Mexican cleaning woman; but her obsessive need to excel carried over into virtually every aspect of her life and Linda felt compelled to do the cleaning, the cooking, everything. After answering all the calls on her phone machine, and making Charles a list of his calls, she would change the sheets, order food for the next two days from the gourmet delivery market, and luxuriate in a herbal bubble bath for an hour, drink in hand, until she felt the tension from the last weeks on the road disappear.

By the time Charles got home, Linda was waiting for him with an ice-cold Bombay gin martini, three olives. The grill was lit, the steaks were ready to be thrown on the fire, the backyard glowed with subdued lights. As Charles joined her in their first drink together, they vowed that one day the joy ride would end.

"I wish I could be home more for you," Linda would quietly whisper into Charles's ear as he pulled off his tie and—exhausted and pale—glanced through the mail.

"I never get to see you anymore," she said softly, as her man began to undress, knowing that Linda would have the hot tub and the sauna ready for him.

"I know, Honey," Charles—a tall, fair-haired, rangy man from Dallas in his early forties—told her, as he listened to his phone messages, by now downing his first glass of champagne, and smoking endless cigarettes.

By the time a late dinner was ready, the couple had finished off their first bottle of Moet & Chandon White Star, the wine was being uncorked, and Charles was mixing just one little martini because he was so glad to be home. Linda was already planning her itinerary for the next week.

Both Charles and Linda understood that it was not a lack of love that kept them so individually driven and away from each other; it was their total commitment to their jobs and successes. It was their inability to spend any time at all together that finally instigated Linda to set up her own company, a company that would be based in their hometown. It would enable her to work as much as she wanted but to be there for her husband when he came home. This was the plan they devised one typically cool, rainy Houston December weekend when their schedules meshed, and they

somehow managed to spend three whole cozy days with each
other by the fireplace. Not that either one was sober. But
the plan for the business was born. And it didn't take Linda
long to implement her dream.

In 1979 Linda left her real estate development office and
her lucrative job to open her own business. She was thrilled.
Charles had not been feeling well for quite a while: he was
having some chest pains and was undergoing a painful divorce after a decade of marriage. The separation from a son
whom he adored was especially acute. Linda was very
positive about her new endeavor, obsessively so. She found
two wealthy Houston socialite women to back her. They supplied the instant capital she needed. One was an old roommate of hers from several years ago, a woman she felt she
knew well. Linda had saved some money from her years of
working, so she had a little cushion to live on until the business opened. She felt very independent, excited, and typically compelled to prove herself capable of running her own
show and making it work, as well as maintaining a full time
relationship with the man she loved.

The drinking did not slow down. She was at home more
often; and the hot, humid summer was upon them. So she
often drank by herself, never thinking for a moment that she
was heading toward alcoholism. After all, she was successful,
had good looks, a house, her own brand-new car, her own
company, lots of fine couture clothes, two master's degrees,
and a very successful man who was in love with her. Everything a little girl from Nebraska could want. Or need.

"Financially, Charles didn't have to be supportive of me. I
wouldn't have allowed that. I lived with him for three years
and for three years we've been married. We got married
after I was arrested, so he knew that I could go to prison at
any time," Linda told me as I continued to take notes. And
why should Charles not have been supportive? The successful woman he loved was setting up her own business to

be near him. He loved her, she was everything in the world to him, and most of the time he was too crocked to question any decision either he or she made. It was amazing for me to discover how many middle-class, ostensibly solid, successful business people are alcoholics or drug addicts. Amazing and frightening.

Linda's business deal went like this. She opened her own corporation with offices in downtown Houston, in Allen Center, on Smith Street. In this case the corporation acted as a general partner for a limited partnership, her two investors. The general partner directed retail product planning and ultimately franchise development. This means that she took a retail concept, whatever retail concept was brought to her, and turned it into a business by developing the product and opening a store. As a general partner she developed a business plan for this concept and started implementing the plan with site selection, model stocks, advertising, store design, construction, hiring and training personnel—all the things necessary to make this new business a turn-key operation. In both the footwear and real estate businesses, she had an incredible record and reputation for excellence and productivity; everyone thought she would be a winner. How then did this blond bombshell end up busted in 1980 for grand theft, corporate collusion, and grand larceny, sentenced to three years in a Western prison for women?

"A lot of this mess came from the fact that everything was done over cocktails, and I should have been much more aware of what I was doing. Because when it came down to the courtroom, all they did was make me out as a total incompetent, someone who did not know what was going on within my own corporation," she tried to explain over the din of telephones ringing in the warden's office where we were speaking. A look of helpless confusion fell over her features like a white sheet. "How did this happen to me?" she seems to be asking. "How?"

Linda was artfully evasive with me about the details of her crime. She spoke in generalities about what had happened, and she tried to blame most of her mistakes on her drinking. I do know that somewhere along the line her husband had a massive coronary and had to be hospitalized in the intensive-care unit at M.D. Anderson Hospital in Houston.

I do know that she did drink a lot. She has been in prison AA for two years, and since becoming sober, she admits that she is more coherent and less manipulative than when she was drunk. But in this day and age, women do not get sentenced to prison for a mistake; and Linda tried to make it sound like the whole thing was a giant error.

"We overstepped our bounds as far as what we were allowed to do in being the general partner," she began the second time I questioned her about what she had done. ("We?" Who was "we"? Linda was the chief executive of the company and the only employee she admitted to was a comptroller.) "We violated the rights of the limited partners, I was kind of under the impression, the way the attorneys had set everything up, that everything I was doing was within the bounds of the law. However, not when it came down to it. The court determined that the amount of the fraud was actually $60,000 from the two investors, thirty from one and thirty from the other. . . . How could I have known that the gentleman who was the comptroller of the company was doing this and this? I was just incompetent."

What does this mean? After questioning Linda five or six times and rereading the transcripts at least twenty-five times, I have pieced together the scenario like this. Linda and her partners had set up a corporation. The contracts were signed—over cocktails. The first retail concept had been brought to her. Let's say someone came to her with a new wrinkle on how to sell stationery. She had convinced those people that she could refine their concept and set up their business. She then worked out all the details of the marketing, the site selection, the projected figures for the future, where the next franchise for the product was to be. She had started implementing the plan up to and including construction of the first unit when the shit hit the fan. And when the shit hit, Linda was at her favorite bar, drinking with her networking friends. The banks started barking because she had got behind on the construction schedule and she had a construction loan. She tells me today that she was undercapitalized. Her limited partners had started to get jittery, and Linda began jiggling the funds. Instead of the construction money going to pay the contractor, it was being funneled past the construction phase, into another place, maybe to inventory requisition and other start-up costs. As far as her partners were concerned, the business kept hitting construction delay after construction delay; and when the two partners requested an accounting, and pulled the checkbooks and all the records, certain monies (she said $12,000; the court said $60,000) could not be accounted for on the company's books. Now, whether she had used this money for personal gain or not is not clear.

Obviously the courts thought she did, otherwise she would not be serving time. She admits that she had a monthly income of $6,000. She claims that only $2,500 came from her salary as general partner to the limited partnership. She says that she had some money coming in from other businesses that she had invested in, so she was not desperate for money. But this was a woman who was obsessed with succeeding. The key to her crime, the key to her self-delusion, lies in her obsessive need to achieve. So it makes sense that if she had opened a business, and four months into its first year there were numerous and unexpected construction delays and the usual holdups with the bank, and with the partners pushing for answers, and the clients worrying about deadlines and their investments, that a woman who is not used to failing on any professional level, ended up redirecting the corporate money into the areas she thought would benefit the business most. To hell with everyone else. It was her baby and she was going to make it work, no matter what.

Linda will not admit that she did anything wrong. It does not fit in with her image of herself. Her denial of wrong-doing is a natural extension of her childhood denial of her mother's alcoholism. She continues to believe that what she did goes on in the business world every day of the week. People take funds earmarked for one part of the project and apply it to another part of the project, hoping that the funds necessary for the first part of the project will come in later. But she never makes it clear whether the funds made it to a facet of the business or to her pocketbook. She claims that most people in business don't get busted for what she did. She was a woman in a man's business world. Where people did business big—Texas style.

She did admit, however, that "I was really in over my head. . . . I didn't have the background. . . . I'm not a business person. I'm OK working for someone else, but as long as I had somebody who could do the follow-through it was easy. I didn't mean to defraud anyone. . . . I'm not making excuses for it because as far as I'm concerned it was stupid. I should not have gotten into it in the first place."

But she did get into it, and she did misappropriate more than $60,000, and her partners did accuse her of corporate collusion and grand theft, which means that the court found her guilty of taking large sums of money from her business. I'll never know if Linda's being sloshed most of the time contributed to or caused the crime. But the little girl with the alcoholic mother who spent her childhood denying her mother was an alcoholic turned into one. Her reference to doing deals over cocktails underplays the role alcohol played in her life and business life and is further evidence of her denial.

Even with Linda in prison, her parents don't believe that she did anything wrong.

"My dad can't understand what happened to me because business goes on this way all the time." She lowers her voice to almost a whisper: "I've had staff here tell me that there's a lot of women in here they don't feel have done anything wrong. . . . The future of women and crime has been opened up, putting us into the work force in the way we have been, giving us the responsibility that we have . . . being placed in positions where we have to make decisions . . . the way the system works, the way you get all caught up in this stuff." She ends her sentence abruptly, realizing the absurd rationalizations she had presented.

Prison is a harsh reality; but often, as in the case of Linda, prison saves a woman's life. Linda readily admits this. Prison gave Linda a chance to put everything in its proper perspective. She may not admit guilt for her crime, but she has a new understanding of her marriage and drinking. Linda's marriage ostensibly was one made in yuppie heaven. Two over-achievers with giant salaries and inexhaustible energy, joined together at the deposit slips, to live happily in gin ever after. Prison, however, enforces sobriety; and sobriety is a revelation for someone who has been an alcoholic for many years.

"When my husband and I came together for conjugal visits here, it was the first time that we had ever had any kind of really sober relationship. It has made our marriage stronger, in the fact that it's opened him up, and these communication skills would have been dead otherwise," she proudly states.

Linda lived with her husband for six years, beginning in 1979. She was living with him until she was convicted. She maintains he never knew anything about the details of her business life. Today he is a recovering alcoholic. He's only been sober for two years, and in the six years they were together, they went through a lot of turmoil waiting to find out if she was going to prison or not. After he had his massive coronary, he lost his job. He got divorced from his wife.

Linda's case cost her a lot of money. She borrowed $28,000 and used $14,000 of her savings to keep the business going after the indictment came down.

"He married me knowing this whole thing could just blow up in his face," she confides, a liberated woman, "but emotionally he's been super through the whole thing. And now there's conjugal visits."

If you are legally married in Linda's West Coast prison, you can have a conjugal visit as often as you can get your counselor to process the paperwork. You accumulate a stipulated number of hours of E time. E time is like a vacation or a paid holiday. It has to do with day-to-day behavior. Following the rules; being good. You can accumulate up to sixteen hours of E time a month, and you can utilize that time in several different ways. One is to have a private, sexual, almost real-life tryst with your man. It takes place in a little trailer by the river, a single wide mobile home, with two bedrooms. Linda appreciates the opportunity, but basically the discomfort, mentally, emotionally, and sexually, makes it almost not worthwhile.

"It's very uncomfortable." She begins reaching for a Newport. "It had been almost eight months since Charles and I had been together the first time, and our marriage was strained before then because I was taken into custody while the probation report was being done; and he had just been out of the hospital seven months after his heart attack, and there had been little sex before then because there was so much turmoil. And then they're pounding on the trailer door every hour and a half to count you at night, and you're in the middle of whatever it is. It's like being on a time schedule; it does not have any romantic feeling, everything's plastic in the trailer. . . . I don't know." She taps her ashes off in the orange tin ashtray sitting on the warden's desk. "My husband's in a high-powered job anyway, and it's hard for him to walk out and leave the office and then to have to come here and absorb himself in this type of environment, which to him is a farce. It's almost surrealistic, like stepping into a picture," she concludes sadly.

The only thing that's saved them is that a certain strain has been taken off the relationship by actually being able to be together physically, to touch flesh upon flesh, to dream at night in his arms, to fantasize that when they walk out the door they're going to go water-skiing anytime, because the trailer is set up exactly like their summer house on the Gulf in Galveston. But these sexual encounters are hardly erotic.

So Linda does her time and follows the prison code, which she learned real quick. "Don't talk, and mind your own business." She has a few friends; as a matter of fact, they call Linda and three girlfriends, the "middle-class white girl gang" because they're all from the same type of background, although their crimes are dissimilar. And she waits to get out, meanwhile making plans for her future. Most of her and her husband's friends are successful judges, attorneys, and executives. But Linda plans to avoid this life when she gets out.

"I'm not going back to any kind of business world again. I'm going to go and do in a completely different direction. I want to go back to something I feel good about . . . like working with ex-felons in the pre-release program here, and putting them through mock interviews, and showing them how to go about getting a job, that's what I want to do when I get out."

Many of the women I interviewed plan to work within the penal system when they get out. Why? For one thing it enables them never to have to face the real world again, the world they committed their crime against. And it makes them a hero in the prison world. A world where they will not have to say no to the temptation of finances again. So continuing to work within the penal system insulates and isolates them. It seems unlikely that most of these women will really pursue this course.

Because how would that ever be enough for Linda? What happens to her obsession to excel, to be the best, the little girl with the alcoholic mother crying out I can save you, family, I'll show you, you'll pay attention to me. I'll never fail, I'll do no wrong, I'll make it. Does being caught in a crime she never really felt she committed mean her criminal life is over? Does it end this whole story?

Some stories never end.

THE CRIME—Grand theft, corporate collusion
THE SENTENCE—Three years

CHAPTER VII

THE HUSTLERS' CONVENTION

It was a full moon
in the middle of June,
In the summer of fifty-nine
I was young and cool
and shot a bad game of pool,
and hustled all the chumps I could find.

Now they call me Sport,
'cause I pushed a boss short,
and loved all the women to death;
I partied hard
and packed a mean rod,
'n' could knock you out with a right or left.
LIGHTIN' ROD—*The Hustlers' Convention*

THE BIG HOUSE is definitely Riker's Island. At least for women, it is the unequivocal epitome of all the horrors you ever saw on TV or read about in connection with prison and time.

The prison is located on Riker's Island, in the East River, and is part of New York City, probably the nation's most cosmopolitan capital. I had to take a bus there, and once there, I went into a security area to have my ID checked in order to get clearance to go through.

It was like a scene out of a Third World manual for survival. Washing the floors were Rastafarian prisoners from the men's side, with thousands of hair plaits and a gone, mountain look on their faces. They had absolutely no fear in their eyes, and their forest green prison garb looked exactly like guerrilla fatigues.

The visiting families were all huddled together in groups, with screaming babies, covered containers of strange foods, chocolate bars, and an assortment of ancient relatives, dark and raisin-faced, living mummies from other cultures, attached to permanent seats grounded to the floor of the prison. I half expected to see chickens fly out of the brown grocery bags that everyone held so protectively between their feet.

Spanish is the main language here. Dark-eyed beauties with bright red lips and tight angora pastel sweaters waited in their skin-tight designer jeans for their old men to come out and kiss them on their wet lips. The noise level was akin to that in an arena of a boxing match. Everyone was waiting expectantly, totally disrespectful of the system.

The guards were hardly disginguishable from the prisoners. They laughed and talked to the families with their guns shining in the air, gold teeth flashing, looking like renegades from Mohamar Khadaffi's merry band of revolutionaries. Everyone looked at me as though I was a white, honky intruder from Bloomingdale's.

"Hello," I meekly told the guard at the check-in point, who was yelling at one of the prisoners washing the floor.

"Hey Bro Jones, cool it on the action of the mop. This is not play time."

"My name is Susan Nadler and I'm here to see Warden Tom Barry," I repeated, wondering why I felt intimidated here. After all, I'd done time, I'd been across the country working at six women's maximum security prisons. I'd even interviewed child molesters. Why did I feel so out of place?

"Walk outside, the first bus with the number two on it," the hipster guard yelled at me over the blast of the loudspeaker, which was announcing the next shift for visiting hours. "Get on and get off at the women's prison."

"Which stop is that?" I wondered out loud, feeling as though I had stepped into another universe here.

"The one where the other women get off," he said sarcastically. One of the Rastafarians laughed out loud. At me?

By the time I got off the bus, which was filled with the most masculine (largest) female guards I had ever seen, I was ready to leave the island. The female half of the prison, or the jail, as I was to find out the facility is called, is located next to the teenage adolescent section of the prison. And I knew for a fact that whenever three young boys sodomized and killed an eighty-six-year-old nun, maybe even carving a few token crucifixes into her skin and dumping her body into a handy dumpster, just for the hell of it, the killers wound up here. Right behind where I was walking.

Riker's Island is not Bedford Hills. Wealthy socialite murderesses don't end up incarcerated here. This is the big house.

Warden Tom Barry was very pleasant to me. A slight, fair native New Yorker, he has been involved in the penal system for the last eighteen years. He worked as a supervisor in the Queen's House of Detention, the Manhattan House of Detention, the Old Tombs, and the men's division of Riker's Island. I asked him, as we drank coffee from the prison Mr. Coffee pot, if he had noticed that in the last decade the number of female inmates has increased? I told him that I've discovered this fact in my research. The FBI Uniform Crime Reports, various Justice Department statistics, and an article in the Miami Herald (11/26/82) had all concluded that in the last ten years the number of women in prison had doubled.

He answered carefully, phrasing his words correctly. But Warden Barry does not try to pass off prison rhetoric or dogma.

"I am not up on the statistics, but I do know that whatever happens in jails is just whatever's happening in the community out there. This is a city jail, for an extremely huge city. . . . If a person is convicted of a misdemeanor offense, they can serve a full year in this facility . . . and if a woman is busted by the state, she will come here until her case is adjudicated."

I pause in thought, a year spent in this rough atmosphere could have a profound effect on a young girl. It could permanently change the way she looked at the world and herself. Prison, especially in the violent world of Riker's, could have an equal impact in the amount of psychological damage done, as in teenage pregnancy, sexual abuse, and incest. Jail is an excellent gauge of what is happening at the exact moment on the street. That is why it often takes some time before the prison population convicted of certain trendy crimes catches up to the equivalent jail population. Most judges, by the time they get to the bench, represent a community perspective, they're attuned to the scene on the street, the current scam, the current new mode of treachery, the current means of murder. And the first stopover for the citizens they detain, put on bond or bail, or need held, is the city jail.

Warden Barry believes that the paternal attitude of the courts is still in effect, reflected in the sentencing women receive.

"There's a propensity on the part of judges not to send a woman to a detention facility, because usually they have families to take care of, children at home; there's still that stereotype out there, and while it's changing on the parts of the police and judges, the female's caring, nurturing role is one that no one wants to disrupt," he concluded. Barry's private lines rang incessantly. There were calls from the guards, from attorneys, from the men's side of the jail, from city officials, from the media. He seemed to slide right through it all with refreshing single-minded purpose. The fact that his prison population is fresh off the streets gives Barry a unique look at the immediacy of urban crime.

"There's a sense, whether it's men or women, when people rise from one level, corporately, to another high level, that they believe they're generally smarter than the world around them, that they're superior in many ways; and consequently they think they have immunity from certain issues and they can get away with things, and if they have the opportunity some do get away with it. . . . Also, a person living in a Beverly Hills type of community where maybe the annual income's a million or two to keep up with the Joneses, if this person is making $100,000, he can feel deprived in this community, and almost feel justified in taking the extra $150,000; and then because they also feel superior, surely they can get away with it. . . . The point is that sooner or later this press for material items in life is a very strong force in our economic structure and it certainly is a key measure of success . . . and since there are less and less marriages occurring today, I think, if you will, that there's a greater freedom for women to be more and more involved in a kind of corporate philosophy that makes you have to do those things in order to succeed. And if they're willing to do it, they certainly have the opportunities today." Today, for example, employee theft—much of it committed by women—is a major financial problem at many companies.

The majority of inmates at Riker's Island are recidivists, career criminals of some form or another, whether their career is purse snatching or murder. A lot of the inmates are street girls, raised in the inner city ghettos, where crime is one of the workable survival alternatives. Not everyone from a poor family is motivated to break laws. Individuals have different reasons for the types of lives they choose. Some do it for the thrill. Some for love. For some it's the only life they know.

Tom Barry told me he had once had the opportunity to deal with an infamous criminal who ostensibly committed

crimes for the thrill. "I once had the occasion as a correc-
tions officer to watch Willie Sutton for a period of months.
That was my job. I sat outside his cell to watch him to make
sure he wouldn't escape. Now at this stage of his life, he was
sixty-eight years old and he had plastic arteries in his chest
from open-heart surgery; and he really wasn't the major escape risk that he was in the 1930s when he was thirty years
old.

"But we had a chance to talk, and I said, 'Geez, obviously
you're an intelligent man; you have a lot of personal re-
sources at your command.' I mean clearly he had charisma,
he had intelligence; he could have put all of those to some
sort of constructive use if he wished. He could read books
very quickly, and as has been evidenced, he could write. I
asked him, why? He told me very simply, 'It was fun.' He
enjoyed it."

Warden Barry grew silent for a minute, perhaps reflecting
how different a man who could see crime as an enjoyable
alternative is from him. "Willie Sutton was considered the
nation's prototype of Robin Hood. He was one of the public
enemies, but clearly he was popular out there. People would
talk about him, and to the working-class communities, he
was somebody. He was a hero . . . but he was not giving to
the poor at all. That was a perversion of the Robin Hood
theory. But we pay for these scams not only in taxes, but in
the prices that we pay when we go to the supermarket; the
prices are adjusted accordingly."

The smartly dressed secretary came into the office at this
point and I was sorry, because Warden Barry had to get back
to work, and obviously my time with him was over.

"Do you think any of the women will talk with me, Sir," I
asked, as I walked him from the coffee klatsch area back to
his desk.

"Well, we'll try to identify some of the women you want
to talk to, see if we have any middle-class women here . . .
white-collar crime. . . . I don't know; we have a lot of street

hustlers incarcerated now. They speak a different language; they have a different perspective."

Starr Pointer was the last woman I interviewed at Riker's Island. She was an anomaly. The most forthcoming about her life and her crime, she was nonetheless unapologetic. Starr does not feel guilty. She grew up in the street, knows the life better than any woman I spoke with, and although she was hardly middle class, I included her in this book because she is unique and because she represents the contemporary inner-city stereotypic woman in crime, one who never had many choices.

Starr was born and raised in Harlem. She is twenty-nine years old. She is currently serving time for possession of stolen property, grand larceny, forgery, and petit larceny. She is a street hustler extraordinaire and spoke a special language used only by players in the Hustlers' Convention.

She is another facet of a good girl gone bad, a girl who never had a chance from the beginning to be good. My general impression of Starr was that she was one of the brightest women I interviewed. Starr knows who she is, she has no delusions about her role in society or from what stratum of society she came. She was tall and lanky and wore more gold jewelry than any of my ostentatious cousins.

I learned that she and her husband existed in a small apartment with their two children somewhere in what we outsiders perceive to be the war zone: the blown-out, haunted, once-elegant townhouses of Harlem that stand as dusty sentinels to our modern cities. Starr is special, an urban warrior fighting a war against poverty and drugs. Her domain was the area of Manhattan where I've always felt the safest, Fifth Avenue between 50th and 70th Streets, and Madison Avenue around 65th Street: the Upper East Side.

Starr has probably robbed people that I know in Manhattan. She probably doesn't have any future at all; she'll probably never change. I probably wouldn't trust her if I met her

on the street, in a club, or in a department store. But she
wouldn't trust me either. It's the old black-white game that
we Northerners play as well as any bigot from Birmingham.
Starr Pointer speaks her own language. She cruises to a different synthesizer. She is not a new breed of female criminal, there have been others, many others, before her—
products of poverty, no dreams, no hopes, no way out, wel-
fare, no dignity, no chance at education. Some rise above it.
Some fall back into it. Starr has perfected the lifestyle, has
fine-tuned the nuances of ghetto life and street crime, how
to move among the rich. These are territories that she owns.
It is a jive-ass world that you may need a dictionary to
follow.

"Now my dad was a scrambler, which means that he sold
drugs, but he also had a square job. He worked downtown
on Wall Street. He didn't have no job too long, he used to
be a courier, then he left there and copped a job with a
place called Caterpillar, where they used to make bulldozers
and stuff—heavy equipment. My mom, she used to work in
Harlem Hospital; she was a RN. Now she don't work no
more. After she left Harlem Hospital, she went into private
practice, nursing, in an old folks' home. I just turned
twenty-nine March first. And I'm in here cause I knocked off
a Macy's. They caught me with possession of stolen property, grand larceny, forgery, and petty larceny. I have lived
the life, Girl. I know the game, I stay sane, I play real
good." Already I like Starr. She is not evasive for one minute.

"The game is second nature to me now. Sometimes when
you go into restaurants, like a lot of those between Midtown
and Wall Street, you go into these plush joints, like I've
been doin' this since I was a jitterbug, you know a chippy, so
sometimes when me and my husband first step into them
joints, the white people they're lookin' at how you're
dressed. You got to be dressed down, and the first place they

look is at your feet, the shoes, the shoes tell a lot about you."
I always thought that too, but for different reasons. "And
we's got to hide from the other dragsters going in there,
stinging out over there, but you can kind of get past all that
because it's all on how you act; cause a lot of the people, the
managers and maitre d's, they hip to the niggers be comin'
in there. They be comin' in there too often. And like this
dude who played with us, his name be Jazzy, like he don't
know how to sting or nothin' like that, so he's just got the
gift to gab. He'd step up and play the maitre d' or the manager while we cased the joint to see what's happening in
there so we can be able to sting. A lot of times, when the vic
wakes up, cause some of those white women be hankty,
leary, so they feel a black person sitting next to them, they
think they're up to no good. I'm up to no good, but I'm
saying all white, anytime they see a black person sitting next
to them in a plush joint, they gonna get hankty. Sometimes I
kick it because the white people that I've been around, as
soon as I sit down next to them, they jump from their seat
and I had to kick them with it."

Starr walks back and forth as she talks, pulling at her hair,
scratching her leg. She is very hyper, overenergetic, almost
manic. Street life is not calm. "So, I walk in, I spot the sting,
the sting is like on the back of the chair, and I sit down
where I can get access to it. I sit next to where the sting is
at, in the lap, on the floor, and the vic might turn around
real quick or something like that, you know, and then I put
her back to sleep. I also look at the plate to see how much
food she got, cause if she ain't got that much food on her
plate, I might not mess with her because soon she'll be
leavin' . . . but sometimes they be the whole way there, you
can steal, they be up and they be just dead. Once I see the
lap and the plate I start into motion that I'm going to do it, it
all depends where the hit is situated. If I talk to the vic, I
ask her what's on the menu, I'll just kick it around with her
about somethin', and I'll just come out of my bag, cuz you

know I can't talk to no white person any kind of old way, you got to use some kind of finesse. I can't talk to them like I talk to them niggers up in Harlem. So, after I feel her out then I just stroke her down, so she'll just ease on back and go to sleep. I'm not going to keep laying on her. Once I get the chance, I going to get it and I'm splitting. You just can't run out of the joint, you got to walk out like you came on in the joint. Sometimes when you walk out they want to know why you're getting up and walking out, and you have to try to play the maitre d' and say well, I really don't feel too good or you kick something to him that sounds slick so you can raise up out of the joint.

"And then, after we get the hit, then we go see what's in it and usually them broads like that, they be havin' it big. They be having jewelry, cash, and what interests me is the checkbooks, a driver's license, and a VISA or MasterCard, cause that's money I can get right away. A cash advance. You can get up to $1,000 to $1,500 off a cash advance and if you got calm enough you can go to another bank and get another grand or so. Sometimes these broads be having their payroll digits in their bag. The only way you can bust a payroll digit, they have a card from where they work and a card with their signature on it because a bank ain't gonna take just any payroll. Don't care what kind of ID you got, you got to have this card from the job where you work, where your supervisor signed it. Some of these payrolls be like $1,500, but these broads have big-time jobs. Cause they be lawyers, doctors, or some type of high profession. Then, after the bank close, you only can get $250 off a personal check from the bank, anything over $250 they're gonna check. I get knocked off if I want to write a check over $250. The only money I could get is like X bank, you can get a whole lot of money off of them, Chase Manhattan, Manufacturers Hanover, Chemical, you take the cards and put it in the computer and you press 5*21, that will kick up the balance of what the broad's got. If she's got fifty G's, you might write for maybe five G's, as long as the nine and the eight don't come up in the computer. Then, the broad is stung. So once you leave X bank, you might have another chance to get another X bank and get another five G's off the broad; but you put the card back in the machine and push the 5*21 and then the balance will come up again. As long as nines and eights don't come up, you're cool. Then you go on to the teller, and you write a personal check for five G's, cause the machine balance ain't showed up yet, and you work on like that. Then after the bank close, you got store work, where you can use the driver's license, a store card like Saks, or Lord and Taylor, or Guccci. Maybe even Macy's, B. Altman, or Gimbels. If you give them a personal check, all you got to give her for ID is a driver's license or another credit card. I like watches. Maybe a nice Rolex for two grand. You can get some fine outfits, some suits, some fly dresses, funky French stuff, silk, something for about $600, that's reasonable today."

I am surprised at how cavalier Starr is about the cost of clothing. I guess when you're spending someone else's money, $600 is not much. "And all you do is put the vic's phone number on top of the check. Then the sales broad writes the license number on it and the other ID, and she calls the teller check, after the bank's closed, the teller check will kick back that it's cool, and, shit, you can do that for up to two weeks, till the first check falls. Once I busted out for a month on this particular broad, but once the first check falls, it's over. Once teller check says it's wrong, it's stolen. The woman in the store ain't gonna tell you that because they're gonna want to lay you over and you're gonna get knocked off. But a pro knows how far to go with it.

"Sometimes, if I have to, I mess with Macy's. I like Bergdorf-Goodman's and Saks much better. I shouldn't have messed with Macy's, cause that's where I got trapped off; and it was a humbug. I had played the salesperson the whole way dead, I had got about $975 worth of stuff, two fine suits, some jewelry, a leather coat, so I'm playin' the dude, he

called teller check, everything was cool, but the broad that I
had stung was a doc, she had a Ph.D., and this broad had it
on her check. Sarah Epstein, Ph.D. I had been in Lord and
Taylor's, Gucci's, I was taking care of me and my old man
and kids, cuz I used that work for myself. I even went over
to Crazy Eddie's and got a $800 color TV, I laid my crib out
and that Sunday morning I got knocked off, January nine-
teenth. That Sunday afternoon my man said to me why don't
you get up and go downtown and hit a few joints, baby. I
said I didn't feel like going to work today. Something told
me not to. But I went. First to Gimbel's for a $450 bracelet.
Then Lord and Taylor's. Then Macy's. Everything was fine
there, teller check said OK. The check went through. He
said I have to have this approved by my supervisor, so he
stepped off. Sometimes they step off, but it's cool, but sometimes when they step off and the shit look raggedy, raise up
and beat away, just raise up and leave, but it was cool. But
when he came back, the supervisor was a black dude; and I
don't like messin' with niggers like that. So the security
guard came back with him, and he said, what's your name?
And I was playin' it, I said, Sarah Epstein. I played them
like a fiddle cuz they weren't sure enough, anyhow . . . they
got me. I guess I didn't look like no Ph.D. No Epstein.

"My family, I had two brothers and two sisters. One of my
brothers went to Howard College in Washington, another
went to state college in Pennsylvania, and so did my sister.
I'm the only one that turned out like this. The only one's
been knocked off, the only one who gave my mother and
father a headache. I don't understand why me, but when I
was fourteen I met these drag players from Atlanta, Georgia,
and something about them and their game turned me on. I
don't know, my immediate family, my brothers and sisters,
they don't talk this way at all. Now my cousins and uncles,
they talk like that. I guess it was the money that turned me
on. The action. The life. I don't know no other way. It all
seems so boring. . . ." I am sorry that a C.O. came in to get

Starr and our interview ends. I had so much to ask her. Like why her brothers and sisters, coming from the same background, didn't end up in crime. And if she ever thought of doing something else. And if she used drugs. I tried to get her to talk to me again, the next day, but I was never able to get back in to the prison. I am sorry her chapter is so short.

I thought about Starr on a recent trip to New York to be a matron of honor in a wedding party. Ten adult couples from the wedding, who consider themselves to be fairly hip, went down to a Greenwich Village jazz club, the Blue Note, to hear Maynard Ferguson play trumpet. And somehow that night, I turned into the vic. My new wallet turned into the sting. Someone stole $150 from my purse and I never saw who did it. And I was knocked off just as easily as any lame at any plush joint. And for one minute I laughed. Because street hustlers are fast. And those of us on the outside, who don't really know the life, we feel superior to it all. And white-collar criminals, especially the ones I interviewed, consider themselves the cream of the crop of crime. But no one of them is even safe from being hit.

To assume that you know it all about crime, or can protect yourself, is an illusion. Because the hustlers, the players, have nothing else to fall back on, no jobs, no future, no prospects, no birthday presents. They have their minds, their tongues, their fingers, their cunning, their wile, their busts, and their early deaths. Ain't that right, Bro?

THE CRIME—Possession of stolen property, grand
larceny, petit larceny, and forgery
THE SENTENCE—Pending

CHAPTER VIII

DREAMBOATS

He's so fine, doo-lang, doo-lang
Wish he were mine, doo-lang, doo-lang
That handsome boy over there
The one with the wavy hair.

I don't know how I'm gonna get him, doo-lang,
doo-lang
But I'm gonna make him mine, doo-lang, doo-
lang.
He's the envy of all the girls
It's just a matter of time.
THE CHIFFONS—1965

"BUT HE PROMISED that he would never leave me," Karen pleaded, as she pushed several strands of blond hair away from her forehead. "He told me that no matter what Marcia did, no matter how she tried to tempt him with money and power, he didn't care," she cried to her friend Leslie, who continued to file her nails and shake her head in dismay at her friend's naivety.

"How could you ever believe him?" Leslie asked slowly. "You have been around, Karen. After Philip and that whole nightmare, how could you possibly think that Marcia's family money and the fact that her father is practically the richest man in the state wouldn't affect Duke. I mean he's been trying to get his business off the ground for so long, and now . . ."

A knock at the door of the summer cottage where the women were eating their lunch interrupted their conversation. Karen, with muscles straight from Nautilus, and a Los Angeles tan that contrasted with her white bikini, shook her long hair, and walked over to answer the door to a tall, thin man of about thirty-five, with curly brown hair and a big smile.

"Hey, Baby, are you alone?"

Karen's expression instantly changed, revealing all of her turbulent emotions at once. "Duke," she turned her head away, "I . . . I wasn't expecting you."

The man she called Duke took a step toward the door and pulled a bouquet of yellow roses from behind his back. He handed them to the now teary-eyed Karen.

"Oh, Dukey," she sighed, "you remembered."

"Aren't you going to invite me in, Baby?" he whispered softly as he gathered her hair in his hands and kissed her teasingly on the neck.

In the background, Lionel Richie was crescendoing with Diana Ross on the chorus of "Endless Love."

"Leslie's here; we're having lunch together. I needed someone to talk to when I got your note . . . I don't really think I should see you. I can't believe that you and Marcia announced your engagement. Oh, Duke, I feel so foolish."

Inside the paneled, rustic cabin Leslie poured herself another glass of wine. What a fool Karen was. Marcia was right, the bitch. Leslie conjured up the hazy transaction between her and Marcia at the bank. Marcia had paid her over thirty grand to stop Karen's affair with Duke. "She's so stupid, she'll believe anything you say, Sweetie," Marcia had laughed, clicking her red nails against the teller's window.

"You'd rather listen to her than have me hold you in my arms." Duke shook his head, as he turned away from the steps of the cabin toward the lake and Hillside Drive. "These women you call your friends are going to destroy you, Karen. All I wanted to do was protect you."

"Is your marriage to Marcia going to do that?" Karen began to cry. "Oh Duke, I'll never be able to trust you again."

Lionel and Diana concluded their duet, the violins were lush. The camera panned to Leslie sitting on the floor, smiling malevolently. Duke disappeared down the driveway, his shoulders held high. The final scene was a long shot of Karen's tear-stained, wistful face.

The television screen quickly changed to a diaper commercial, with appropriate pediatric music, and Darlene stood up to finish preparing her son's lunch.

"God, that Duke Langston is a dreamboat." She smiled. "I don't blame poor Karen one bit, but if I looked like her, I'd figure out a way to get rid of Marcia, what do you think, Mom?" She asked the older woman, dressed in a floral print, who was sitting on the sofa, a strand of dark garnets around her neck.

"I think in the old country such nonsense wouldn't be on the television and that actor playing Duke would be working in an office somewhere, and you would be happily married to some man, like your first husband, Darlene," her mother carped, "not worrying about some dreamboat on the television."

"Listen, Mom, I can't talk about Christopher any more. He was my first love, I did everything you and Pop wanted and it just didn't work out. Now I've already been through another marriage, and my second husband's left me, and I have a son and I'm back living on top of you and Pop in the apartment you should be renting out, and I need to forget the past, because, Mom, the past's gonna kill me, I swear to God, I just can't take it anymore," she finished, on the verge of tears herself.

Darlene's mother looked over at her only daughter, the once hope of her life. The dreams she had had for this girl. Darlene lit a cigarette. Her mother made the sign of the cross and stood up. She looked at her antique eighteen-karat gold watch. It was almost four o'clock—time to go downstairs to begin dinner for Joseph. In less than a month it would be Christmas. Time to buy presents for the family. Time to begin baking the traditional Yugoslavian cookies, the apricot and maraschino cherry strudels, the heavy whiskey fruit cakes, time to get the tree ornaments down from the attic and call the church to organize the dinner for the poor. Maddie had a lot to do. She tried to run her fingers over the antique secretary in the corner of the apartment without her daughter seeing her. There was a minuscule layer of dust on it. And Darlene hadn't lost weight since the baby. She looked heavy, stocky almost. It was no good. Maddie shook her head to herself. Who would marry a young woman with two marriages behind her, a young infant child, no husband around to give the child his name, and a figure that was becoming too full?

"Look Mom," Darlene tried to be gentle, "I saw you run your hand over the furniture. What can I tell you, Mom? I'm trying to be clean. I'm doing the best I can. I have a job now, I can't take care of Joey, cook, work, take care of myself and be the balabusta you want. Give me a break, Mom, please, or I'm goin' to have to move outta here, so help me, God."

Maddie walked over to her daughter and held her in her arms. Darlene was a good girl, she just had some back luck. She would be all right. "All right, my darling," her mother comforted her, afraid that if Darlene moved out of her parents' home they would lose contact with not only their daughter but their only grandchild as well. "Dinner will be at six-thirty. I'm making stew and bread, salad, the way you like it. But no dessert for you tonight, you seem to have put on . . ."

"Mom, I know what you're gonna say. Don't say it." Her mother was still as slim as she had been when Darlene was ten years old. Dinner was still at six-thirty. There was nothing new in the Podic household. Nothing new in twenty-five years.

"All right, Darling." Maddie understood she had best not push it. Joseph had told her a million times in the past six months.

"Leave Darlene alone; let her be."

"I'll see you later, and Darlene," she knew how much Darlene would hate what she had to say now, but she couldn't help herself, "don't smoke in the baby's face." Maddie opened the door.

"Mom, good-bye," Darlene was anxious to get her mother out and rejoin her soap opera. "I love you, Mom," she added. Her mother was old, she was not going to change her ways. It was up to the daughter to forge a new life for herself and her son. Her mother only said those nagging things out of love. Pop had told her that since she was five years old. And it was true. But it didn't make things any better. She kissed her mother on the soft cheek that smelled of rose water and glycerin. Maddie had the perfect skin of a woman who had never been in the sun, the poreless skin she had inherited from the Slavic gene pool of Eastern Europe. Maddie's garnets shone gentian-violet in the hallway light.

My mother will never understand me selling my jewelry for Christmas, Darlene agonized to herself as she closed the door. She made a mental picture of all the jewelry she had received as presents over the years: the matched pearl necklace upon confirmation, the opal pendant for straight-A report cards, the diamond-and-sapphire earrings and bracelet, the heirlooms from her great grandmothers in the old country. Darlene felt a sharp pain in her stomach when she envisioned the smirking face of the shyster jewelry dealer she was trading with. She was effectively getting rid of all the love she received as a child. But when her baby cried, and she seated herself in front of the television, she knew it was worth any price for Joey to have a good Christmas, any price at all. Even if she had to do without her beloved jewelry forever.

*   *   *

The camera panned in on Marcia's tightly honed cheekbones as the soap opera continued. Marcia and her brother were planning her wedding to Duke.

"We'll all have to wear designer dresses, David," Marcia told her brother, who nodded his head in agreement and looked with love at the raven-haired, arrogant beauty who was his sister. "After all, I can't allow Sarah Ferguson to outdo me. I think I'll get Galanos to do my gown in champagne color. And all the bridesmaids can wear peach. So fitting, considering the new wine we're bringing out, don't you think, David?" she asked, inhaling deeply on her emerald cigarette holder.

"Let's not get too carried away here, Honey," David said as he touched her face lightly. "Let's try to keep the ceremony to a minimum of pretension."

"David," she acted offended for a second and began to laugh at him as the doorbell rang, "I never act more pretentious than I am."

Darlene lit up another Marlboro and looked at the calluses on her hands. She never thought she would have to clean so hard again. She had thought that once she was married to Christopher, her life would be like all the fairy princesses she had read about in the magazines. The life of love, with servants and presents and negligees, and vacations and tenderness and doing things because she wanted to. Instead, it had turned out like a nightmare, somebody else's nightmare. As the soap opera music lapsed into the familiar, trite melody Darlene knew so well, she reminisced about her wedding to Christopher, how happy she had been, how beautiful she had looked, the light streaming in through the rainbow-hued stained glass windows in the church . . .

Darlene Podic grew up in America, but her values and her sensibilities were impressed upon her when she was still in the womb, values the people lived by in Yugoslavia, where her parents were born. Her father had done well in America. He owned his own business, a very successful hardware store in Lincolnwood, Chicago, with two branches. Darlene and her younger brother were raised as strict Catholics. Darlene was so bright, so quick, and had such an aptitude for learning, that at the Catholic girls' school she attended, she had graduated with honors, at age sixteen. As the oldest daughter, she had been extremely spoiled. She was given everything—except personal freedom.

She never realized what was missing from her life when she was a young girl, because she was raised in Berwin, a largely European section of Chicago. Berwin is a middle-class to upper-middle-class suburb twenty-five minutes outside the city. Most of its residents, whether wealthy or just comfortable, are descendants of European ancestry who form a tiny cultural ghetto in this mid-Western city.

Darlene's father was so anxious to do well that he worked sixteen hours a day at the store, commuting back and forth twice a day from Lincolnwood to Berwin. But he always had time for his little girl. Darlene was a lot closer to her dad than to her mom. Her mother was very demanding of her. Darlene was supposed to be skinny, smart, clean, know how to cook, and end up by marrying a nice educated, wealthy Yugoslavian man who would take care of her and her children.

In effect, she was expected to continue the tradition and values of the old country at home, an American on the outside, an expatriot Slavic in her soul. As a child she loved to play the guitar and sing old folk songs in perfect Slovene, which she was able to speak and write fluently by the time she was ten. All her cousins and friends loved to hear her play at holidays. Darlene also listened to country music. Her favorites artists were Loretta Lynn and George Jones. She was a beautiful girl, tall for her age, with golden thick wavy hair, a wide forehead, high cheek bones, and extremely large blue eyes that were always flashing and merry. Aside from a minor acne problem that temporarily scarred her face as a teenager, Darlene looked a lot like Frances Farmer, intelligent and well bred, but with the heavy, creamy features that harkened back to ancient Slavic stock.

Darlene had everything that any teenage girl growing up in the sixties wanted. She had jewelry, including the opals and garnets from her mother's trousseau, and the finely wrought treasures that had been sneaked out of Yugoslavia and Czechoslovakia in the folds of women's clothing and in their mouths. She wore expensive clothes from Marshall Field's and Carson's. She had a car, a brand new Mustang, when she was sixteen, and a solid gold watch when she was fourteen. She went to Europe a lot in the summers, Yugoslavia and Paris, Rome and Portugal. It was her choice where she wanted to spend her vacation. What she said, went. She didn't drink or smoke dope. She was a model child.

When she was sixteen, she began college at the University of Illinois, Circle Campus, in downtown Chicago. She was the youngest freshman. When she finally received her BA in business, her professors agreed that she had a good career ahead of her in business management and finance. Her Poppa was proud.

But even when she was attending college, Darlene was not allowed to date. Her mother didn't want her to spend her free time socializing with certain kinds of people, people she thought would negatively influence her daughter and bring to her sheltered world the so-called American forms of rebellion: drugs, drink, and promiscuity. Darlene grew up spending her time in Yugoslavian and European atmospheres, choosing to travel back to the motherland for vacations, and socializing at a Yugoslavian club in Berwin. She wasn't permitted to attend school dances, but every Saturday night, from nine o'clock until two in the morning, Darlene went to the club with her cousins and was permitted to dance and laugh with older men. It was the European atmosphere that Maddie approved of, the fact that everyone knew everyone else, that everyone spoke Slovene, and when Darlene was there she felt Yugoslavian, rather than American. She loved the music, the ethnic polkas and waltzes. And in her stylish dresses from Carson's, with her high heels and red lipstick, she was often the belle of the ball, twirling around madly on some strapping young man's arm, lost in the beat of the mountains and the sea of Yugoslavia.

As the soap opera broke for the last commercial before the conclusion for the day, Darlene remembered how it would go back then. Maddie used to say, when her daughter got home from school in the afternoon, "Wash the floors and wax the stairs; make this house a place where anyone could eat off the floors, and you'll go out this weekend." And that is what Darlene did, that was her reward and she loved it. At that point Darlene didn't even like hard rock. She preferred the singers who used to come from Yugoslavia to perform concerts at the club. One windy Chicago evening, she remembered now, changing Joey's diaper and kissing his perfect little buns, she had sneaked out to the school dance on a Friday night and discovered that the only excitement there was drugs. Drugs just weren't her thing. She got a natural high just from being with the people she liked, laughing and having a good time. She didn't need artificial stimulation.

"I still don't," she thought to herself, "even after all I've been through."

Darlene was working part time as a secretary for an attorney in the Loop area and going to college when she met the love of her life, Christopher, her first husband. Darlene had met him ten years before that night at the club, but she had never gone out with him. The night they came together, a great Yugoslavian folk singer was performing. Darlene was wearing a long white silk skirt and pale yellow silk blouse with high-heeled open-toed sandals. She smelled like violets and wore a sprig of them in her hair. The wind was blowing outside, spring was coming to Chicago. In the parks the lilac trees were opening up. Christopher was mannered and gentle. He had a degree from Oxford University in England. He asked her to dance that soft May evening and held her lightly in his arms, waltzing with her into the wee hours, staying close to the shadows, smelling her hair, commenting on the herbal essence that floated up from her neck, telling her that she was more beautiful than any violet.

Darlene was enchanted. He was older than she—by fourteen years. He owned his own tool and die refrigeration shop in downtown Chicago. He had money. He began to bring Darlene bouquets of flowers every night. He took her dancing and out to dinner, the movies. He brought her violet perfume he imported from Paris and antique lace mantillas. He was her dreamboat.

Maddie and Joseph loved him. He would be the one to bring security to their little girl and legitimize her. She could have the kind of family life that they had, the kind of secure, cozy home like the ones all of her cousins reveled in.

Darlene was not frightened of sex with Christopher because he never tried to do more on any date than hold her and kiss her passionately. His arms were powerful, his tongue held the secret of rituals she had only read about in books. And Darlene decided, together with Christopher, to wait until after they were married to lose her virginity. It wasn't anything her mother forced on her. It was her choice.

The wedding was like a fairy tale for Darlene. It was held at St. Kiri and Methodija Macedonia Church in Berwin, the reception was given at the club. There were over five hundred guests. The bride and groom broke a crystal glass after the ceremony under an arch of violets and greens to ensure years of love and luck. Darlene wore a heavy lace-and-brocade gown that was made for her by Yugoslavian seamstresses. It was white on white, shimmering, white as the mountain peaks where she and Christopher would honeymoon in the Alps. Christopher looked handsome in his black tux, his thick dark hair slicked back from his face, his cheeks red and flushed with anticipation, his face smelling of Lilac Vegetal. His eyebrows were heavy and dark, but his hazel eyes shown with love for his young bride, who danced the polka with her uncles, squealed with her girlfriends over all of her presents, and breathed heavily as he held her malleable, manicured hand and together they cut the tiered wedding cake.

The food was rich and buttery. There were Yugoslavian roasted meats, potato pancakes, and loaves of steamy breads with cooked vegetables inside. The accordian was the featured musical instrument, and the father of the bride provided the toast for the couple with fruity wine he imported directly from Belgrade. The bridesmaids, dressed in powder blue, screeched under the colorful paper streamer decorations to see who would catch the bouquet. Large-boned men who worked hard all week danced gracefully with their rolypoly wives, whose fingers were coated with sugar from the deserts. Mikey and Pete, the bridegroom's best friends, passed out cigars and slapped all the relatives on the backs. Darlene thought she had died and gone to heaven.

Darlene dressed quickly in her rose-colored suit and matching hat and gloves for the honeymoon. The trip was to begin in Paris and continue on to Germany, Italy, Switzerland, and Yugoslavia. She was taking too many clothes, but she didn't care. Her mother kissed her over and over again on the cheek and pressed a pair of diamond-and-pearl earrings into her hand. Her daughter had made it. They were in America, they had all the good things that money could buy, the tradition would not be broken.

On the jet from O'Hare to Paris, Christopher gave her his wedding gift, an antique cameo necklace from his mother, who was dead. Darlene cried, whether from exhaustion, love, or the champagne, she never knew; but she took off the gold link chain necklace that her father had given her for her thirteenth birthday and put on the cameo and swore never to take it off. Christopher was her first love, the man of her dreams, she would have done anything for him.

The next morning, at 7:30 AM, they arrived at their hotel in Paris. The bridal suite was waiting for them. Darlene couldn't wait to take a shower and put on her white peignoir set with matching white satin mules. Her wedding night outfit. Christopher insisted she bathe first, while he unpacked for them. When she emerged, forty-five minutes later, clean and expectant, he was lounging in a velvet smoking jacket. All of her clothes were put away. She went to sit by his side on the bed. He had ordered a bottle of wine, and two crystal glasses for them. Outside the window, the Seine River rolled along the left bank of Paris. She was with her man. She was ready to open up and give all to him. He turned to her. She parted her lips for the kiss that would begin the most important ceremony of her life, her deflowering. Christopher kissed her softly on her lips and then put his arms around her neck, slowly slipping his tongue into her wet mouth. Then his hands felt her throat, and suddenly he stopped. "Where is the necklace I gave you, the one from my mother?" he asked in a harsh, unfamiliar tone of voice.

"I took it off, Darling," she answered, using the unfamiliar but sophisticated term of endearment she had longed to use.

Suddenly Christopher slapped her across the face. The shock sent her spinning off the bed and hurled her onto the floor. He grabbed her arm and slapped her again, bringing blood to her mouth.

"Never, never take that off again unless I give you permission," he yelled into her face, ripping her gown off, lifting her up, shaking and frightened, onto the bed. He quickly took off his robe and without so much as kissing her again, he pulled her hair roughly in his hand as she gasped in terror. This was to be the most important moment of her life. The moment when the two joined as one in the universal act of love, coming together before the mother, the virgin, God, and the Lord Jesus. She had never seen a man naked before, and her husband's giant reddened penis scared her beyond belief.

"Wait a minute, Christopher, Darling," she tried to stop him.

There was no explanation for his violent anger. "Don't you interrupt me." He slapped her again and, too excited to contain himself, he entered her immediately. He was unmindful of the pain, the physical and spiritual pain his young wife was feeling as blood burst forth from her virginal penetration and the man on top of her pushed back and forth violently, never noticing that she was dry and crying, not excited, only afraid, and sick unto death. Who was this man, this cruel and vicious man, riding her so fiercly, pushing his giant penis into her, causing her to bleed? Where was the music, the stars, the tenderness? She would never know.

Christopher beat Darlene the entire honeymoon. She never knew what happened or how she had displeased him so continuously. But she came to know that sex was a nightmare, and nothing she ever did was right. She later found out that he had had two, not one, previous wives. One was in Yugoslavia, the other in California. Her mother's network of spies had never uncovered them. And he had beat them, too.

After the honeymoon, Darlene moved back with Christopher to Berwin, near 27th Street, into a large house, with beautiful furniture and lots of charge accounts. Christopher was not just a good provider, he was a wealthy man.

But Darlene lived in fear of him. Too afraid to leave, too frightened of disappointing her parents, thinking and praying every night that the beatings would end, Darlene never told her mother what was going on. She was too embarrassed. Her life was hell. She had become his property, she was no longer her father's daughter, she was Christopher's to do with as he pleased. He went out; she stayed home. If she cooked a meal and there wasn't enough salt for him, she'd get a beating. If there was too much salt, she'd get a beating. If she didn't look the way he wanted her to, she'd get a beating. If her lipstick was a little too red, or her nail polish a little too bright, it was an automatic beating.

Her eyes lost their glow, she finally lost enough weight for her mother to consider her skinny, and her father to worry. But she couldn't tell her father what had happened. He would kill her husband and that thought confused her. She was ambivalent about what action to take.

The marriage lasted eight and a half months. When they took a cruise to Freeport, on the deserted island with all the other cruise passengers gone, Christopher beat the shit out of her. It was the end. Darlene passed out, unconscious, and he took this opportunity to burn her inert body with lit, orange-tipped cigarettes. When I interviewed Darlene in prison she showed me burns on her back that will never go away.

"It was his need to dominate me, not to let me have my own free will," she explained in a voice whose meter sounded more like the old country than that of a contemporary American woman. "He still lived in the eighteenth century. The man was king, and I wasn't raised that way. He wouldn't even let me work. My father never hit me and I don't know how I took it. I guess because he was the love of my life. There were times when he beat me and I'd get up and disappear, and then I'd get a double beating when I got back. It was hard for me to leave him, because I felt I had gotten married for life. I loved him, but I did leave one day. My husband went to work. I kissed him, I made him a beautiful breakfast and packed up my clothes, took the money out of the bank, and went to San Francisco. I never told my parents that he beat me."

When Darlene returned from San Francisco, she immediately filed for divorce. The cigarette burns on her back were positive proof of how cruel and abusive her husband had been. Her divorce was quickly granted. She returned to college to complete her degree at night. Daytime she worked for a well-known Chicago attorney. In two weeks time she met her second husband, a short-order cook who owned a restaurant. He was Czechoslovakian, which is as close as he could be to a Yugoslavian. He was not as wealthy or educated as Christopher had been, but he seemed to love Darlene; and that was all she cared about, love. Protection. A man who didn't beat her.

In the interview room at the prison, Darlene pulled her yellow sweatshirt down to hide her stomach and hips. She has gained weight behind bars. She had bitten off the bright red lipstick she had had on at the beginning of our talk.

The past is very painful for her. "I got married again very quickly after my divorce. I wanted to prove that I wasn't a failure. I got pregnant in a month and had my little boy in 1979. My husband decided he didn't want to become a father. Right as I went into labor. He told me he needed to buy cigarettes, he went out to get a pack of Marlboros and he never came back. I never saw him again. That was another big blow to me, especially with the family I came from. I just couldn't seem to do anything right and I didn't know what I was doing wrong." There were to be no real dreamboats in Darlene's life. None that lasted. None that mattered, but she would continue to search for one as long as she could.

After the second divorce she went back to live in the large five-bedroom apartment that her parents owned upstairs from their home. Darlene insisted on paying rent. She didn't know who she was, she had a little baby that she wanted and loved, and a husband who had walked out on her and she didn't know why. Her life was not going smoothly. The soap operas she watched so compulsively every day only reflected back to her how far away from love and the dream of the white knight on the horse she really was. There were no princes coming to rescue Darlene.

When she finally received her degree, she moved out of her mother's house because she needed time to breathe. Her mother wanted to protect her. Consume her was more like it. Darlene wanted to open her own business—be independent. That final Christmas in her mother's house, Darlene sold all of her jewelry to make a nice Christmas for her son. Her mother almost killed her when she found out that she had sold so much for so little. Darlene's son was only eight months old, he didn't even know what Christmas was. But that was Darlene. Ritual was of utmost importance to her.

"Finally," she told me, ravenously eating a huge sandwich, the mayonnaise dripping down her chin, as she delicately wiped her mouth, "I decided to forget opening my own business. My father developed cancer in his throat. He had to have a total laryngectomy, and I went to work for a burly man in the Northside of Chicago, on Lawrence Avenue, who had a commercial kitchen repair service."

At first Darlene was only answering the phones and doing the billing. But after a few months she saw that the owner, Steve, could not handle the pressure of business, and that he was not as good as she was in management and planning. By the sixth month she was running the business. She did all the book work, paid the taxes, scheduled the repairmen and installation department, ordered the parts, checked out new products, and collected on old unpaid accounts.

"I fell in love with him." Of course. "And he was married. He was married only six months when I met him, and six and a half months when we started our affair. I only was with him on the grounds that he was going to get a divorce because he loved me."

As we sat in the now chilly interview room, Darlene pushed the last corner of the white bread, yellow cheese, and tiny pink tip of remaining ham into her mouth and chased the whole sandwich down with a large swallow of Coca-Cola Classic. Then she wiped her mouth carefully, cleaned off the table, and neatly folded up the sandwich wrapper before throwing it out. Her meticulous home training showed, even in prison.

I told her it must have been difficult for her to break her strict religious training and have an affair with a married man. I knew she must have been lonely and desperate. She said that her self-esteem was so very low that she was willing to settle for a man who was not too romantic, heavy set, and older than his years. He had married his wife for money and offered Darlene no future for love.

"To make a short story shorter, six and a half years later, he's still married to her, and we're still going together." They could only meet secretly. Darlene pretended, especially to herself, that they were married. She fantasized that her small but clean apartment was their home. She spent her hours and most nights waiting for him to call. On holidays she was alone, or at her parents' house, making excuses to them why she still hadn't found a new boyfriend. A classic case. A classic heartbreak. A beautiful, vivacious, and educated woman who sold herself short because all the men she had chosen in her life had rejected her so thoroughly.

At age twenty-seven, she had given up. She was afraid to leave her old neighborhood in Berwin. She was afraid to leave her mother's territory, the familiar smells of the corner bakery, the butcher shop she knew since she was four, the tiny park with the tree she had carved her initials in when she was only thirteen. Darlene stopped shopping at Marshall Field and Carson. It wasn't that she didn't have the money; she did. She earned an excellent salary and her father continued to help her and her son. Her lover constantly bought her presents. But the little part of her, the part that danced till dawn, wore violets in her hair, and smelled of herbal essence, was gone forever. Demoralized by the inappropriate choices she had made. The foolish men she had given her heart to.

"Steve still comes here to visit me religiously, but at this point, my love for him has died. I really have no feelings for him except maybe contempt and guilt. The reason I'm here is because his business was going badly and he needed money. My way of getting even with him for the way he was treating me, and for not leaving his wife, was to take his American Express Card and go to California with my son." And Darlene went first class.

She and Joey stayed in a two-bedroom suite at the Beverly Wilshire. Darlene had her hair done at Jośe Ebars, where Victoria Principal and Farrah went. She went shopping on Rodeo Drive, at Giorgio's, and Charles Jourdan; she bought expensive shoes, satin teddys, silk outfits for Malibu nights that she would never wear to the office on Lawrence Avenue, let alone on her clandestine dinners with Steve in the out-of-the-way restaurants they chose so that no one from his wife's rich family would ever see them. She rented a white Lincoln limousine with a driver, and ate at the Palm and Chasen's with Joey. She bought ounces of expensive perfume that she later gave to her mother; she bought Joey a leather jacket and a heavy gold chain. She lived it up. Alone. "Steve was going to hell, but I wasn't going to suffer that Christmas. I wasn't going to feel lonely." Everything was fine until he got the bill. It was $8,000.

It happened right after an afternoon quickie on the back of an Amana refrigerator lying on the floor of the storage room. Steve's bill arrived. Darlene pulled up her pantyhose and skirt, fixed her makeup, ran a comb through her hair, and met the mailman who brought the bill. Steve practically had a coronary. He was wealthy, but American Express had to be paid right away. He didn't have that kind of cash available that month. He was afraid he was going to be arrested and put in jail. Darlene was not a criminal. Not yet. All she knew was that the man whom she currently adored was in deep trouble, trouble that she had caused. And as he sat in her apartment that night, on her Castro convertible couch,

Darlene rubbed his feet in that special way she had. She lovingly put a cold compress on his worried brow. She knew she had to help out or lose him. And if she lost him, what was next for her?

Darlene devised a complex plan to make up the money to Steve. It was based on her business acumen and courses that she had taken in college. At this point, she was running the business. Steve was the figurehead. Usually he sat at the office, in his chair, read the track results, the ball-game scores, and made phone calls to his bookie and his father-in-law. She took care of him at work like she couldn't at home. Like she had been trained to do. Like she was dying to do.

The plan went like this. Steve was putting immense pressure on her to come up with the eight grand. Darlene had a momentary realization that like the other two main men in her life, he was going to sacrifice her for himself.

He might even turn her into the police because he was so afraid of going to jail. She couldn't sleep at night. She drank warm milk, liquor, nothing helped. What would happen to Joey? Her parents? Finally Darlene went to an attorney. She set up a phony corporation, Illinois Chemicals. Then she went to a factory where a friend of hers worked and he helped her to set up what appeared to be a business. She had a few contacts in business, people she met through Steve, plumbers, electricians, who said that they bought soap from her, chemicals, supplies, and so forth, on a regular basis. Thus her phony business would look real on paper, with legitimate customers. The factory friend called the plumber friends, and they verified the purchase orders. This all transpired in a two-day period over the phone. Darlene took a bus to an out-of-the-way stationery store, bought the invoices, filled them out correctly with order numbers, taxes, and so forth, as she well knew how to do, forged signatures, and went back to the factory and gave her friend the phony invoices. He gave her a check for the products she had supposedly sold for him, she cashed the check, and then took the $15,000 she had supposedly made to her lover. He asked no questions. She sacrificed herself for him. To make sure that he would never leave her. She wanted a man so desperately that she never thought of the consequences. All she cared about was love. She wanted to be cared about, like her cousins who had homes and husbands and children. She was sick of carrying on like some little tramp in cheap dives with a married man. Maybe now he would leave his wife. Maybe now he would be hers. Maybe she would be able to make up for all the hurt she brought upon herself.

She got found out very quickly. And she stood trial alone. The judge didn't care about her romantic record of pain. All he saw was that she had deliberately and carefully committed grand larceny in the first degree. She could have borrowed the money from her parents. Her father was a very wealthy man. She had a substantial enough salary to make a bank loan. But she chose the criminal route.

Today Darlene claims that when she went to the factory she had every intention of really starting a company, really becoming legitimate, taking part of the fifteen grand and reinvesting it back into the phony company to make it real. It seems unlikely to me that these were her actual plans. It seems more likely that because of her desperate need to have a man, any man, even someone else's husband who obviously wasn't going to leave his wife, that she acted on the moment, never thinking of the future.

When she gave the money to Steve, she threw it on his desk dramatically, and told him that she never wanted to see him again, that she had got married. And to drop dead. He was so shocked that he called her mother, who knew him well. Maddie said that Darlene must be having mental problems because she was certainly not married.

Darlene also told me that her mother knew all along about her relationship with this married man. Steve had helped to raise Joey; he bought him gifts, he did his homework. Steve had been coming to Darlene's apartment for six and a half years. Darlene's mother who didn't approve of dust on the table tops, or alcohol, or Americans, actually condoned this relationship with a married man. Perhaps she was as desperate for Darlene to find a man as Darlene was.

Darlene and I walk through the visitors' room of the prison to stretch our legs. It is gray and sleeting outside. Darlene looks bloated. "I never thought about being caught while I was committing the quickest crime in history. All I thought about was that I had to help Steve because I loved him so; and if I didn't help him, he was going to borrow money from his wife again, and it would be another loan from her. He already owed her a hundred thousand dollars on one loan, and he'd never pay it back and we'd never be together. She owned him. He owed her so much that he even owed his in-laws fifty thousand dollars. There's no way in my lifetime that he's ever going to pay her back. And now today, the business is closed. Without me he can't run it. He's just a stud for his wife. I called him today and asked if he had collected any of the money he had on account. He hadn't. Meanwhile, I have very little money in the commissary. He has a roof over his head and somebody who's going to feed him. And when I committed my crime, factoring those phony invoices, he never even knew that I did it for him." For him, but really for herself.

The lover still comes to visit her, out of guilt or pity, she doesn't know. He comes up and brings her cigarettes and puts money into her commissary account. She feels he owes her something after six and a half years. She feels he owes her more than that.

After Darlene was caught, which was within two weeks of the crime, she jumped bail on her case. She didn't have $10,000 to pay her bond, she didn't want to ask her parents, and there was a warrant out for her arrest. She went into hiding at a sleazy hotel on State Street, a hotel with rats and hookers. A place like she had never seen. Then on May 16, after she had missed her son's Holy Communion, which was what she had lived for since the day he was born, Darlene tried to commit suicide.

She knew that she was going to go to prison for a crime that she didn't make one penny from. She figured Joey would be much better off without the humiliation of a mother in prison. The hurt in her parents' eyes was overwhelming. They had paid the attorney and bailed her out of jail. She couldn't bear to look at her dying father. Her guilt, her sense of despair for her senseless crime, overwhelmed her. She had gone to a doctor shortly after she had been arrested. He had given her a prescription for sixty Valiums, ten milligrams each. She took thirty of them and four shots of scotch and decided to call it quits. But her mother found her and rushed her to the hospital where they pumped her stomach. She lived.

"I wanted a full-time lover, not somone who was part time. I'm a three-time loser, I knew I'd have a one-and-a-half to three-years sentence on my back for the last love of my life. I don't think I'll ever trust a man again. I don't think you'll ever find me in love again. It's very hard. It's hard having my lover come here telling me how difficult life is for him. But I tell him, wait a minute, Mother Fucker, it's harder for me than it is for you. You're out there."

Darlene is not sure if she really wanted to kill herself or if she wanted to escape her shame and humiliation. She never thought she was strong enough to live without Steven. And she wasn't. Her parents have moved to Louisiana; they have a beautiful house there on several acres of land with a gorgeous bedroom waiting for her. Joey is happy there. Darlene can get a job in New Orleans. But how will she be able to have a relationship again? How will she be able to break the pattern of finding her identity through her relationship with men?

"Right now all I want is to get out of here and go live with my parents and my son for a while and take them on vacation. My parents don't go on vacation. Cancer is a very expensive disease. I'd like to take my son to Yugoslavia. Let him see his past. To my father, I'm still his little girl. I call home once a week. I get packages. They can't send me vegetables, but I get cans of delicacies, cigarettes. Their only concern is that I survive, that I don't have any major mental problems. My father, he lost his voice, it's very raspy; all I can hear on the phone is just, 'Please come home.' I want to say all those things to my father before he dies that people wish they had said. I don't want to say I wish, I want to say I did."

Darlene concludes as Patsy Cline's true grit country voice comes singing out of a radio in the visitors' room. "Crazy, I'm crazy for thinking about you," she croons.

Darlene may be a convict, but she is not a murderer. "There is no mother's son in this world that is worth me dirtying my hands with his blood, because if there was one, it would be my first husband, who'd be dead at this point . . . to kill someone and come and do twenty-five to life . . . never . . . I'll never be back again. . . . If you work here they pay you forty cents a day and work you like dogs. . . . They're supposed to rehabilitate you, but they don't. . . . I'm sorry I committed a crime; you know the classification counselor told me, what are you doing here, you don't belong here, you have almost a genius level IQ, you have an education. Well, it doesn't say if you're poor or black you come to prison; if you're white and middle class you don't. I'm not ever coming back." Darlene gets up and walks around the small interview room. Our interview is over.

She still dreams of the club in prison. She still dances the polka in the stardust and wears violet perfume. She would have been married ten years last June. She considers Christopher the love of her life—and the turning point. Call Darlene down on the farm in Louisiana. Ask her how terrific her lifestyle is. Ask her who she's in love with today. She'll probably tell you no one. Men aren't worth it. No man is worth doing time for. There is no such thing as a dreamboat? Is there?

THE CRIME—Grand larceny, first degree
THE SENTENCE—One and a half to three years

CHAPTER IX

THE BEAUTY

To be beautiful is to be isolated
To be beautiful is to be a gardenia
With your flower growing underground
Your Roots pointing to the sky
Alone, with grace upside down.
S. B. N.—1976

MTV WAS BLARING loudly out of the giant TV screen that stood alone in front of the marble fireplace. It was the only furniture in the living room of the brownstone on 72nd Street, where Amber lived.

Amber was in the bathroom, performing her daily ritual. "Sometimes," she thought, "this damn ritual actually consumes more of my time than anything else . . . but work."

Michael Jackson was singing and dancing "Thriller" on the screen. She plucked the last stray eyebrow from her left brow, wiped the area down with witch hazel, and checked her avocado and elastin facial mask to see how the peel was doing. Underneath the green mask, her perfectly creamy skin was waiting to be washed down with warm milk and sprayed with ice water to close the pores. Her hair was wrapped tightly in a plastic bag, heavy conditioner coated every strand of her recently straightened long new style.

Michael Jackson tapped out intricate steps, in complete control of his pelvis; and Amber rushed into the living room, almost slipping on the recently waxed parquet floor, to catch his chorus with the line of monster boys, who were gyrating madly in beat to the pounding rhythm.

"Music hasn't changed that much," Amber announced to her best friend, the mirror. "Why, when I was growing up in Nashville, it was only country music and Motown." She remembered dancing the bump with Alvin Jones in Hillsboro High School to the music of the Four Tops. "Sugar pie honey bun, you know I grow weak for you, can't help myself, I love you and no one else."

Amber laughed, singing the old lyric, running the water in the bubble bath hotter and hotter. Back then, she had let Alvin feel her perfect little titty in his grimy wet hand. And just that, that stupid little boy's grubby advances, had made her wet between the legs. But the Four Tops weren't really erotic. The Four Tops were foreplay. Just like the Supremes. Ol' Diana Ross sang about Baby Love, but she never told you about the act itself.

Amber hummed along with the Cindy Lauper song, "Girls Just Wanna Have Fun."

"Ain't that the truth." She smiled, thinking about her evening ahead with Michael. Dinner at the Four Seasons, a show, and then a night of love-making that only Michael could give.

Amber stood, warm white bubbles running down her long cocoa-colored thighs. It wasn't really until Donna Summer that anyone really sang about doin' it, the ol' down and dirty, and when Donna sang "Bad Girls," you just knew she was talking about the girl gettin' on top for the ride of her life. Girls like to do it on top. She had finally admitted that to her first boyfriend whom she had gone all the way with, when she was sixteen, and that was in 1972. She had gone all the way a number of times since then—and ridden on top as often as she could.

"What it is," the black radio DJ named Elroy had intoned in the late sixties. "This is the boss with the hot sauce, the man with the plan, the top of the line, the candy man, the cat with the platters, the geeter with the heater. Welcome boys and girls, to the hour of love."

Amber could still recall exactly how she had felt after she lost her virginity, how sophisticated, and urbane, wanton, wild, just like a heroine out of a James Bond book, just like Pussy Galore.

"Shake your money maker," Michael always told her. Amber stood up now and turned on the shower full blast, careful to keep her face out of the water, wanting only to rinse the conditioner out of her hair. The water felt wonderful, beating against her skin. It was so hot, her long black nipples stood erect, at attention. Amber felt herself becoming excited. The tingling sensation that began in her breasts and worked on down to her thighs was starting.

She grabbed a soft pink towel from the towel rack and began rubbing herself down vigorously. She looked at her toes and her fingernails carefully. She didn't like the new color Diane was using—it was too dark, purple was passé. Out. Lionel Richie's mellifluous voice was crooning on MTV now. Ahh, Lionel. It was only since him that music had broken through to pure sex.

Amber looked at her gorgeous reflection in the mirror.

"The most beautiful face I've ever seen without makeup," the modeling agency on Fifth Avenue had told her. She might have had a successful modeling career. Her eyes were huge, the color of topaz. A lower lip to suck all night. Amber rubbed collagen cream on her face and hummed in harmony with Lionel. She applied baby oil to her buttocks and thighs and put Elizabeth Arden Perfection Cream on her face. That's what Amber wanted, perfection. She needed a massage. She'd have to call Joel and ask him to bring over his board for a long session. She threw off the towel and examined her exquisitely formed breasts and hips. She was magnificent.

"Ain't I gorgeous?" she taunted her friend the mirror. "Mirror, mirror on the wall, ain't I the fairest of them all?

Ain't I the prettiest little nigger girl you ever did see?" And
Amber laughed. And laughed. And laughed.

Amber had always been beautiful. When the obstetrician
in Louisiana had brought her mother the tiny baby girl,
wrapped in a pink swaddling blanket, Annie had looked at
every feature of her new daugther. Especially the eyes,
which were topaz, a strange combination of yellow, green,
and hazel. Unusual eyes for a black baby. Annie decided to
call her Amber.

"This little girl's gonna be another Elizabeth Taylor," she
told her husband, Arthur, who sat by her hospital bed already studying his schedule for the next two weeks.

"That's fine, Dear," he answered by rote, not paying particular attention to his young wife. He was thirty years older
than Annie, and an excellent provider. She was used to his
detached attitude by now, after the first child. He would be
a good father to his new little daughter.

Although Annie was never quite sure what Arthur did up
there in Washington, D.C., she knew that he visited the
Pentagon twice a month. The trips entailed more than his
just being a mathematician, but he kept his business life private. And Annie respected that.

As they drove the baby home, in the black Pontiac coupe,
Annie saw that spring had come to the South. The crocuses
and tulips were bursting forth around her tiny home. Soon
the forsythia would bloom and the honeysuckle would se-
duce lovers of all ages. Any day now sloe-eyed summer
would wind its way around the countryside.

Annie hummed an old Billie Holiday tune as she placed
little Amber in the large wicker basket that would serve as
her cradle. Annie's girlfriend Nettie had brought over a
baked ham and cornbread for dinner, and as the late afternoon light poured into her kitchen, and Arthur went out to
drink lemonade on the porch, Annie once again realized how
lucky she was to have so fine a man for a husband. He might

be strict, and he might be religious, he might be older than her, and he might not be an experimenter in the marriage bed, but he performed his duty well.

A large hawk circled the driveway as their little son Albert burst through the door, glad to be home, glad his mother had had the baby and he could leave his granny's house. "Mom," he threw his tiny arms around her neck and kissed her on the bosom, his small glasses slipping down to the bridge of his nose.

"Hello, Sweetie," she crooned, touching him lightly on the forehead and nodding her head to her mother, who was examining the baby.

The old woman's eyes made instant contact with the eyes of the infant. "She's got devil eyes, Annie," Cornelia told her daughter, putting down her bag of preserves and relishes. "She's got devil eyes and I'm tellin' you she's gonna be trouble for you."

Annie ignored the admonition. She would be glad to leave the Deep South. It was full of old women with their negative outlooks on life. Amber would have a new start in Nashville, where soon blacks would be equal to whites, and education would be available for everyone.

Amber wore a slinky silver evening gown with rhinestone straps that night with Michael. The dress had cost $1,200 at Henri Bendel. Michael liked her to doll up. She had bought some new eye shadow to match her heels and bag. But Michael would be happiest when he saw how much money she had beat the Japanese businessman for that afternoon. Fifty grand was not an uncommon profit in her line of work. But it was not that easy to come by, either. You had to be a pro. You had to be a silver-tongued fox. She grabbed her silver fox coat, the one she paid for herself last year, the one she was so proud of, and called her service to tell them she'd be out for the night. Then she threw her moldy, ancient lucky rabbit's foot from old Grandma Cornelia in her four-hundred-dollar bag and laughed.

"I guess I'll never lose that ol' country superstition," she realized as she gave the room a final survey. "I guess my ol' grandma would have something to say about me tonight," she whispered quietly, thinking all the time of Michael's hands and mouth on hers. If only they could skip the formalities and come back home and smoke their base and make love. It was all she cared about in the world. Except making money, of course.

Michael was waiting for her at the ground floor entrance of the Seagram Building where they would have a white man's dinner at the Four Seasons.

"God, he is handsome." Amber couldn't help but notice again. His black silk Italian suit fit perfectly. His gray silk shirt hung exactly right. His three-hundred-dollar alligator loafers glowed. Michael's curly hair hung past his ears in a fashionable length. His swarthy skin was almost golden. And his mouth, she adored that mouth, that mouth that knew every way, every word that could make a girl feel like shit, but could also perform the motions to make her come in a minute.

"Damn that Dago," she thought to herself as Michael watched her get out of the taxi and stared at her appreciatively. She was some dish. And incidentally, the best con artist he had ever met, or trained.

"How'd you do today, Doll Face?" He kissed her on the cheek, not wanting to disturb her perfect lipstick.

"Not bad," she answered, standing back so he could see the swell of her perfect breasts. From Alvin Jones to Michael, men loved her titties. They could just not keep their hands off of them.

She opened her purse for Michael to see all the cash inside as they entered the exclusive, expensive restaurant that

Michael loved. He really didn't care so much about the food, preferring the steaks at Peter Luger, it was the smell of the wealthy he wanted—and needed.

"Not bad at all." He smiled, noticing that all the bills stacked in Amber's purse were hundreds, and there were hundreds of them. "You've been a good girl." He rubbed her on the behind, knowing how much she loved it, "and we're gonna have a good time tonight."

When Amber was six months old her family moved up to Nashville, Tennessee. The family bought a cozy little house in Green Hills, one of the wealthy suburbs where a few blacks had moved in. It was a far cry from a dilapidated Southern black ghetto, and Annie's dreams of living in a free state were recognized. Arthur's mathematical specialty was physics. He was sent every other week to the Pentagon. No one in the family ever knew exactly what he did there. Annie was instantly hired as an executive secretary in the governor's office. Both of Amber's parents had been educated at Fisk University, an excellent black college in Nashville. Her father had his master's degree as well. Over the next several years there were two more children born to the couple, a son and another daughter, who was very pretty, but not nearly as exotic looking as Amber.

The family house was located in a woodsy suburb, with a border of tall pine trees around it. Cornelia came up to visit and was amazed and curious about the vegetation in Tennessee, which was so different from that of Louisiana. The winters here were cold, although there were few major accumulations of snow. The temperatures often dropped below zero. Amber lived for the January snowstorms that brought enough snow that school would be called off. Then she could stay home and daydream.

After the birth of her fourth child, the youngest son, Annie had stopped working to stay home and take care of the children. Annie was up at daybreak, along with Arthur, who was becoming more and more religious and got up early to say morning prayers. There were many other Pentecostals in Nashville and Arthur drove to his church in North Nashville every day to talk to the pastor who was conversant in his specialties: speaking in tongues, the coming apocalypse, Revelations. Arthur began to teach night courses in calculus and physics at Vanderbilt, and he also opened a hotdog stand near Opryland that was going quite well for a while. The Fairchilds were very successful financially. They had a comfortable house with a huge fireplace, access to a tiny cottage on Old Hickory Lake where Arthur and his sons could fish, and high hopes for the children's scholastic future. Mr. Fairchild was a very respected citizen.

"My dad made sure we would get good grades," Amber remembers today, "my parents went to all the PTA meetings and if I didn't get good grades I'd get a beating for the week." Amber liked science and math especially, which pleased her father who thought she might have a future in one of the new industrial math-related fields. The computer industry was just a tiny futuristic part of the American economy then, but Arthur saw its potential and spoke to his children about it.

Although in the early 1960s, civil right's issues were exploding on the American scene, Amber never paid particular attention to them. Her brother and her father did, but she was a self-absorbed teenager.

"I was sort of tomboyish back then," she recollects, although looking at her in the prison interview room it is difficult to believe this. "I loved to play with the guys and wrestle at the high school gym. I basically liked swimming the best, I was a profesional swimmer," she proudly says, showing me the well-developed muscles in her back and upper arms. "I won trophies and everything in high school. My life was pretty straight. You know, Nashville was sort of a small town, lots of trees and hills. I didn't like to read too much, mostly just magazines and stuff. I went to sleep-over

camp every summer for thirty days, and I came back and
had a little job in the last part of the summertime working
with kids in the nursery, teaching them how to swim. I had
to be back in the house before the street lights came on,
because we'd all have dinner together every night. My
grandma and grandpappy were living with us by then. I
never used drugs, I never stole, my parents wouldn't let me
play with a lot of different types of kids, mostly we had to
stay in and study. And read about weather, my dad's really
into that. He never liked the guys I brought over to the
house, he was pretty strict, even for my mom."

Amber's life seemed very ordinary. Small town. Confined.
No real future that seemed glamorous. But over the radio
waves, direct from Detroit, there was that music, that
Motown sound, that visceral beat that every teenager in the
country, not just the black ones, was listening to. And Amber listened hard. Sometimes she sneaked her tiny white
transistor into bed with her at night, after her dad turned off
the bedroom lights. There was Smokey Robinson and the
Miracles, the Temptations, Solomon Burke, the Supremes,
Dionne Warwick, the Marvelletes. And as she lay in bed,
tired out from a day of school, or camp, her body exhausted
from competitive swimming, she knew that somewhere in
America there was more to life than math and swimming and
weather. There were parties, and clothes and jewelry, and
dating, and big houses and traveling all over, and men. Definitely men.

Michael held Amber in his arms, her eyes almost rolling
back in her head from the long drag of freebase she had
taken from the pipe. Around the kingsize bed dozens of candles flickered. Somewhere in the background Teddy Pen-
dergrass sang.

"You like that, baby," he whispered into her ear, knowing
that she was still in ecstasy, still writhing from the hit that
had blown the top of her brain off, sent her on a voyage to

paradise, put her right in the midst of dreamland waking. He reached his hand down to touch her soft, soft thigh, and she moaned. She wanted it now. "Come on baby, don't tease me," she stretched her hand between his legs, still in a fog, but never too stoned to arouse him. She had studied all the sex manuals and erotic literature she could get her hands on when she first came to live with him in New York, including the Kama Sutra. She knew how to titillate a man with a glance of her eyes, her breathing, her smile, how to arouse a man to passionate heights, and then stop, let him build up steam again, and then plunge him back to passion. Amber was an expert, there was no doubt about that. And she knew it. She was as good a hustler on the street as she was in bed. Although she'd never try to hustle Michael. He was her teacher. He knew all of her tricks. As he began to stroke her stomach in small circles, he thought again how angry Amber would be when he told her that he wanted Georgia, the ripe Southern peach, Amber's blond equivalent, to move in with them. But if Amber got high enough, and Georgia performed well enough, Amber would agree. She licked her lips and Michael, streetwise Michael from Greenfield, P.A., home of the steel mills, and the hunkies, and the Steelers and the Pirates, and youse guys, was struck once again by how beautiful she was, how exquisite. The most beautiful black girl he had ever had. Amber's mouth nuzzled his thighs in that unique way she had as he took another hit of the freebase pipe and forgot where he was. Amber already didn't know.

Amber Fairchild was the most gorgeous criminal I ever saw. She is beyond gorgeous, she is breathtaking. In the dismal atmosphere of Riker's Island, where the guards are butch, and the prisoners gray and medicated, or hostile and clothed in fatigues, Amber strode into our interview in an electric blue-and-black print two-piece pants outfit by Jean Muir, her hair pulled back from her face in an elegant chig-

eye shadow light, but perfectly coordinated with her clothes, her cheeks matte and blushed and her lips outlined, filled in and glossed over with a subtle rust color that sparkled. Her long legs ended in a pair of high, high heels. Her nails were perfectly done, and her laugh was amazingly fresh. She was also the best hustler I have ever met. Amber is sly, savvy, and sexy. A tough combination to beat in a con artist.

"I wish I had a friend like you. I wish I could really trust you," she cooed, staring straight into my eyes with a true look of sincerity.

"Why can't you?" I asked.

"Well, it's hard. I wish I could work for you," she added, changing the subject like a pro. "Your shoes sure is fly, where did you get them?"

"In Miami, close to where I live. I . . . ." I found myself suddenly being interviewed by her, flattered, questioned, and ultimately expected to pity her, which was difficult to do.

"What crime were you accused of, Amber?" I asked, try-ing to steer the interview back on track.

"Have you ever done anything illegal?" she answered sweetly, offering me a Marlboro, which I desperately wanted but felt I must refuse at this point. I remain silent. If I had told Amber about my past, any professionalism I wanted to maintain would be instantly over. She would have taken ad-vantage of me.

"The charge is grand larceny," she finally answered, "that's the only thing I've ever been arrested for. I have a one and a half to three years running concurrently to a one and a half to five in Tennessee because I absconded from a correctional institute there. The first time I ever went to prison in my life was in 1983, for the con game. That's the only thing I've ever done. So I went to prison and I stayed there two months and I guess they checked my records and the counselor told me I was low risk because I'd never been arrested before. She recommended a halfway house. I stayed there maybe thirty days. I had my own room, my own key, I had to live in there, but I could sign out to go look for a job; and one day I got tired of it and I just walked away. They didn't use to prosecute people for walking away, but so many do nowadays. I just left and came back to New York, and I got arrested here and got bailed out by my daddy, and then I got arrested in the late summer of 1985, at 59th and Columbus Circle, and they found out about me walking away from the correctional institute, so now I'm serving concurrent sentences." She pauses and smiles. "You sure are pretty."

What does Amber want from me? I can't get her out of jail, I'm not going to testify on her behalf; it is just her habit now to hustle everyone and anyone she meets. She cannot stop. I wonder if she was a hustler when she was young. I wonder if every time she smiled she thought the skies were going to open up for her.

Amber decided she wanted to become a model when she was fifteen. She and her sister Julianne had modeling portfolios compiled in Atlanta by a famous fashion photographer. Their father approved of that, and he paid for them both to travel there, with Grandma Cornelia as chaperone. Grandma gave Amber the rabbit's foot that summer for good luck. Although she hoped that her granddaughter would find success, she never lost her intuition that Amber was trouble. The sisters spent one summer going on tour for a publishing company, which published fashion and style magazines. They had small walk-on parts in a movie the company was making, but when the school season started, both girls had to go home. Amber didn't want to, but she had no choice. She wanted glamour and fame, her reward, what she deserved for being so beautiful. Her father didn't see it that way.

Almost immediately upon her return to Nashville, two very important things happened to Amber. She lost her virginity, out of spite against her father or a true passion, it was not clear. And her aunt was beat out of half of her life savings by two con men.

Amber was furious when she got back from Atlanta. She had seen the future and it included black limousines, fur coats, diamonds, champagne, and lots of attention. Her second week back in Hillsboro High she stayed out all night with a high school senior. She was just a sophomore then. In the back seat of his parents' 1970 Chrysler she lost her cherry. Amber was punished but she had learned the power she had over men. All she had to do was smile her rich chocolate smile, and doors opened for her.

"One day," she would tell herself over and over again as she lay in her single bed at night, under her grandmother's hand-sewn down comforter, "I'll have more than any of these little white girls can even imagine. I'll have it all."

It was in the spring of Amber's fifteenth year that her Auntie Louann, her mother's sister, went by herself on a trip to Atlanta to see the sights and get swindled.

"Louann told my mother how two guys had swindled her of all her thousands, and she asked my mom not to tell my dad or uncles or nobody. It was a big secret. But I heard her tell it. And it was very interesting to me. It was amazing; she didn't know these two guys, and they came along and convinced her to go to the bank branch up there and withdraw all her money. Really, they told her she'd end up getting twenty thousand dollars from them, and she didn't want to report it to the police because she said it was her own fault because she thought she was getting over on the guys. And they got over on her. And my mother kept on saying, 'I don't know how you could let two strangers you've never seen in your life convince you to go get your money.' She told my mother that the story made so much sense and it was so convincing, and she was there all the time and she doesn't know how they switched the money on her. When she came home, she thought she had all the money in a newspaper. And I tell ya, the expression on her face was like she had seen a Frankenstein."

What interested Amber so much about that story? The point that really caught her attention was how greedy her aunt was to fall for such a scam. Amber tried to imagine herself pulling this scam on people. But her plan was just a dream, a distant dream of the future. Sometimes, with dreams, if you want them badly enough, you can imagine your life and it will happen that way. That is what transpired with Amber Fairchild. She thought long and hard about her auntie and the con game. And the man who would teach her the game was just around the corner. Like she had wished him into her life.

Women are looking in through the glass window in the interview room that Amber and I are using to talk. Some are laughing, some are serious and menacing looking. They have a profound curiosity in what we are discussing. Word has spread through the prison in a matter of a few hours that I am here doing work for a book. Everyone wants to be in it, to tell her tale. Amber ignores all the knocks and exclamations of the others. This is her show and she is running it. The longer we speak, the more positions I see her face in— full profile, three-quarter profile, smiling, pensive, sad, sarcastic, hustling—the more beautiful she looks. She is not someone whose looks fade on you.

"I was hot on the trail of fashion and I decided to go to college in New York, at Parsons School of Design. I was still pretty naive then, and I just met this guy that I liked and I didn't really know that he did anything wrong, that he was a crook or anything, because at first he tricked me." You can only hustle a hustler, the best of the con women told me. If you don't want to be hustled, you can't be. If you are looking for it, it will come to you. "Once I got involved with him for awhile, he told me. I mean I ran across some of his stuff that he had, read it, and I thought he was like a hit man or something until my sister came to visit and I showed it to her and she said, nah, he's a con man. So then he explained to me what he did for a living and he said he thought I would be pretty good at it, and I left school. I thought I would be good at it too because I always wanted to be an actress."

Amber picked up and left school, with Michael. Michael was a young, handsome stud, who seemed worldly, wise, and sophisticated to the young girl from Nashville. Michael was Italian, had connections, and recognized in Amber a little goldmine. With her looks, her sex appeal, and her savvy she could hustle the pants off anyone, and did, quite frequently. Amber and Michael stayed together for years.

Amber never explained to me how her parents reacted to her leaving school. I thought that her very straightlaced father would have been quite upset by it, but apparently they did not come to the Big Apple to find her or try to stop her, because her life as a con artist began immediately.

She and Michael moved to the Bronx, into one of those shabby apartments, in a building owned by one of Michael's friends or associates. The Bronx was very rough. The streets were composed of whole blocks of tall brick buildings that once housed new American immigrants. These buildings are now exploded from the inside out by years of occupation by the poverty-stricken soon to be homeless of New York City. The dwellings originally designed for a five-member family were crammed with two or three dozen people, drug addicts, often violent. The furniture had mostly disappeared, the windows were broken, filthy curtains hung aimlessly from the glassless frames. There was often no heat or running water in these places, so fires were started on the floor to keep the people warm. The whole block looked like Dresden, Germany, after its World War II bombings.

Amber and Michael lived in this area, but not in a totally devastated building. Theirs was shabby and certainly not glamorous, but it was not filthy. It was just dismal and used. The white, white heat of the New York summer sun beat down upon them mercilessly as Michael showed Amber the script—the plan—the way to pull a con. He instructed her daily about how to dress, in dresses, sports jackets, not too much jewelry. He practiced her in the mirror on how to smile demurely, how to speak with an African accent, the psychology of the hit, how to pick out a good victim, how to fake Swahili or Jamaican, the difference between white and black victims. And always, what they would do and buy with their profits, the jewels and furs, travel, the new apartment in Manhattan they would have. The quicker Amber learned, the quicker Michael could get them out of the Bronx, where she might be beautiful, but she was just another nigger on the make to most of the blacks who knew the scene so well.

So Amber quickly learned how to play the con game. She forgot about fashion and modeling. Instead, she studied the streets of Manhattan, learned what corner was the best to work, learned how to avoid a compromising situation with male victims, and who could be the most easily conned. In the evenings she read sex manuals that she took out from the 42nd Street Public Library, and old pictorial instruction guides she and Michael found in the grungy second-hand book stores of Greenwich Village. Late at night, the desultory city breeze falling through their windows, they smoked some reefer, or sometimes even snorted a little cocaine, which was relatively unknown in the mid-1970s, except by a cadre of the most experimental. Michael would make love to her until dawn and tell her how beautiful she was and convince her how well she was going to do and how easy it would be to con most people out of their life savings. Amber laughed in his arms and followed his instructions as the summer wore on. And then it was the day to hit the street.

It seems remarkable that Amber was not aware of apartheid when she began her con days. Maybe she was, maybe she didn't care that by using this particular con and accent that she was exploiting the entire race issue. Maybe she was so self-absorbed that she was not even cognizant of how blacks were treated in South Africa. But Amber's disguise, when she hit the streets of Midtown Manhattan, was a South African accent that was word perfect. When we spoke, she explained how she was turned out in the streets, and how she was perfectly able to imitate the South African dialect. She actually performed her entire rap for me in the accent. And it was so good, the cadence so perfect, the tone so humble, but proud, the dialect so clipped, that not only did she sound like a native, but I realized that instinctively Amber could have become a truly fine actress, at least as good at accents as Meryl Streep.

In Manhattan, Amber preferred the Upper East Side or Upper West Side to find her vics, chumps, suckers, or lame—all the terms of endearment she uses for the people she beats. She claims she has extraordinary judgment when it comes to people, because everyone doesn't go for her con. She claims that she meets some of her victims because people stop her on the street, interested in a unique article of clothing she wears, ethnic items not too flashy, not too prim. In her African pose she would wear a dashiki. Using her Jamaican accent, she wore their colorful native dresses. "I don't know," she told me pensively, "there's something about a person that you can just see, something there that says come and get me, I'm the one.

"I would say, 'Excuse me, Mon, today be my first day here in America. I don't read or speak the American language very good. I'm here in America because my brother got killed here, in a train accident, about eighteen months ago, you must have heard about it in the newspapers. I meet someone at the airport and I pay the mon two hundred and fifty American dollars and he tell me he's going to give me a place to stay and he tell me to wait fifteen minutes and he don't come back. He told me he had a little brownstone place, hotel. He gave me a receipt, and I give him the money.'

"Of course, this never really happened. I show her a receipt. So she doesn't think I'm a bum or anything, I show her my own American dollars, I have ten thousand dollars with me, I show them my money. Now here it depends on how I play that day. I might really have a couple of thousand in cash so I make a mish, with real money on top and on the bottom. And I tell him or her that I'll give them fifty or a hundred dollars if they just come back and look this residence up for me in the Yellow Pages. Then they'll go to the phone booth and look it up for me and the operator will tell them that there's no such place, the Brownstone Hotel, because it doesn't exist. And then I say, 'Wait a minute, Miss, Lady, maybe you should ask another American person like yourself.' And by chance my partner Michael will be walking down the street, and the lame, will tell him what happened and that they think someone is trying to rip me off because there are a lot of swindles and stuff like this in this country, and I just got here and I don't have anyone, and I have an awful lot of money on me. Then Michael might suggest that since he's a cab driver, or whatever gig he pretends he has that day, that we should all go together and find me a place to stay. He has a Christian lady he knows that rents rooms to foreigners and exchange students, so he'll write the address down, and he'll ask if you could see to me getting into a cab and getting there safely. The lame says yes. Then I say if the both of you put your heads together and take me to this place, I can't make you rich, but I can give both of you something for your time and trouble. Everyone's time is worth something. So then, the both of them, the partner and the lame, will end up taking me around to this place he's talking about, but we never really get there. Instead we go to a restaurant, and he says he thinks you should explain American customs to me so that when you drop me off and I do get a place to stay, I'll know a little about America.

"So we sit at the restaurant and have a cup of coffee and they tell me about America, and that I shouldn't walk around with this large sum of money on me, and then Michael will

ask the lame, Where do they think is the best place for me
to keep my money, Ma'am?' And they say, why the bank. So
then I say I don't know anything about banks, cause where
I'm from, Johannesburg, South Africa. I work for a multi-
millionaire. I live on a yacht and do domestic work for my
boss, so I don't know about finances. I'm afraid to put my
money into the Jew Man's dollar house because if I put my
money in there, how will I get it back? They'll stick dogs on
me, and the lame, will be trying to convince me that it's not
like that, then they'll explain the procedures, how to open
an account. I ask if I put my money in there, because by this
time I tell them that the man I work for he had his lawyer
help me, and when my brother died he left stocks and
bonds, and the lawyer told my boss that I have to come to
America on my own, and I have to have somewhere to stay
for ninety days till the taxes and everything is cleared up on
my money so I can go back to my country. So if they let me
put my money in there, what will the bank give me to know
my money from your money? Then the lame will show me
what they'll give me, by showing me what the bank gave
them, a bankbook, and I'll ask what does that mean. And
they'll show me what that means, and then I'll pretend that I
don't believe that you can do anything with a meat and potato book, and at this point some people get a little hostile,
because I tell them oh, you're nuts, you must be trying to
get my money, you don't have anything and that's less than a
meat and potato card, so I'll pretend like I was going to get
up and leave and then some people call me back and say
miss, we're not going to try to fool you. And if after today we
picked up a newspaper and read that something bad had
happened to you, we'd feel it bad on our conscience. So at
this point I gamble it all.

"They keep explaining to me bank procedures, and I say if
I give you four thousand dollars for a gift could I see you put
that on your meat and potato bankbook, then I would know
it would work for me. Then I try to give them part of my

money, and they say they don't want it. Some people say OK, but I never give them my four thousand dollars. Then they tell me to wait, they want to see how much currency they have in their account. And they tell me if I put my entire fifty thousand dollars in the bank, and I wanted it back in case I wanted to leave this country and go back to my country, I could get it. Then they tell me right now they have fifty thousand dollars in CitiBank. If they wanted to right now they could go to their bank and get ten thousand dollars without anyone stickin' any dogs on them. It's their money and this is America."

I realize now that Amber likes mainly to hit wealthy white people. She explains to me that she really doesn't like to be bothered with black people because they give her too many hassles after they hear the rap. Some people feel sorry for Amber and take her to the bank and show her that the banks in America work. They think they're only taking their money out for five minutes to show her how the cards work. Some people tell her that they don't believe in accounts, they prefer safety deposit boxes at the bank, and they go and take their money out to show her how life is in a democracy. Some people tell her they keep their money at home, and they take her to their house and show her what they have and she tells them aside from the money she has that she's worried about keeping in the country, she has lots of jewelry, valuables, and more money at the airport. She only brought a certain amount with her. The deal is that she tricks them into thinking that she's worried about keeping her money safe here, and they show her how safe their money is, in the meantime taking their money out of the bank, or the safe deposit vault, or their home safe.

"Then they end up keeping my ten thousand dollars for me, which is mostly fake, on the pretense that me and my partner are going back to the airport to get my personal belongings. And the lame either gives me their home address and phone number, or if they're near the bank, they take my

money with their money that they showed me and got out of
their account. Some people have the tendency of waking up
a little bit when they have their money in hand and then you
can rock them back to sleep. Some people turn all the way
and say, look, and they show me they got all their money in
hundreds and fifties, and they ask me to count it down for
them, so that when they hold my money while I go to the
airport, I'll feel safe, because the man at the airport that
gave me the address of the Brownstone Hotel, he saw me
counting my money down, and maybe he has some other
friends and they're afraid that I'll get robbed if I go back to
the airport with all that money on me. So, the deal goes, I
met you first, you are my first friend and my best friend in
this American country, if I let anybody hold my money for
me, I'm going to let you hold it. Not even the man that's
trying to help me (who is really my partner). So then the
money the lame already has, from the bank or the home or
wherever, I never ask them for anything, I just give them
my ten thousand dollars so they put it up for me, safe like,
and me and my partner are pretending like we're getting
ready to go to the airport, and then it dawns on me. I come
back and say no Mrs. Lady, or Mister, please don't keep my
American dollars right out here, I say where will you keep
my money at? They'll show me, they've got it right here,
nothing's going to happen. And I say wait a minute, something just struck me in my head. I say back in my country,
the mon I work for sent me to the store one day and I carried his money here, and I had my money there, and I lost
his money but kept my money, but he always tells me you
can watch one pile better than two. The lame says, well, that
makes sense. So I say let me show you how to keep my
American dollars, then this way I know it will be safe. The
lame says OK, so they let me show them, so I show them
how to keep my money, I say where do you keep your
money, and I say keep mine side by side with it, so if anything happens to my money it's going to happen to yours

too, you're going to watch it, you're going to put the same protection you put on your own, on mine. Now maybe my partner comes up and gives me an envelope, and we put the money side by side, so it won't get mixed because mine has a money wrapper on it. So we put it side by side. I seal the envelope up and put it back down in my purse and I say keep it down deep like this, deep in your bag, because they have long finger men in this country, and the partner says oh she's talking about pickpockets, they do have them. And as I put the envelope deep in my purse, or deep within my bosom, I switch the envelope with one we have prepared that looks exactly like the one I just prepared. So I talk all the while and tell her she knows about stuff like this, and the lame never looks at the dummy envelope again because they've seen me do the whole transaction, and then I put it deep inside their pocketbook, or briefcase, or bosom. So then the lame grabs a cab to go on home, or if we're at their house we leave and tell them we're going back to the airport to get my belongings, and they just go up the stairs and put the money in a safe place, and I say I'll call you and meet you in the lobby as soon as I get everything, because I don't want your husband or you to say anything or anyone to think anything about it. And she promises she won't mention it to no one. And I be gone."

The first time Amber ever pulled a sting, she found herself back in the Bronx, in Michael's arms, lying in their stinkin' little apartment bed, counting the money, which came to $7,200, and crying and laughing at the same time. She was exhausted.

"Man, I feel so sorry for that lady," she had told her man recalling the trusting look on the small Jewish woman's face who had led them up to her East 57th Street apartment, and made Amber, dressed in a red-and-white dashiki, a cup of tea.

"Well, don't," Michael told her, stroking her hair, watching a large gray rain cloud pass outside, high above the Manhattan skyline. "We didn't take everything she had. She is one rich bitch, Baby, did you see the artwork in her pad? There looked like a real lot of valuable things there. No person's ever going to give you everything that they have, people don't gamble with everything, especially the people we hit. Stick with the rich ones, Baby, and pretty soon, not too far away, we'll be living in places you can't even imagine now. Trust me, Baby, trust me." He began kissing her wrist softly, licking the tiny brown mole on the underside of her elbow.

Amber only had to make a few more stings like the first one and they were gone, out of the Bronx. Sometimes Michael worked with her, sometimes he introduced her to other women, never as beautiful nor as flamboyant as Amber, who would act as the other partner, the silent con. Sometimes, after they moved to first the Lower East Side, and then to 23rd Street, a two-bedroom apartment with a built-in kitchen and white walls, Michael would disappear for weeks on end, trusting Amber to deposit the money in their safety deposit box, knowing that he left her enough coke to last the duration of his trip, knowing that she was slowly gaining confidence, slowly building up the strength to live on her own, but not quite yet.

At first Amber was so overwhelmed by the amount of money she was making that she was afraid to spend it without Michael by her side, Michael telling her what to buy, what to wear, how to act. But that quickly wore off as she realized that it was really up to her to pull off the job, and it would be only her ass to go to prison.

"The thrill of the crime was strong," she explained to me, a big nostalgic smile breaking over her face. "You can have a lot of fun pulling the sting. Sometimes I'd be happy to beat these people, because they'd be so greedy and arrogant; and they'd be telling me all this stuff about their business, and how they got involved with lawyers, and they got swindled out of this and this, and how I should be careful. And we'd eat together, I'd have dinner with them, you have to spend a little bit of time with people when you swindle them."

As Amber became more and more expert at pulling the cons, she moved on to acquiring more and more cash. She found out that men fell for the brother who just died rap, and she devised her own particular story that would most affect the women. She maintains that the best, easiest people to swindle are Chinese men, because they don't believe in banks, and the Japanese, because of their love of secrecy. She says she got $100,000 on her biggest sting. Immediately after that she and Michael moved to the brownstone.

"I bought Cadillacs; I bought expensive designer clothes; I gave my mom thousands, jewelry; my sister, too. I traveled a lot. I had a condo in Hawaii, Colorado, Reno. We used to go to these ski tournaments in Colorado, because Michael had a lot of friends there, some other Italians that own their own businesses. They swindle legally in Reno. After a while, especially after Michael had the white girl Georgia move in with us so we could all have sex together, I started staying out in hotels a lot. Hiltons, the Plaza. It was like I got up in the morning and went to my nine-to-five job, then I was finished. I came back from work, cleaned a little, changed my clothes, got on the phone, jumped in my car, went shopping or partying. Michael was gone so much. He's a con man too, and he participated in another type of con, a terrible one, impersonating police. They go in and tell people they're police, all dressed up in uniform. . . ." She stopped short of telling me too much about Michael. She is still protective of him. Like many of the other middle-class women I interviewed, she never turned her man in when she got busted. Michael remains free—out on the streets.

Amber admits that her mother knew for a long time what she was doing. "One day I went to visit my mom and I had a lot of cash, and she asked me where I got it from. Did I rob someone? And I just sat down and explained it all to her. What could she do? But my dad, he'll talk to me, but he'll never help me, because he came and bailed me out once, and he told the police everything, my real name, and then they rearrested me for using a false name. He told me that it was my auntie who had been swindled who asked him to bail me out. But he will never approve of me. Never."

It is a long way from Reno and Colorado ski matches to Riker's Island and the final prison where they will send Amber. The next place will not allow her to prance about wearing her own clothes while she is incarcerated. She will have to wear more subdued outfits, or prison garb, depending on the prison. But she will be beautiful and she will still not have changed. She feels no remorse for what she's done, no sorrow, and has no plans to reform.

I pity the first person she hits when she gets out of prison. It will be an honest, hard-working citizen, who is taken in by the beauty and the fragility of her face, the sad story she has to tell. To be beautiful might just be to have been cursed by the gods, always looking for more love, more reassurance, and confidence that you have more than beauty—brains. But to be beautiful is not to be invincible.

THE CRIME—Grand larceny
THE SENTENCE—One and a half to three years,
                        concurrent with one and a half to five
                        years.

CHAPTER X

A LONG WAY FROM HOME

*Alone in L.A. I continued my search for the Holy Grail.
And to being really hip—I mean to make the scene—was to
live next door to Yvette Mimeiux in a four bedroom house
with a pool in Benedict Canyon, wear old denim, and drive
either a funky pick-up truck or an old Rolls. And when you
pulled out a diamond coke spoon everyone knew, oh man,
she's one of the enlightened ones—let's all go out and eat
salads in the smog on Sunset Strip and buy $150 shirts to
wear with our faded dungarees so everyone knows that
we're not materialistic . . . and go home, shoot heroin and
talk about moving to the country and getting on with the
simple life . . . and whole wheat bread, a lot of vitamins, a
lot of mystical, astrological, numerological, Brotherhood of
the Light, cosmological, full-on-in-the-divine, jive-ass talk.*
THE BUTTERFLY CONVENTION—1976

IT WAS FOUR AM in La Paz, Mexico. The sky was dark blue,
blue like the Pacific Ocean fifty miles from shore, blue like
the imported cashmere sweater from Beverly Hills that I
would never wear again, blue like Andrew's eyes the last time
we swam at the beach. A falling star drizzled past the bars on
the windows of my hospital cell. It had not shot out of the
night like a free-wheeling cosmic dancer, but had fallen dejec-
tedly behind the row of houses where Andrew and I had
lived. My heart was beating in my throat. I faintly heard his
steps coming down the corridor, padding softly on the outside

217

strip of linoleum, the strip that didn't squeak, the silent strip he tried to stay within on his nightly visits to my cell.

Somewhere outside, a lone radio played. I recognized the plaintive melodic voice of Armando Monsinaro, one of Mexico's famous composers whom I had come to love since being in prison. He was singing my favorite song, "Yesterday It Rained." Julio was standing outside my cell door now. My solitary confinement cell door that was made entirely of corrugated iron bars. It permitted every guard and policia to look directly at me no matter what I was doing. I could already smell his scent of lilac from several feet away, and I quickly made out the outline of his giant sombrero in the velvet blue of night air.

Tiny Francisco, my beloved guard and friend, my companion in card games, my teacher of comic book Spanish, the provider of homemade tortillas, was unlocking my cell. I heard him whisper, "Si, Julio, yo soy aqui por todo el tiempo."

And then my cell door opened and Julio entered my world, my world of panic and heat, of memories and fears of never leaving, fear of a twenty-seven-year sentence, and my final fear of being let out to return to a world where I no longer belonged.

My eyes adjusted to the muted light and I saw he was wearing one of his several pale purple shirts. He was so clean and smelled of lilac cologne and Clorox. Julio was tall, perhaps six-five and large framed. He was the sublieutenant of the Baja Mexico Federales, an arm of the police that rode horses and acted like the Texas Rangers. His moustache was thin and black. He was so handsome, so virile, and from such an entirely different culture that I momentarily quivered. What was I doing?

"Hello, Baby," he whispered to me in his sexy voice, using the only two words he knew in English. Then he threw his sombrero on the table beside my bed, slipped his thirty-eight under my pillow, and crushed me in his arms.

"Baby, Baby, Baby," he whispered again as Francisco mysteriously disappeared from sight, down the hallway to

guard for any errant nurses or interns who might mistakenly
slip down the hallway and catch me, Susan Nadler, the so-
called dangerous prisoner, the gringita, the drug smuggler
supreme, the supposed head of the gang, and Julio, the gun-
packing Federale, the Mexican who had killed over thirteen
prisoners, the man who had captured renegades high in the
hills of Durango, a hero of the police, catch us, two unlikely
lovers, in each other's arms, hear our sighs and cries, our
moans of passion and laughter, our attempts to communicate
when neither one of us spoke the other's language. It was
not safe what we were doing, not safe as he unbuttoned my
snow-white hospital gown, my bata, and ran his fingers
slowly down my thin chest, kissing the individual ribs that
stuck out, massaging my back and wide shoulders, running
his thumb over my thighs, which were covered in goose
bumps despite the fact that it was at least 94 degrees outside
and inside my cell. It was not safe as I grabbed his thick,
pomaded black hair and forced his lips onto mine, felt his
tongue run over the outline of my teeth, kissed his eyes and
his neck as he tried to unbutton his shirt and I unlatched his
belt, the one with the notches in it, the one with the mark
for every man he had killed. And as Julio stood naked in the
early light of dawn in the isolation cell in the hospital where
I was confined, and he climbed gracefully into my bed, de-
vouring my lips, my long hair, the mole on the side of my
face, we knew that we had to hurry, because the soft light of
morning was just beginning to break over the mountains,
and soon would envelope the town of La Paz.

Somewhere, not far away from the hospital, a rooster
crowed. "Ac-a-pul-coo," they all seemed to say. "Ac-a-pul-
cooo," the bird welcomed the new day out of force of habit.

I knew that I would never see Acapulco again, would never
swim on the shores of Las Brisas Hotel, or eat a fine meal at
Carlos and Charley's. And I wept for my lost past and my
stoned-out dreams of freedom. Julio caught his breath when a
tree branch fell on the roof of my cell, because he thought he

heard someone approaching. But nothing could stop him from cojoining with me. I pulled him on top and spread my legs slowly, inhaling the danger and culture of Mexico. Julio tasted of life, life outside the prison. He tasted of horses and guns and laughter and the sea and freedom. And I tasted to him like America and womanhood and forbidden fruit and tears and the future he would never know.

We two moved together in the narrow bed, on top of the stiff hospital sheets in the glow of the morning light, holding onto each other for dear life, coming together from opposite planets, understanding everything and nothing of who the other is and was, what the other wanted and dreamed. The rooster outside heralded the morning and Julio's heartbeat quickened. He had to leave soon. Or get caught by Adolpho, the head of the Federales, and lose his life.

"Baby," he whispered into my soaking wet hair. "Baby." He kissed the back of my neck and I held him tightly to me, never wanting to let go but knowing that we had been doomed before we had begun.

"Acapulcooo," the neighborhood bird crowed, "Acapulcooo," he warbled, to the sky and the sea and the air and the misty rays of the tropical morning.

"Acapulco," I cried to myself after Julio had left me, and I smelled the pillow where his head had lain and our hearts and souls had met. "Acapulco," I sobbed at my realization that today, August 19, 1972, Julio was my only contact with the world around me, and the mighty Mexican policeman might be my last, my last lover, my last man, my last touch with freedom and passion. My last dance with life as I had known it. I lay back in the damp humid hospital sheets and allowed the past to invade me.

I guess my real scenario with stepping over the edge began the first time I ever smoked marijuana. It happened in Greenwich Village when I was sixteen. No one in Squirrel Hill, the wealthy Jewish section where I grew up, or anywhere else in Pittsburgh that I knew, had even heard of marijuana. It was 1963 and my mother had taken me up to New York City, to the Plaza Hotel, for my birthday present. It was a great gift that I didn't appreciate. Back then I wore my hair short, my face was scrubbed clean, and I had on the de rigueur short white gloves. My mother's best friend Bunny had moved to New York City several years ago, after her gorgeous husband had died of Hodgkin's disease. I was definitely not prepared when her son Larry answered the door of Bunny's large West Village apartment. I was dressed all in white, short white dress with blue smocking, white gloves, bone-colored heels from B. Altman. And Larry was dressed all in black: black turtleneck, black pants, vest, even black gloves. He was almost handsome in a soft way. He had long brown hair that framed his face and green eyes that looked at me like I was the most conservative girl he had ever seen. I felt very awkward.

Larry was obviously part of a lifestyle I didn't know about, not even from all the books I read. Dinner was difficult; Larry and I tried to pay attention while our mothers, best friends for years, talked about old times, new jobs. Bunny was now involved in television production in New York. Neither one of us ate the charcoal-broiled steak and salad. Right after dinner, Larry asked me if I wanted to go hang out in the Village with him and meet some of the members of his band. Larry was a full-fledged musician. I played the classical flute. My teacher was the first flutist of the Pittsburgh Symphony. Larry knew the "Zombies" and Peter Gallagher. He was cool. I wasn't. My mother was nervous about my going out with hip Larry into the Village, the late night den of jazz musicians and Billie Holiday. But she consented even if Larry was dressed all in black.

I'll never forget the way the air smelled in New York that spring. It smelled of excitement and unfamiliar stimulation. The Village was another world. There were restaurants and coffee shops at every corner. Lights flashed. People hung

out. A man was reading poetry on a corner. Larry gently
held my arm and guided us to a downstairs cafe, where the
skinny Armenian bartender seemed to know him. Two other
members of his band were there, also dressed entirely in
black. Larry walked up to them and their dialogue began.

"Hey, Man, I wanna cop a skinny one so the chick here
from P-burg can burn with me, you got?" Larry seemed to
be talking a foreign language. I really felt out of it. The wait-
ress had long blond hair and wore a peasant skirt. Her ankles
were adorned with beads. She had a look like she knew
something that I didn't. In one moment I decided that I
wanted to be in with these people. I was already a mini rebel. The past year I had been suspended from my private
girls' school for harassing the librarian.

My suspension had been the humiliation of my family.
There were very few Jewish girls permitted into this school,
most of the members of the board of trustees were gentile,
wealthy, influential business associates of my father. My rebellion had been a little thing, but the headmistress blew it
way out of proportion. And my name became synonymous
with trouble. My parents considered my suspension a momentary aberration. But I was completely embarrassed when
I returned to school after two weeks. Certain girls, the key
ones, the cool ones, never talked to me again. I had had to
learn to hang out with the intellectuals. Something I would
later be thankful about.

Larry copped a j, and we took the key from George to his
pad, which was a block away. I desperately wanted to act
like I was not afraid to try to smoke marijuana, but my heart
was pounding in my eyes. Larry was very nonchalant. He
opened the door to George's apartment and proceeded to
tell me it was a "crash pad." The place was a mess. I had
never encountered this kind of atmosphere before. A curtain
of beads hung between the bathroom and the combination
living room and bedroom. Pictures of Indian gods covered
the walls; the bedspread was a dirty piece of madras mate-

rial. Filthy glasses with cigarettes floating in them and old pizza cartons littered the floor. The one lamp in the pad was covered by a long, embroidered black scarf; so even when Larry turned on the light, it was not too bright.

"Sit down," he told me in his soft, soft voice. I carefully looked around. It was a far cry from my parents' large house, with its priceless antiques, oriental rugs, sculptures, maids, and classical music. I tried to find a seat where my white dress wouldn't get dirty. Maybe that was why Larry wore black. He turned on a radio.

"You like Miles?" he asked me as he took the long thin white cigarette from his vest pocket.

"Sure," I answered. I didn't know who Miles was.

Larry lit up the joint and inhaled deeply. I could not get comfortable on the bed, which squeaked no matter where I sat. There was a pair of dirty men's underpants on the floor next to me.

"Now, take a toke and hold it in as long as you can," Larry instructed as he passed me the joint, a ritual that was to become an emblem for my entire generation.

I was not entirely a novice in deceit. I had tried the conventional forms of rebellion. I had smoked Camels with Carly, my best friend, while we hid in the bathroom and opened up the window to get rid of the smell. We coughed a lot from the unfiltered tobacco, but I was not prepared for the pungent, sickly sweet taste of reefer. I looked at Larry in the diffused lighting, he was looking at me, and I decided to ask no questions and be cool at any costs. I took another long drag of the joint, and focused all of my attention on it. What I really wanted to do was to ask if the smoke would hurt me, or how I would feel from it, or if I was going to get sick. But I was too afraid, too afraid to appear not with it, so I sacrificed my feelings of anxiety and decided whatever would happen would happen. At least I would not seem to be a fool. This was a pattern that was to dominate the next decade and a half of my life. Try anything, no questions asked,

rather than admit how frightened I felt. Never let anyone
know how you really feel.

Larry took the joint back from me and turned the music
up. He lit one of the giant, perfumed candles that sat beside
the bed.

"You like incense?" he asked as he handed the joint back
to me.

"I guess," I answered, never having seen real incense before in my life. I filled my lungs with the smoke and listened
as the street noise of New York City became background to
Miles's music; horns honked like tubas, cars screeched like
violins, peoples' voices sounded like reed instruments. Reality was growing hazy.

I handed the joint back to Larry and watched his lips as he
deeply inhaled. By the time he handed it back to me I felt
very happy, laughing, light, young, but knowing in a way far
beyond my years. After I handed the joint back, the first
thing I did was take off my little white gloves and lean back
on the dirty bed. The apartment no longer felt strange. I
sensed that I had been here before. Everything seemed
deep. I felt an overwhelming hunger that I would later identify as "the munchies."

"Hey, I wish I had eaten that steak now," I told Larry who
looked like moving liquid.

"Well, we could order in a pizza," he gestured to the half
dozen Gino's boxes on the floor, "or," he rubbed his hands
through her hair, "we could stay here and . . ." Larry leaned
over to kiss me at the same time than I leaned forward to
touch his face in a way I had never touched a man before. I
might have been rebellious according to the upper-middle-
class values of Pittsburgh, but I had never allowed any boy
to go further than feeling me up. I really had no idea what
sex was all about, although I had read all the right books,
like *Summer Place*, and *Parrish*. It sounds naive today, but
what I was experiencing as Larry's lips engulfed mine in a
wet kiss was a drug-induced passion, a passion that was just

beginning to awaken. Passion that was timid, but overwhelming. In a few minutes, after we had finished the joint,
I never wanted to leave Larry again, and when he unhooked
my bra, I allowed him to touch my young breasts, knowing
in my heart that perhaps I was going too far. But I didn't
care. I laughed hysterically at everything with him. There
were tears in my eyes as we talked about how we were both
stifled in our homes, and how we both wanted to write poetry, and demonstrate for civil rights, and go to the Left
Bank in Paris, learn about meditation and live forever. I did
stop him when he tried to unbutton my dress. That was a
little too much. But I felt closer to him in a shorter time than
I had ever felt to any of my adolescent boyfriends.

The next morning when my mother tried to get me to go
for my birthday haircut at the world-famous Kenneth's studio, I pretended that I had a headache. I told my dis-
gruntled mother to go on by herself. I couldn't bear the wait
for Larry. He sneaked up to my room at the Plaza and we
smoked another reefer. We laughed and made out for hours
until it was time to meet my mother for lunch at Schrafft's. I
would not be so turned on by a man again for years and
never quite with the same intensity. My little white gloves
soon became a symbol of the past, dance classes, coming-out
parties, Sunday School.

For the next two years marijuana was not accessible at all
in Pittsburgh. Country clubbers and their children were not
turned on. In the slightest. The biggest decision most of
those women made was what dress to wear to the high holiday ceremonies at the Temple. Or how to redecorate their
living rooms. Or where to go for the summers. It wasn't until 1966, when John, my closest friend, returned home from
Columbia University for the summer that I even saw a joint
again. Johnny spoke about nickel bags, and copping a buzz,
being mellow, all the terms that the so-called hip crowd
knew. After I smoked my next joint I became a regular toker
for the next twenty or so years. I depended upon marijuana

to alter my consciousness, to take me away from a reality that I later discovered was not so very bad. And always I tried to repeat the innocent and sensual high I had felt in Larry's arms, laughing my head off in Greenwich Village. A few times I thought I had it. But not really.

College was a very important issue at my house. Where would I go? Where would I live? What would I major in? I was finally accepted into the University of Wisconsin, in Madison. The decision was a family one. There were many arguments with my parents. My father was an extremely soft-spoken compassionate man, whose anger you could perceive only because his voice got softer. He was a very successful businessman. He didn't watch sports or drink with the boys. He liked to spend the weekend with us, his children, his three daughters, and Sundays he would take all the neighborhood gang to the museum to look at the dinosaur bones, and go to Isaly's for ice cream shakes. He and my mother seemed to have a perfect marriage. They never argued. He wore his pink Brooks Brothers shirts, and his Gucci loafers, and presided over our long mahogany dining room table, carefully carving the meat as the maid served the vegetables. My mother was a beautiful woman who had once sung opera and danced on the stage with Gene Kelly. She had given it all up to marry her college sweetheart, my father. Although World War II and family complications made it impossible for either one to finish their BA's, education was the issue in the house. How you scored, not how you felt. My mother had an art studio on the third floor of our home where she sculpted. She was quite good. She ran a perfect household, sometimes with three in help. The house was her showplace, the food was extraordinary, her clothes were the chicest, and her daughters the most cultured. Culture was also very important in my family. I had taken art, ballet, tap, eurythmics, and recorder and flute lessons all of my life and had fought constantly with my mother about practicing. My middle sister played the violin, and my youngest sister was a child prodigy on the piano.

All seemed perfect on the outside. A fairy-tale life with vacations to the Cape, family trips to the ballet and museums, books discussed, and ideas tossed about. But something was not right. I was rebellious from a young age. First of all I was a compulsive shoplifter, stealing little things, cheating on school exams, trying so hard to live up to my parents' expectations, which were nothing short of perfection.

After my suspension from private school, I appeared to get back on the track again, teaching Sunday School, winning the prestigious poetry prize in junior and senior year. But at night I had terrible insomnia and in the morning I never quite made it up for breakfast.

When I turned sixteen, I began to have horrible fights with my mother. These lasted into the wee hours of the morning. No one in the family was permitted to have anything wrong with him. If I liked Bob Dylan, they took that as a personal affront to their values; if I couldn't score well in math, it was because I wasn't trying hard enough, not because I didn't have the aptitude, which was really the case. I had very few opportunities to make my own decisions. Everything was decided for me. I wasn't asked how I felt, where I wanted to go, it was decided for me. I don't think I ever made a decision in my life until I was twenty-nine. I tried so hard to fit in with what my parents wanted that I had to lie to please them. I spun such phanta-magical scenarios of lies that sometimes even I didn't know what was the truth and what wasn't. And everything was based on how you looked on the outside.

By the time I was getting ready to go to college, it was decided that I would grow into a beauty. But I never cared much about clothes; I never wore makeup. I spent most of my time reading and writing poetry. I never even had my own style of dress until I was in my thirties. My mother sent me all my outfits, except my college uniform of turtle neck, boots, jeans, and peacoat.

The night before my big trip up to Madison, I sat in my third-floor room—my giant room I will remember all my life—and I looked out of one of the row of tiny windows. I could smell fall's arrival. Below me was the oak tree that David Glazer and I had carved our initials on. Next door Carly's mother, a world-famous concert pianist, was practicing the Brandenberg Concerto late into the night. I had just finished reading the *Alexandria Quartet* by Lawrence Durrell. I wanted to find that type of exotic existence for myself somewhere in the world. I knew that I was not meant to live the expected life, which was marrying a rich Jewish attorney and having children, settling into a routine of shopping and lunches and boredom. But what was I destined for? I had no idea, I never knew what I liked at this point, not even what I didn't like. I had no identity. I was scared to death to leave home, and yet I knew that if I didn't I would drown in my family. On my stereo, Joan Baez sang on about the "black haired boy." Suitcases of new clothes, still tagged, lay all over the brown wall-to-wall carpeting. And below, in their newly decorated bedroom, my parents were in their nightly positions.

Meanwhile, out in the world of the mid-1960s, events were conspiring to sweep me away into a storm I had no idea existed. Events that would seem to change the world, give people freedom, bring sanity back after the assassination of the beloved president John F. Kennedy. Give blacks equality. End the war in Vietnam. Give peace a chance. I was a tiny cog in this wheel of fortune. I would be an activist and a participant. And a flower child who never quite fit in. A searcher for identity. For attention. From my family who never knew who I was or what I wanted.

But I would find out.

The University of Wisconsin in the 1960s was one of the hotbeds of political radicalism. Wealthy middle-class sophomores in expensive boots and down parkas from back East ran chapters of SNCC, Score, and SDS. I lived in a very cushy plush dormitory, in a suite with living room, maid service, and a millionaire's daughter from Chicago as a roommate; but my tendency was to gravitate toward the dope-smoking rebels who gathered daily in the student union and talked about the inequality of life in America.

Sororities and fraternity boys weren't for me, homecoming was boring, and LSD was happening. However, Uncle Tim Leary never explained that to turn on was easy, dropping out only required a little guts; but tuning in, that was the trick. When in rapid succession Martin Luther King, Jr., and Bobby Kennedy were assassinated, I felt the urge to leave America, to go far away from the nightmare of Vietnam and torn-apart families and arguments with my father about integrating the unions.

Like most wealthy postwar American Jews, my parents had assimilated to the point of joining a Reform Temple. The precepts of my religious education required minimal attendance and were based on intellectual principles. Judaism was an ethical value system where integrity was foremost, and emotional attachment to a historic and often inexplicably unjust God was secondary.

I wanted something stronger in my life. I decided to take the money my grandfather had left me, savings he had accrued from years of operating one of the first scrap metal yards in Pittsburgh, and go to Israel the summer of my junior year in college for an archaeological dig at Ashod, one of the five holy cities of the Old Testament. I felt totally out of touch with my college roommates' idea of how they wanted to live their lives. So when I left the country in June 1968, I never had any intention of returning. Somehow, I didn't specifically know how; but in some way I knew I would find the means to stay in Israel. I managed to get a full scholarship to the Hebrew University by late August, based on my records from Wisconsin; and I found that housing was not a problem. Israel encouraged *Alia* (emigration)

for bright young Americans who might contribute something
to the growing nation.

By November I had dug in the ruins, had a small affair
with a soldier, realized that almost all Israeli men looked
better in uniforms, swam in the Sea of Galilee, been to Mas-
ada, and come down with pneumonia. Then I met the hip,
handsome, Israeli Joel, who spoke seven languages and was
a photographer, cameraman, painter, artist, student, and
soldier—and who became my husband. What did I know
then? I had an orgasm the first time we made love, and he
was gorgeous and funny and intelligent and listened to Bob
Dylan. I never knew then you could live with someone and
not marry them. Nor did I know that marriage between two
cultures is almost impossible.

The marriage was doomed from the beginning. I had no
idea what living with a man or taking care of another person
was all about; and Joel, one of the machismo Israelis who
live as if each minute was his last, could not believe that
marriage meant giving up one thing that he wanted to do.
We took gobs of LSD, and I found myself mysteriously dis-
contented for reasons beyond my control. I was desperately
looking for my spirit—which was nowhere to be found.

Living in a foreign country had great merits, however, despite the fact that we argued every day. We took tiuls, or
excursions, every weekend. We saw where Samson met De-
lilah, where King David was buried, and we spent a lot of
time at a strange small pyramid right outside of Jerusalem
where Absalom was buried. We ran from bombs and sym-
pathized with the young country of Israel. I watched as my
husband became more and more sympathetic to the Pales-
tinian guerrillas because we had many Arab friends in the
Old City where we lived. But as I became closer and closer
to God, I got further and further away from my husband,
who was more interested in painting cemeteries and distorted figures groping in hell. We smoked a lot of hashish,
moved to the Armenian section of the Old City, and bought

opium from the laundryman called Jacob's father. The Old City smelled of camels and pita bread and spices and exotic herbs like myrrh and cumin and rugs and Bedouins and tension.

My little *Alexandria Quartet* species of existence became harder and more confining. I wanted to get closer to Judaism, Joel wanted to get further away from the religion that would never let him forget the Holocaust nor the fact that his neighbors were his enemies. We hung out with expatriot hippies who lived in the Old City, and every weekend we had parties on top of the roof of the Petra Hotel, where we roasted legs of lambs and I made hash brownies. We traveled to London, Paris, Dublin, and Cyprus, smuggling hashish in giant tubes of shampoo and shaving creams—unafraid of being caught. We had no fear of the law. We were going to live forever. We took too many drugs, we had acid confrontations and there were occasional slaps for me. My husband used to tell me to go away for a while and not bother him.

One night in the Old City, at a party, I met Ivan, a seventeen-year-old Californian who talked to me of freedom and health food and sunshine and music and making love not war and tenderness, all the inexperience of youth and mescaline mellowness of LA—which was vacuous and good-vibrationed out with Jesus freaks, Krishna freaks, drug freaks, health freaks, and fuck freaks, but mellow man, very very mellow. And my husband, who was always too busy being productive to talk to me, told me to go talk to Ivan and his mystical rabbi friend. And so I talked to Ivan and his friend Rabbi Saul, the twenty-three-year-old Cabbalist. And Ivan and I talked and talked until we saw it rain from the same cloud, and I got divorced, and Ivan and I went to live on a mountaintop high in Jerusalem. But instead of studying spiritualism, we read Marvel comic books and marveled at love and methedrine. I copped morphine in Bethlehem from an Arab pharmacist who traded the vials of pure drugs the British had left after Israel's independence for ten trips of Purple Haze. I watched Ivan inject me with drugs. Maybe I hoped to find something, some grain of purity in my arm and instead I retreated further and further from reality into a psychedelic mist. Life is so simple when your parents support you.

I finally received my BA from the American College in Jerusalem, managing to write my papers stoned out on either seconals or methedrine. But Ivan had to return to the United States. There was a five-year age difference between us. Ivan was worried about how he would support me in LA. We wanted to continue our dream in California and all that we knew how to do was smuggle hash. So I sold my car, a Fiat my parents had given me as a wedding gift, and we found an Israeli Interpol official to send out the hash that we bought in Beersheba inside religious books from a Jerusalem yeshiva, because the rabbi who ran that yeshiva also wanted to smuggle. Everyone was doing it. It was the fastest way to make cash. I remember driving up to Mount Zion in a terrific desert storm, a khamseen, or sandstorm, and seeing this Hasidic rabbi, with his peyos and fur hat flying, yelling at us because of the sloppy way we were packing the kilos in the Gommorah, and the Mishna, the Jewish books of law and commentary on the law. The rabbi was afraid we were trying to screw him. He was standing in front of King David's tomb, near to the room where Christ supposedly held the Last Supper; and here we were in the holiest of all cities in the world, overlooking Jerusalem, and the rabbi was yelling at me and Ivan because he thought we were cheating him, yet he was smuggling drugs. It was too surrealistic.

By the time we arrived in LA, Ivan's mother, a mad, impassioned survivor of Auschwitz, also an Orthodox Jew, had called in a rabbi from the Eastwood division of the Khabad house to help her because she had found the first hash shipment, which we stupidly had sent through the mail in hardbound copies of *The Godfather* and *Huckleberry Finn*. The rabbi called in a California official, who appeared at Ivan's mother's small pink West LA house with several FBI men, and they met us there. I was dressed in a multicolored cape and long Bedouin dress, I had blond hair, and Ivan was wearing a Bedouin shirt and had hair down to his shoulders. Because the official from the state was Jewish, we were never formally arrested, just scared. Ivan's mother called my parents in Pittsburgh to come help. They were so shocked by my blond hair and gaunt appearance that they didn't recognize me when I came to meet them at LAX. They were also shocked by the facts that I had left my husband for a young hippy, and was totally involved with drugs. My father was always very law abiding and he didn't want to do anything to jeopardize his integrity, especially if pay-offs were involved. He did help me out. But my parents judged me and what I had done.

My parents finally left LA when they realized I wasn't going to jail. And I was left with a dingy apartment on Olympic Boulevard behind a Chinese restaurant, dark roots in my hair, Ivan, no money, and the reality of working. This was all too much for our flimsy relationship to bear. We broke up, penniless, without our mountaintop. Ivan died about ten years ago from a drug overdose.

Between 1970 and 1971 time was of very little importance to me. I worked a series of offbeat movie-related jobs, script girling, delivering sandwiches, jobs I acquired through friends. Then I finally hit cocaine, the rich kids' drug. I discovered rock stars in Rolls-Royces collecting unemployment, and all the beautiful people who worked so hard to be mellow. I moved up to Benedict Canyon Drive with a coke dealer and made the scene. Sometimes in my travel from bed to bed or from city to city I would stop and say, wait a minute, what the hell, how did I get from twenty-one on a dig in Ashod, ban the bomb, at least reading a book, to twenty-five, still a lot of jive, Quaalude madness? Sometimes I thought if only I had enough money, I would buy land and not have to work and get straight and find God, the quest of my generation. But I never thought in terms of why not now, because when you fool yourself enough into talking about spiritualism, you start to have delusions of grandeur. You know, a little knowledge about Egyptology, a few joints of Acapulco gold, a few male reinforcements and I just knew I was Cleopatra this lifetime. I was divine. And when the Messiah came, which is sooner than anyone thought, I would be the one to walk in a white robe beside him and he would shine his everlasting light on me.

So I made the rounds of hipdom and ultimately ended up on a beach in Acapulco, in 1972, getting an airmail telegram from my attorneys that my long-forgotten automobile accident of two years ago had finally paid off. Please fly back immediately and collect $15,000. Do not pass go.

I returned to LA, split the money with my attorneys and physicians, and felt I was left with options for the first time. As it turned out, that same night I went to a party in Hollywood and ran into an old friend, a blond-haired, definitely full-on-in-the-divine, upper Hollywood bro, Gemini, songwriter, ex-Laurel-Canyon redwood lover. And he says to me, he says, "Hey sister . . ." And in Los Angeles, as in practically no other city in the world, relationships start very casually. The slightest raise of an eyebrow or candid smile smacks of invitation, the slightest sign, such as a rainbow reflection in the toaster behind you, and you know that you two are meant to be. So Andrew and I, we received our cosmic OK to begin a life together. We moved to an apartment in Hollywood, surrounded with mandalas and tie-dyed sheets, fur coverlets, and $200-a-pair sunglasses and a circle of friends who always included some fringe movie stars, some has-beens, some Sufi mystics, some health food addicts, and of course, some drug dealers. In our case, it was us. And we made plans to invest my money in a drug deal that would originate from Morocco and move on to La Paz, Baja, and Los Angeles. I imagined more and more that I was the living representation of Mata Hari. Everything felt glamorous and exciting, Technicolor and cinematic. Sometimes late at night, lying on Andrew's huge bed, smoking a giant joint, looking up as Venus seemed to kiss the moon, I would think of my father and mother, worrying about me in Pittsburgh, listening to my nasal telephone conversations and asking me what drug I was taking. They had just recovered from getting me out of trouble in the Jerusalem-LA caper. But I assured myself, Jackson Brown playing plaintively in the background, my parents would never know about this deal, they would never be a part of the La Paz scenario, I would never, ever be caught again. I was far too careful, sniff, sniff, pass the joint, my life was on the upswing now; there would be no trouble in paradise. All I had to worry about was making sure that I had the cash ready for Andrew's partner Ted, so that he could buy the hashish in Morocco, and have it built into an armoire there, and shipped to La Paz, which was a duty-free port, and pick it up at the tiny airport, where everyone would be too sleepy and languorous to notice, and have it built into a boat, to speed up the coast to Los Angeles, sell it to the distributor, collect my $40,000 and be home free. What could be easier?

Finally, Andrew got the telegram to leave. His job was to wait in La Paz for the package. I spent two lonely weeks in LA. I did a lot of dieting, smoking, writing, reading, and laundry. Then the phone rang and it was Andrew, whom I barely remembered. He told me to get on a plane the next morning; there was a ticket waiting for me at the airport. I was to bring a little money, some dugee, and some coke.

I carefully planned my travel outfit. I wore a large silver-and-turquoise cross some of the Sufi brothers had made, carried a tan leather case from Georgio's, checked to see if all the dope was in my makeup case, took two Quaaludes and fell asleep as the Air Mexico plane left LA.

The last words I remember hearing before I fell out on the plane came from a wealthy California real estate dealer who was going to deplane in Puerta Vallerta. "Baby," he laughed, taking off his shades and adjusting his collar, "people who love rock 'n' roll will never grow old."

The minute I stepped off the plane in La Paz I felt a wave of tropical desert heat that was overwhelming. I started sweating between my breasts. I immediately spotted Andrew, in his straw hat. He looked a lot like Richard Chamberlain as he crushed me in a sweaty embrace.

"Hey, Honey, que pasa with my baby?"

The La Paz airport was very clean, unlike the other Mexican airports where I had landed. I was painfully aware that despite all the years I had spent in Mexico, I had never bothered to learn any Spanish. I had been too stoned and too preoccupied. We jumped into the Safari Jeep that Andrew's so-called company rented. As we drove off I reassured him that I had brought along the dope. We drove past beaches and restaurants, down immaculate, steaming streets and my eyes searched La Paz for a beggar with an outstretched hand, so common in other parts of Mexico, but there were none.

The beach road was spectacular, the sand white and clear, the Sea of Coromel, aqua and teeming with fish. I would spend many days at this playa with Andrew.

Because La Paz is a duty-free port, much of its money comes from importing low and making marginal profit on perfume, sweaters, Oaxaca straw bags, Taxco silver, and mainland embroidered shirts. Large packages, such as the one our hashish was coming in, arouse very little suspicion. The tourists who frequented La Paz were primarily WASPy boating types. There were many yachts moored there, and an entire subculture of inbred fishermen scooted from boat to boat in small-water crafts. The town had no university, so most of the young people either left for Guadalajara University with dreams or stayed home with the reality of becoming busboys at one of the four hotels, waiters at the restaurants, fishermen, or police. Life was very simple there. The natives were friendly to Americans, not out to hustle them. The older sections of town, with the roosters that crowed to the tune of Ac-a-pul-coo, and the mud houses of red and ochres and browns looked like "Desolation Road" from Dylan's song. The city proper was small, but slightly sophisticated. The one modern building was the Hospital Salvitorre, across the street from our apartment.

La Paz literally translated means peace. It was calm there. It had an aura of some of the old Western towns of Utah and Wyoming. The crime rate was very low; no American had ever been busted for drugs; the police were the highest paid of the civil servants; there were a few tourists; a few orchata, or rice water, stands; a central *commercial*, or supermarket; many fresh fruit and tortilla stands; and much serenity and peace. But not for long.

Our apartment was modern, had two bedrooms, bathroom, kitchen, and dining room and living room combined; it smelled clean and like the sea. The decorations were from Morocco and India, left over from another dope shipment. Mandalas covered the walls, a little plastic sculpture of Krishna and his pals playing various instruments sat on the dining room table, and the doorways held chimes and mobiles from Tangiers and maps of Mexico. It was really like a cleaned-up version of the crashpad where I first got high. Andrew and I were a wealthy couple in land development; we went out to eat frequently, swam, stayed on an occasional yacht, and kept to ourselves. I wondered how long we could keep up that image. Then we started to get loaded and didn't care. Andrew told me that all the dope came from Mazatlan, and was good, the farmacia had all the Mandrax (the French equivalent of Quaalude) that we could eat, and with my good looks, who knew what else we could score. We had an all-expense paid trip to the hotlands, a beautiful apartment, all the drugs we wanted, we dug each other, and I had an assured forty grand coming. What else could you want, but a little brains, common sense, foresight, and self-respect?

Life for us went immediately downhill once I began to score drugs on a regular basis from the farmacia. The next month was one of oblivion. We swam and nodded out all day at the hot beach, drank fish soup, went home, made love, woke up, got high, planned what restaurant to go to for the evening, ate, and loaded on our asses, headed out to a steamy discotheque, drank banana daiquiris, and sensuously danced with a group of young Bajans clapping around us as if we were heroes. We had a certain charisma that all conspirators had: we knew something that no one else did.

And in the heat of the anticipation of the deal, under the influence of drugs, which we were now injecting, in the warmth and somnambulism, the lassitude of the tropical paradise, we soon began to fall into a romantic daze. We got lazy and sloppy. We wore out our welcome at every drugstore, we nodded out at all the restaurants, sometimes we were so stoned that we yelled at each other and the waiters. We wrung out our bodies and minds on methedrine, thinking we were organized, staying up all night writing lousy songs that we imagined were going to make us famous. We drove around town defiantly as if we owned it. We didn't obey the traffic signals, and we began to forget why we were there in the first place.

Three weeks had gone by and still no word from Ted about the package. Finally, with much trouble trying to walk straight, we made a long-distance phone call from one of the fancier hotels to Aero Cargo, the small national airline that was supposed to be flying the package in from Mexico City. The administrator told Andrew, one muggy afternoon, that the package had been sent four weeks ago from Morocco. We should have received it by now. This fact should have alerted us—we should have become suspicious, but we were far too stoned and far too confident in our divine protection. This date, approximately May 15, or around the day George Wallace was shot, marked the beginning of our descent from Lower Level Boogie to Looney Tunes. We ignored a warning from a friendly neighbor who was getting us heroin that strange men had been around asking questions about us. We were so zonked out that when Ted arrived, in his three-piece suit, and looked at me, sick from shooting so many drugs, and Andrew, who was babbling about our music, Ted tried to get me to leave. If I had left, I never would have got into trouble. But I didn't want to miss out on anything. I wanted to be there for the action. Despite my premonition that all was not right. I was afraid to act uncool.

Two days later, slightly cleaned up, the three of us went to the airport to pick up the package. Ted immediately noticed that the bottom of the armoire had been opened and reclosed. All the Mexican workers at the airport were staring at us with intense curiosity. We should have realized that the gig was up. But we didn't—or couldn't, or weren't meant to. And that afternoon, the armoire safely in our living room, the lifters well tipped, we were on our way to the travel agency to pick up my ticket back home. I had decided by now to go back to the states to see a doctor. Suddenly, like in the movies, there was a big knock at the apartment door. All I could think about was hiding my tiny remainder of coke and heroin on top of the closet. When I opened the door downstairs, I saw a huge Mexican (who turned out to be Julio), with a moustache, a sombrero, and a machine gun pointed at me. I looked at Andrew and he looked at me and I looked at him and I said, "Do you believe this?"

Suddenly there were thirty Mexican police and thirty machine guns pointed at us. I was thrown against the car and frisked; and people were racing back up to the apartment, breaking open the door. Two of the hombres identified themselves as FBI men and casually said to me, "Congratulations, Girlie, you are part of the first drug bust ever in

Baja—and yer in fer the longest and hottest summer of your life." Andrew was handcuffed. There was nothing but commotion. I was coming on to my Mandrax and getting belligerent. But I managed to stash the joints from my purse under the mattress of the bed. I denied over and over again that I had any idea what was in the armoire (only the best hashish any of the Mexicans would ever see). An older man, a Mexican who spoke English, checked my arm for track marks. I thanked God that I was so tan he couldn't see any of the abscesses.

Another man identified himself in all the tumult, with half of the excited neighborhood children at our front door and Federales breaking open the armoire with hatchets, as the district prosecutor. He told me (and I wondered how he knew my name and then realized that they had been watching us for God knows how long), "Susan, do you know how serious this is?"

And the tall, skinny FBI man in the hat told me as I began to cry that we had to have someone's name in the States to call to get help for me, and I spat out, "I don't need any help!"

Clothes were thrown all over the apartment, music and books were on the floor, and the other FBI man kept repeating to me that in Mexico you are guilty until proven innocent.

Then Andrew and Ted and I were hustled into police cars where we all swore to keep our mouths shut. Ted tried to reassure me, "Don't worry, we'll be out of here overnight. The brothers in Los Angeles will take care of everything."

Then suddenly we were at the jail, the Edificia M. Sobarzo, an old hospital with thick walls and a lot of police hanging around. They took us out of the car at gunpoint, in the hot noonday sun, and Andrew was dragged away toward the men's side and I was led away to the women's cell, in my cutoffs and transparent halter top, with at least forty pairs of male eyes following me.

There were no provisions in Mexico for female prisoners—only for prostitutes. The women's cell was small. The police pushed me into a hole about fifteen by six feet, very dark, dank, and filthy. And all there was, once the huge cell door slammed shut, was a cement slab as a bed, a broken-down table, lice, huge spiders, and where the bathroom should have been, there emanated an unutterable stench. There was no toilet, no sink, no shower, just a small dripping faucet. Sitting in the corner was a woman in a long nondescript dress, pregnant, holding her knees. Her face was Mongoloid, she couldn't speak, and was apparently severely retarded. She sat there, in this huddle, with a few scroungy boxes around, which contained her clothes, and some old bread.

I was completely panic stricken. This couldn't be happening. The deal had seemed perfect. I again realized that I spoke no Spanish, and if this woman proved to be violent, I had no way to communicate with her or even to call for help, since the guards had disappeared.

I had to urinate very badly, but aside from there being no toilet, and appalling sanitary conditions, there was no way I could go in the presence of that woman.

The incongruous fact about Juanita, as I quickly discovered the woman's name to be, was that she had hung a clothesline in the bathroom to hang up some clothes she washed in the dirty water. She was determined, in her bizarre condition, to remain clean, even in her perilous situation, and despite the fact that the dampness never permitted anything to dry. I walked out of the bathroom with Juanita's eyes following me. Carefully, I sat down on the floor in front of the cell door. From this vantage point, I could see the large and beautiful flowering tree that grew in front of the cell. As the months wore on, I would adopt this tree as my own, because it was the only sign of free and growing life around me.

Outside, the huge wall to my right bounded the men's

side and had a guard on top of it, and a policia wandered to
and fro. I was petrified.

By half past five a group of thirty policia was marching
back to my cell. Maybe it was the gang rape the FBI man
had predicted. I literally peed in my pants—hot urine ran
down my leg. I ran to the bathroom and threw up in the
hole. But no one came to my cell; they were only practicing.

The sun was setting behind the tree, and I knew that the
ocean was in that direction. Suddenly, from behind my cell
and through the door I had spotted, I heard pounding on the
wall and yelling. Louder and louder. I was still frightened,
and the effects of the drugs I had taken that morning were
wearing off. Who was back there? Maybe Andrew. I ran and
started pathetically pounding on the huge metal door in the
middle of my cell wall, screaming, "Andrew! Andrew!" The
louder I pounded, the louder they pounded, until I was crying and screaming and working myself up into a frenzy; and
then the outside cell opened and four policia walked in. I felt
my knees start to quake, and the policia looked at me
quizzically and they motioned me aside and I moved back.
The largest policeman took a giant key from his chain and
opened the metal door. I rushed past him to see if Andrew
was there and was grabbed by a small policeman with a
moustache, who looked kindly at me with his huge brown
eyes as if to say, I'm sorry, Señorita.

I tried to question the police to find out who was behind
the door; and the fat tender policeman pointed to his head
and made the universal sign for crazy. "Los locos," he kept
saying. "Los locos."

I later found out that La Paz had no facility for the mentally disturbed. They were kept behind the women's cell in a
huge area, where they were restrained and where their families could occasionally come to visit. But I didn't find that
out then. After the police left, I was alone with the pregnant
retarded woman. Then darkness came.

I was starved and huddled on the floor, afraid of the lice

on the bed. When the sun set, it turned slightly chilly. It was still May, and the evenings were breezy; the stars outside my cell were thick. My legs were covered with goose bumps and I felt nauseous. Suddenly, I heard a radio come on very loud and a rapid Spanish voice droned on and on—the news—and then my own name, Susan Beth Nadler, followed by the names of Ted and Andrew. I realized that we were big news. I was to hear my name every night for the next month, until I began to think they were talking about someone else. A guard came to my cell door to bring me a plate of food that my ex-landlord had sent over. I could not eat at all.

I sat on the floor shaking and began to doze off, the heroin and Mandrax beginning to leave my system. I was just beginning to drift away into memories when the light in the bathroom went on. I heard singing. Juanita came floating through the cell, naked—her long stringy black hair floating behind her and her thin, black-nippled breasts swinging, her pregnancy huge and somehow comforting. She danced and sang as if she didn't see me, which she probably didn't. She hummed to herself as she gracefully choreographed her own special dance of joy and impending motherhood. She wove her way back into the bathroom, where she set the tired red bucket under the faucet and sang to the droplets of water that fell slowly into her hands. Apparently night was the only time water came out of the faucet. Juanita produced a small bit of soap from her hand and washed herself, always singing, until she was clean. She used her dress for a towel, and combed her hair with her fingers. Then she shyly walked up to me and offered me the soap, which I refused. The dancer shook her head, danced back, put on another faded dress, turned out the light, and huddled into her corner to fall asleep. She was to repeat this eerie and somehow religious dance every night for the next month until they took her away, half crazed with pain, to have her child. The dance

added some circle of continuity to my strange life in the
Mexican prison.

I was repeatedly questioned by the district prosecutor
over the next several days about what had really happened.
They would come to get me when I was asleep on the floor
or at midday. When I was led outside, I wanted to run away.
But I didn't. I couldn't; I was guarded by the armed policia.
I denied ever having any knowledge of a drug-smuggling
plan, or of drugs themselves. The two FBI men told me before they left to return to San Diego to report back to the
newly formed DEA, and that if I gave them all the information I had, I would be let go. But that admission itself would
have been tantamount to admitting guilt. And the cops and
robbers' game seemed absurd at this point. I refused to talk,
somehow believing that Andrew and Ted would get me out,
somehow believing that I was not meant to spend the next
twenty-seven years of my life in prison. Twenty-seven years
was the potential sentence I would receive for my crimes:
acquisition, transportation, possession, and importation of
250 kilograms of hashish. In two months' time, another 250
kilos of hashish, addressed to Andrew, arrived at the airport.
It strengthened the case against us.

I stuck to my story. Andrew was a legitimate businessman.
I had gone with him to see legitimate real estate dealers
about land development for his and Ted's company. No, I
had never even smoked a joint in my life. Yes, I had a degree, a BA from the American College in Jerusalem. No,
Jerusalem was not the capital of Morocco. And then I was
taken, filthy and ill, back to jail to wait for my food and the
note that Andrew would pay one of the guards to bring to
me.

I spent most of my first three weeks in prison dreading
the phone call I knew I would have to make to my parents. I
couldn't put them through this ordeal again. I knew by now
that when you are in prison in a foreign country, you are

totally at the mercy of your captors, their laws, their language, their judicial system (or lack of system), their impression of who you were, what you did.

I received the phone call from my distraught parents one Saturday. My father told me over the static line, "The FBI just told us you're in one helluva mess. We're going to try to help you."

And then my mother: "You are killing your father. You are a whore."

And with that little bit of guilt, enough to last a lifetime, the lines went dead.

For the rest of the time until my parents arrived, I met with a hip LA lawyer, Alan Laughlin, whom Ted's people had sent to help us. He engineered several daring escapes for Americans in Mexican prisons. He also tried to pay off my judge's clerk, so my father refused to use him.

I sat in my cell in the evenings and lit a candle from the supplies that Ted's LA attorney had brought for me. Joni Mitchell sang on my tape recorder.

At about nine o'clock, a rather handsome face appeared at my cell door. It was Julio, the sublieutenant of the Federales, one of the men who had busted me. He stood there looking at me and finally asked, "Tu tienes miedo?"

I did not understand. I immediately raced over to get my new Spanish-English dictionary. *Miedo* meant "fear." I looked at the handsome man in the pale pastel shirt, wearing a giant sombrero and a .38 pistol at his waist. He looked like a leftover extra from Wyatt Earp. He motioned me over to the cell door and gave me a flower, a gardenia, through the cell bars. It smelled intoxicating, heady, exotic, free. I began to cry, and Julio tried to explain to me in sign language to smile, be happy. I walked away from the door and sat down on the cement bed. He finally left.

The next day I was brought some of my own clothes and told to prepare for court. I felt very sick, strangely tranquil, as if I was floating in a bubble. I was marched to an office, where Andrew and Ted were standing with Laughlin and a small Mexican man they identified as Mr. Gonzales, our new Mexican attorney.

He told me not to worry, I would be out by the afternoon. My hair was pulled back from my face in a ponytail. I had lost over ten pounds in the time I had been incarcerated. My arms were so thin that the trackmarks from the weeks of shooting drugs were standing out clearly.

"You look yellow, Baby," Andrew said, trying to break the silence.

"After the trial, the judge has twenty-four hours before pronouncing sentence," Laughlin told me during the nerve-wracking ride to court.

The judge greeted us at the door; he was late in arriving and was just opening up the courtroom. He was about five-one, was wearing a filthy short-sleeved gray shirt, and there was egg lodged in his moustache. He was approximately seventy years old and moved so slowly that Ted thought he was senile. I wanted to throw up. My life rested in this man's hands. He sat down at his desk and read through all the notes Laughlin had prepared; it took him about fifteen minutes.

Laughlin was taking a lot of pictures with his Nikon: the courthouse, the ride over from the jail. It was obvious to me that he was planning a breakout. I had put Band-Aids on my nipples to keep them from showing because I had no bra with me. I felt sure that the judge could see the Band-Aids.

Finally, my time to talk came. I felt like I was adrift. I told the judge, as Mr. Gonzales interpreted, that I had never known that Andrew was involved with drugs, that we did not live that type of existence, that I was an educated and responsible woman from a fine family. Obviously my arrest was a mistake.

The judge thanked me. Court was dismissed.

I rode back to the jail alone in the police van. I fell asleep exhausted that night. At three in the morning, I was awakened. A huge guard turned on the naked light bulb in my cell and threw a young woman on the floor. She was small and dark and dressed in a short, sleazy red dress. She was also drunk and belligerent as hell.

She threw up on the floor, and then she saw me. She grabbed me and started to kick and pull my hair. The cell suddenly stank of liquor and vomit. I had been paying the cleaning man to use Lysol. She was my first introduction to Mexican prostitutes. I spent a hideous night on the floor. What was going to happen to me?

Then I became very ill with typhoid fever and hepatitis (and I've never really recuperated from those diseases). I was sick a long time and went untreated. A local doctor diagnosed the typhoid and when the commandant found out what I had, he sent me to the hospital detention cell. It was located in the deserted tuberculosis ward of the hospital. I was feverish and hallucinating. The judge determined that we had to stay in prison for one year before we were to be sentenced. The newspaper headlines were the most unbelievable part of it all. The local reporter covering the crime beat, whom I never met, decided that I was the head of a crime ring that somehow encompassed the Mafia. I was in fact the head of the Mafia.

After they moved me to the hospital, one late night, the infamous commandante of the Federales came to visit me. He was a huge hairy man, dressed immaculately in a pearl-gray silk outfit. He was also incredibly educated. I was reading *Steppenwolf* at the time, and the first sentence he ever spoke to me was about his great love for Herman Hesse. It was difficult to reconcile this image with the facts that I knew about the man. He tracked down criminals with a vengeance, he himself rode up into the hills to shoot them down, he ran the prison with little compassion for criminals. He was unmarried and was said to like mainly prostitutes. He came racing into my cell at about two AM. At this point I had guards twenty-four hours a day. Each one had an eight-hour shift. So I grew to know these men well. Francisco, the tiny fat wonderful policia was on duty that night. The commandante blew in with five of his closest guards, including Julio, and woke me up, which was not difficult considering that I barely slept. He began to question me. I was sweating profusely, and was very weak.

He said, "Susan, we have information that you are head of the gang, a Mafia woman." I didn't know what to say. I realized that he had been reading the paper. He continued. "Your passport says you were in Morocco." I tried to reason with him, he was an educated man. My passport said Jerusalem. He wouldn't believe me. He continued to question me for over two hours, with his men around him smiling and agreeing with his every word. It was sickening. Apparently my parents had just left. Before leaving they had met with the judge, and my father, through a business associate in Mexico, had found me a new attorney, the best criminal attorney in Mexico City. The judge thought that my parents were a plant sent down by the Mafia. It was all so hilarious, and hideous. I told him that they were my parents.

"How could such nice people be related to a big drug dealer like you?" he concluded. I didn't know what to say. "Tell me the whole plot, Susan, and you'll be let out soon."

I had nothing to say. I knew by now that I would have no life with Andrew. I had hardly seen him during the last month since I had been moved to the hospital. My parents were insisting that I separate my case from his. It was their plan that I act as if I couldn't stand him, to make the judge see how outraged I was by my involvement in the whole matter. And I had constantly to lie to my parents and tell them that I didn't ever know what was going on, I was innocent, to placate them, yes, I am really who you raised me to be.

The commandante finally got so incensed by my attitude that he left. The next morning there were two armed guards at my door. The newest rumor was that I was trying to es-

cape. For the next three weeks there were Federales, with
loaded machine guns, at my door day and night.

There was no way for me to discern the truth about who
was who or what was what. I received cryptic notes from
Andrew saying one thing, and then a telephone call from my
parents, who were back in Pittsburgh preparing to return
again, telling me something else about what was going on in
La Paz. I was totally confused. I became prepared to accept
insanity as an alternative to spending my life in prison.
That's how my whole affair with Julio began—it was a life-
line to reality. I knew I had no future with him, and I felt
guilty about being unfaithful to Andrew—guilty about that.
That's how unstable I was. But Julio came to visit me every
night, with little presents: books, flowers, ice cream. He
smelled wonderful, like a man. He looked at me with such
wonder in his eyes.

I spent the next four months in a Mexican prison, from
June until the end of September. This was the hottest time
of the year, dog-day afternoons by anyone's standards. I ate,
slept, cried, prayed, lied, and learned Spanish in an open
cell, with only a windowless bathroom for privacy. When I
took a shower, I never turned on the hot water. The water
heater was on the roof, and the sun-heated water was blis-
teringly hot. My father bought me an electric fan, but all it
did was move the hot air around. I lived in a constant state
of anxiety. Francisco, the little guard, taught me Spanish by
using comic books. One night I was listening to the radio,
and the announcer, who was giving a lesson to Americans in
simple Spanish, used the word *arbol*. I tried to look it up in
my dictionary, but I couldn't find it. Francisco became very
animated, and ran over to my cell door with a comic book,
pointing madly to a tree. *Arbol*, he squealed, his little sau-
sage fingers dancing, "*Arbol*, Susanna," he repeated. Until I
realized that *arbol* meant tree. And so I became proficient in
street Spanish. My new attorney, who claimed he looked
like the Mexican Marlon Brando, used to tell me that I could

speak with the best of the people on the street. And it was the people of the street I grew to love.

The guards who spent eight hours a day with me all had families and these families all became a part of my life. Francisco's wife brought me food, home-cooked tortillas, refried beans, cooked pork with avocado, flan. And his children all brought pictures to my cell. The interns in the hospital, some of them poor young men who had worked their way through college doing manual labor, taught me to appreciate Garcia Lorca, and spoke to me about the green wind. I wrote poems for the judge in my new Spanish and read the daily newspapers slowly. Time passed.

My father came and stayed at the hotel where Andrew and I used to eat. He was very confused by the language business and the Mexican penal system. He had to rely on his attorney completely. He continued to maintain that he did not want to compromise his values by having to pay anyone off. He didn't have to worry. I was probably the only American prisoner in Mexico who had no one to pay off. No one. My fate remained in the hands of the judge. So I passed the days playing Mexican gin with my father and the police, eating ice cream, trying to regain my health and waiting. My attorney had decided the tack to use. He would make it incumbent on the judge to prove that I indeed had knowledge of the crime. The burden of proof was up to the seventy-year-old man with the egg in his moustache. All was calm until I discovered that the judge and the clever district prosecutor had written to Interpol to see if I had a record. I knew that I had an international record from my Israeli caper. My father had never told the attorney about it because he would not have taken on my case had he known. When I found this out I went into the bathroom and threw up. Caught in another wave of lies.

By September an unusual, natural La Paz phenomenon began. Millions of butterflies came to molt by the La Paz ocean. Every day several of the lilac or bright green ones

would fly into my cell through the bars and aimlessly fly
from wall to wall looking for an escape. I learned to stalk
these silent creatures, and form a net with my hands, catch-
ing the butterflies within, and helping them fly free outside
again. I had once read an old Greek myth that when a man
dies it is as if his soul emerges as a butterfly, his pure life
essence bursts forth and flies high in the sky, free of the
body and physical problems. Maybe all the butterflies who
were hovering over the hospital were really souls who had
come to help me see that to truly live is to be free in the
physical as well as the spiritual, and not to worry. I knew
that if I ever got out, an old me had to die forever. The me
that thought I could scheme, dream, and lie eternally, playing the big joke on everyone, thumbing my nose at the
whole world of laws and discipline, and incidentally, peace of
mind.

Of course I did get out. The record from Interpol didn't
exist; even if it had, Mexico was too disorganized to get it
through the proper channels. The judge couldn't prove that
I was guilty. I was sprung loose. The first night out I stayed
at a hotel with my attorney. While shaving, I gouged my leg.
Suddenly I wanted desperately to run back to my cell. What
lay ahead for me in life? Prison seemed safer than Pittsburgh.

Julio came to visit my hotel room, dressed in civilian
clothes. Suddenly, he didn't look romantic at all. I couldn't
make love with him. It seemed foolish and frightening. I just
wanted to get out of the country. Ted was let go a day after
me, but Andrew remained in jail for over a year, until
Laughlin broke him out in a dramatic escape involving the
death of a policeman. One of my old guards. A friend lost
forever.

When I look back on it today, I could blame the whole
thing on my parents, or the political and moral climate of the
1960s; but it was me. I couldn't bear to be the same as everyone else, I wanted my parents to notice me so badly, I

wanted to do anything to get attention, and I was young, pretty, rich, educated. I believed that I was immortal. I didn't recognize death—or fear. I was raised in a break-through generation of dreamers. We made fantasy come true. I had no idea of who I was, or where I was going to go. Perhaps my parents didn't properly prepare me for the future. Perhaps they never understood the world that they had created, the world that I was to be a part of. I wanted action and excitement. I rejected everything successful and rich, because inside I felt like such a failure. But the experience set me free. I broke out of drug use and shady deals. I came to face myself. I was a good girl gone bad. But I went good again. The past is permanently over for me. I was one of the lucky ones.

THE CRIME—Acquisition, transportation, importation, and possession of 500 kilos of hashish
THE SENTENCE—A potential twenty-seven years
Actual time served—Four and a half months